ꓕꓴLLꓭBꓭLꓴꓴ
IN THE KITCHEN

Dallas A&M University Mothers' Club
Dallas, Texas

All proceeds from the sale of this cookbook will be returned to Texas A&M University for scholarships and student activities.

Library of Congress Catalogue Card No. 83-072179
ISBN 0-9612446-0-7

Additional copies may be obtained by writing:
HULLABALOO IN THE KITCHEN
Dallas A&M University Mothers' Club
P.O. Box 796212
Dallas, Texas 75379

First Printing, November, 1983 - 7000 copies
Second Printing, May, 1985 - 7000 copies

Taylor Publishing Co.
Dallas, Texas

INTRODUCTION

It is appropriate that Dallas Aggie Moms are publishing this cookbook, because our organization was founded for the purpose of taking food down to the "boys" at A&M for a "spread."

Mrs. H. L. Peoples of Dallas had a freshman son at Texas A&M, when she gathered together eleven mothers of Aggies to form the first A&M Mothers' Club in February, 1922. Their objective, "By individual effort to contribute in every way to the comfort and welfare of the boys, and to cooperate with the faculty of the college in maintaining a high standard of moral conduct and intellectual attainment," is still being followed. Of course, today that includes girls, too!

To determine how they could best achieve their goal, the eleven mothers made a trip to A&M to speak with school administrators and to visit the boys. In their caravan of Model T Fords traveling on gravel-topped roads, the trip down to College Station took nearly all day, but it was worthwhile. They carried plenty of food for their sons.

On March 3, 1922, with Mrs. H. L. Peoples as President, the Dallas A&M Mothers' Club was formed. The A&M Mothers' Club idea spread rapidly. At present there are 70 Mothers' Clubs in the State of Texas and three in Louisiana.

The Dallas A&M Mothers' Club serves Texas A&M University in many ways. Working together, Aggie Moms have established a fund for a President's Endowed Scholarship and, in addition, have contributed approximately $11,000 each year to various campus organizations, such as the All Faiths Chapel, the Hospital, the Singing Cadets, the Corps of Cadets and the library. Moms baked and delivered hundreds of dozens of cookies to the campus for bonfire workers at TAMU. In the summer a reception honoring freshmen and transfer students is held in Dallas with speakers from the campus to welcome new Aggies into the fold and to greet their parents. Workdays are held all year to make boutique items to be sold at meetings and on Parents' weekend. Moms come together to make "Aggedy Ann" and "Andy" rag dolls and share some of the Aggie spirit. Our meeting year begins in September, and throughout the year various speakers help Aggie Moms become better acquainted with education and social life at Texas A&M. In December the club holds a Christmas Tree Sale at TAMU Research & Extension Center. Many families with current students and former students come from far and near to buy an Aggie Christmas Tree. In the spring the Singing Cadets present their annual concert in Dallas. Moms and Dads provide lodging and meals and a party for the group after the performance, making a festive weekend for everyone. On Parents' weekend we join in activities on campus with our students, as well as participate in the Federation of Texas A&M Mothers' Clubs annual meeting and boutique sale. At the Awards Day Program, the club proudly presents one of the outstanding senior cadets with a saber signifying his achievements during the year.

For many years tradition has held that each monthly meeting is followed by a luncheon or reception, where Moms can share with each other the latest happenings of their students at A&M. This has proved to be a joy and a help to many freshmen mothers. In an effort to extend the benefits of our culinary delights that light up these luncheons and receptions, these recipes have been collected over the years with the hope of producing a cookbook. **Hullabaloo in the Kitchen** is the result. It is a collection of tested recipes served at luncheons, receptions and parties, as well as to our families in our homes. To all of our Aggies, we lovingly dedicate **Hullabaloo in the Kitchen.**

Mrs. George D. Neal
President 1982-83

Mrs. William Heaton
President 1983-84

ACKNOWLEDGMENTS

The Dallas A&M University Mothers' Club Cookbook Committee wishes to sincerely express its appreciation and thanks to the following individuals:

Art Design
Bob Haydon

Color Photography
Rick Cook, Interior & Floral Designer, The Perfect Setting
Michael Wilson, Photographer
Mrs. Cynthia Jubera, Food Stylist
Mrs. Rosanne Greene, Food Stylist

Sketches of Texas A&M Buildings
Allan Weghorst '86, Texas A&M University

Texas A&M University
Ms. Patricia Bode, Library Assistant, University Archives
Mrs. Mary Helen Bowers, Director of Educational Information
  Services
Dr. Dymple C. Cooksey, Food & Nutrition Specialist
Jerry Cooper, Editor, *Texas Aggie*
Paul Glenn, Manager, Photographic Services
Ms. Susan Hopkins, Receptionist, Association of Former Students
James L. Johnson, Lecturer of Floriculture Sciences
Everett D. Laird, Manager of Administrative Services
Donald B. Powell, Director of Business Services
Jim Reynolds, Director, Memorial Student Center
Samuel R. Sciullo, Jr., Publications Director, Athletic Department
Lane Stephenson, Director of Public Information
Dr. A. J. Turgeon, Former Resident Director of Research, Texas
  A&M Research and Extension Center

COOKBOOK COMMITTEE

CHAIRMAN   Mrs. Sam C. Laden, Jr.
SECRETARY   Mrs. Jack McAuliff

FOOD EDITORS

Mrs. Frank S. Covaro
Mrs. G. Wayne Evans
Mrs. S. Ward Hughes
Mrs. John J. Jones, III
Mrs. Jack McAuliff
Mrs. George D. Neal

Mrs. Charles D. Price, Jr.
Mrs. Lee R. Radford
Mrs. Clifford V. Slagle
Mrs. Jay D. Smith
Mrs. Jack Starry
Mrs. Glinn White

Mrs William Heaton
Mrs. Bruce Johnston

PROOFREADERS

Mrs. Bobby Fletcher
Mrs. Lloyd Jones
Mrs. George D. Neal

Mrs. Ralph Plumlee
Mrs. Jim Thompson
Mrs. Herschel Wilson

Our sincere appreciation is expressed to our members, celebrities and friends who graciously contributed their favorite recipes.

To our husbands, children, relatives and friends who have sacrificed generously their time, energy (and waistlines), we give our heartfelt thanks for making this cookbook possible.

We wish to express our sincere appreciation and gratitude to the following friends for their generous support in making our **Hullabaloo in the Kitchen** cookbook possible.

Cookbook Committee

CONNOISSEURS
Mr. John A. Arnold
Mr. H. R. Bright
Mr. Thomas R. Frymire
Mr. Sam C. Laden, Jr.
Mr. George D. Neal
Republic Bank Corporation
Mr. E. F. White, Jr.

PATRONS
Mr. Warren A. Gilbert, Jr.
Mr. J. L. Huffines, Jr.
Mr. J. R. Latimer
Mr. & Mrs. George A. Linskie
Mr. Bill McCord

DONORS
Mr. & Mrs. J. M. Abernathy
Mr. Frank J. Bergman
Mr. J. A. Crichton
Mr. Al Davies
Mrs. L. C. Eubank
Mr. R. A. Goodson
Mr. John R. Hill, Jr.
Mrs. Jo Ann M. Hodges
Mrs. Jack McAuliff
Mrs. Ralph Plumlee
Dr. & Mrs. Lee Radford
Dr. Dan R. Sutherland
Mr. A. G. Wallace

CONTRIBUTORS
Mr. Andy Briscoe
Mr. Joe B. Byrd
Mrs. Donna L. Clack
Mrs. Mary M. Collins
Mrs. A. B. Conant, Jr.
Mr. Rex Corey
Mrs. J. Michael Cornwall
Mrs. Maria Dellinger
Mrs. F. T. Domas, Jr.
Mrs. Alberto G. Escobedo
Mr. Jerry L. Ewing
Mr. Robert W. Fredrickson

Mr. Bill Fuhrmeister
Mrs. Barbara B. Groom
Mrs. Jean Gross
Mrs. Bill Hall
Ms. Kim Hall
Ms. Vickie Hall
Mrs. Janice Hamblen
Mrs. Marjorie Harwell
Mrs. Joan G. Heye
Mrs. Laura Hobbs
Mrs. John Iacoponelli, Jr.
Mrs. Mary E. Johnson
Mrs. John J. Jones, III
Mrs. Lila M. Jones
Mrs. Betty J. Keeling
Mrs. Margaret M. Levy
Mrs. James D. Maines
Mrs. Ruth Long Mayrath
Mrs. Karen Meriwether
Mrs. Young Bok Mirkin
Mr. James P. Newberry, II
Mrs. James W. Phillips
Mrs. C. Durwood Pickle
Mrs. Charles D. Price, Jr.
Mrs. Anton A. Pustejovsky
Mrs. Charles E. Rogers
Mr. Robert P. Schafer
Mrs. Leslie Schreiber
Mrs. Fred D. Sewell
Mrs. R. W. Sexton
Mr. C. W. Shouse
Mrs. H. Peyton Smith
Mrs. Vera L. Smith
Mrs. Betty K. Solomon
Mrs. Alverda M. Squires
Mrs. Dorothy Starry
Mrs. Pat Greer Stonecipher
Mr. Floyd D. Trimble
Mrs. Delores J. Uhri
Mrs. Sheree Starry Wagner
Mrs. O. B. Williams, Jr.
Mr. Walker Williamson
Mrs. Marilyn J. Withey
Mrs. Eugene Zachary

CONTENTS

Flavors of Aggieland

FLAVORS OF AGGIELAND

Texas A&M, the state's oldest public institution of higher education, was established in 1876. The Morrill Act passed by Congress on July 2, 1862, provided for donation of public land to the states. By resolution of the Legislature of the State of Texas in November 1866, Texas agreed to provide for a college under the terms of the Morrill Act, but no institution was organized until the establishment of the Agricultural and Mechanical College of Texas by the Act of April 17, 1871. As the State of Texas grew, so did its land-grant institution. The main campus at College Station includes 5,142 acres and is the largest campus of any major institution of higher education in the nation.

Texas A&M was established as a military institution and the Corps of Cadets has played an important part in its history and development. The University is one of only three institutions with a full-time corps of cadets including all four branches of the service - Army, Air Force, Navy and Marine Corps.

In keeping with the diversified and expanded character of the institution, on August 23, 1963, the 58th Legislature of Texas changed the name of the Agricultural and Mechanical College to Texas A&M University.

Today, Texas A&M has established itself as a leader in many of the newer technological areas, such as the space, nuclear, computer, oceanographic and marine resources fields. Added emphasis has been placed in areas such as liberal arts and business administration and has enhanced its prominent role in other traditional fields.

The University's enrollment now exceeds 36,000, including more than 5,000 graduate students. To date, Texas A&M has awarded more than 116,000 academic degrees including more than 4,500 doctorates and almost 17,500 degrees at the master's level. As evidence of the recent growth and development of the University, more than one half of the advanced degrees awarded have been conferred in the last decade.

Taken from INROL 83-84

FIGHTIN' TEXAS AGGIE BAND

Precision gridiron performances are legend by the military uniform-ed Aggie Band, consisting of over 300 members. All who have witness-ed their spectacular and unique split-second precision performances agree they are without equal.

Bandsmen place practice and the Aggie Band's needs ahead of individual comfort and convenience, thus making the most of five to six one-to-two hour rehearsals each week. Their dedication is ably demonstrated on the gridiron.

Marching in rows of 12 men wide and 24 deep behind the senior-booted bugle rank, the Aggie Band starts its gridiron performances with a classic flourish and style which brings chills of pride. Critically timed maneuvers are integrated throughout the performance, attesting to the skill of the Band Director, his staff, the drum majors, commanders and members. Drills traditionally end with the block "T," with an excellence which makes Aggies and friends stand even taller.

The Fightin' Texas Aggie Band assures that we always win the halftimes!

THE SPIRIT OF AGGIELAND

Some may boast of prowess bold
Of the school they think so grand,
But there's a spirit can never be told,
It's the spirit of Aggieland.

(Chorus)
We are the Aggies — the Aggies are we,
True to each other as Aggies can be.
We've got to fight boys,
We've got to fight!
We've got to fight for Maron and White.
After they've boosted all the rest,
They will come and join the best,
For we are the Aggies — the Aggies are we
We're from Texas AMC.

(Second Chorus)
T-E-X-A-S A-G-G-I-E
Fight! Fight! Fight-fight-fight!
Fight! Maroon! White-white-white!
A-G-G-I-E
Texas! Texas A-M-C!
Gig'em Aggies 1-2-3
Farmers fight! Farmers fight!
Fight! Fight!
Farmers, farmers fight!

THE AGGIE WAR HYMN

Hullabaloo, Caneck! Caneck!
Hullabaloo, Caneck! Caneck!
Good-bye to Texas University,
So long to the Orange and White.
Good luck to dear old Texas Aggies,
They are the boys that show the real
* old fight.*
"The eyes of Texas are upon you. . ."
That is the song they sing so well,
So good-bye to Texas University,
We're going to beat you all to —
* Chig-ga-roo-gar-em!*
* Chig-ga-roo-gar-em!*
Rough! Tough!
Real Stuff! Texas A&M.

MEMORIAL STUDENT CENTER

". . . Here their memory shall remain forever fresh — — their sacrifices shall not be forgotten."

Dedicatory Tablet, MSC Entrance

Located near the center of the Texas A&M campus, the Memorial Student Center stands as a living monument to former students who made the supreme sacrifice in the defense of their country. As a part of the University Center complex, the MSC offers students and visitors vibrant activities, scrumptious dining, tasteful shopping and secure lodging. Adjacent to the Rudder Center, the handsome structure is only a few steps from the Theater Arts Center, Exhibit Hall and Rudder Tower.

The elegant soft tones of the MSC's Westminster chimes are a constant reminder of the beauty of the Texas A&M campus and the gratitude due those who made it possible.

A. WEGHORST '83

CORPS OF CADETS QUAD ARCHES

Symbolic of blending of modern beautification and traditional Aggie heritage, the Corps of Cadets Quad Arches provide an impressive entrance to the familiar Corps dormitories. The arches were added as a part of campus beautification coinciding with the 1976 Centennial celebration.

The Corps Dorm area provides countless memories and stories for Aggies who have been residents over the years. From this part of the campus, Texas A&M has provided proven leaders in the defense of the nation in war and peace time. The Quad Arches serve to remind all of the dedication of Aggies everywhere to the values of excellence in defending our country's democracy.

SYSTEMS ADMINISTRATION BUILDING

Changing the main entrance of the Texas A&M campus from the west to the east side to accommodate re-routing State Highway 6 demanded erection in 1932 of an impressive building facing east - the Systems Administration Building. Pride and dignity characterize the feelings of Aggies and friends driving the tree-lined esplanade toward this familiar and finely detailed structure.

Housing the offices of the Texas A&M University System, the building's grandeur is etched in the mind of the visitor reliving Texas history via the brass and terrazzo map on the main entrance hall floor. Add to this memories of the Corps of Cadets' "outfit" portraits, made on the steps of this monumental structure, and it announces "home" to Aggies everywhere.

A. Wieghorst '82

RUDDER TOWER

University activity abounds at the beautiful and modern Rudder Tower and Conference Center, named in honor of General Earl Rudder, Class of 1932, esteemed military leader and President of Texas A&M University, 1959-1970. The tower offers a panoramic view of the Texas A&M campus, which is a living statement of President Rudder's visionary planning and leadership for Texas A&M University and the State of Texas.

The Rudder Conference Center hosts distinguished leaders from throughout the nation and world attending a wide variety of conferences each year. Professional and cultural activities, continuing education and entertainment are provided in a setting of functional charm, characterized by its bubbling fountain. This area is a favorite meeting place for Texas Aggies, University Faculty and Staff and visitors to the campus.

ACADEMIC BUILDING

Stately and prominently within the Texas A&M profile projects the Academic Building rotunda atop four floors of classic design. In the plaza to the west stands the familiar bronze statue of Lawrence Sullivan Ross, President of Texas A&M and revered as "Soldier, Statesman and Knightly Gentleman."

Since its construction in 1914, the Academic Building has been the home of numerous administration offices, academic departments and classrooms. The beautiful rotunda section provides a vivid focal point for the natural beauty of large surrounding trees and enhancements by landscape design. The Academic Building represents the dignified heritage ingrained within the pride of Texas Aggies.

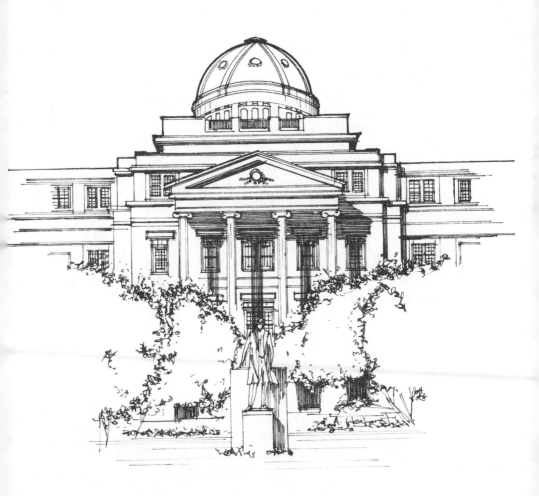

ALL FAITHS CHAPEL

Beautiful and inspiring as it blends in harmony with its surroundings, the All Faiths Chapel provides a place for Aggies and friends to find a moment of quiet meditation and communion with their God. The Chapel serves to enrich the spiritual life of the campus and is a cherished symbol of a tolerant and humanitarian institution.

Dedicated in 1958, the Chapel is the result of gifts of former students and friends who responded to the call: "Few or none of us could build a chapel alone; but the gifts of all of us together can make it a reality." It is the site of thousands of weddings, baptismals, services of all faiths and religious activities serving Texas Aggies.

THE COMMONS

An innovative living center known as "The Commons" is formed by four dormitories bounding a central courtyard. The Dunn-Krueger Aston-Mosher complex is a unique concept in student housing, offering modular integrated facilities for study, dining, relaxation and entertainment.

Constructed over a period from 1970-75, The Commons provide modern housing and services for approximately one thousand students. In 1972 the original units were designated the first women's dormitory on the A&M campus.

A. WEGHORST '83

ZACHRY ENGINEERING CENTER

Home of the largest engineering school in the United States, Zachry Engineering Center houses the largest and most advanced laboratories and teaching facilities. Built in 1971 and expanded in 1981, the facility is renowned worldwide for excellence in research and in the quality of its graduates in diversified engineering fields.

The Center is a veritable beehive of activity as it includes an efficient complex of facilities for classroom, laboratory, study and relaxation, as well as offices for faculty and staff. Thousands of Aggies consider it their "home-away-from-home," as they pursue rigorous engineering curricula demands.

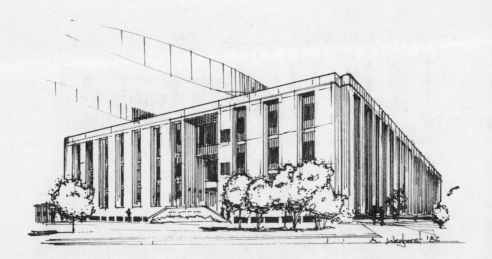

SBISA DINING HALL

Built in 1913 and named in honor of Bernard Sbisa, resourceful and beloved Steward who served Texas A&M for 50 years, Sbisa Hall has been a dining place for thousands of Aggies and their guests. Also its spacious accommodations have been the site of numerous dances and banquets which remain vividly in Aggie memories. Recent modernizing and renovations have made available a wide variety of foods, served rapidly and efficiently in response to students' active schedules.

Besides serving numerous Aggies, each of whom are celebrities in their own endeavors, Sbisa Hall has also served such dignitaries as Dwight Eisenhower, Franklin Roosevelt, numerous governors and prominent guests.

HARRINGTON EDUCATION CENTER

Completed in 1973, the eight story Harrington Education Center was the first of the high-rise buildings to grace the growing Texas A&M University skyline. The facility provides an ideal setting for excellence in education, as it contains the most modern facilities for the Colleges of Education and Liberal Arts.

Sophisticated equipment and arrangements are available to professors and students to ensure catalytic effect on curricular programs. The facility is dedicated to Dr. M. T. Harrington who served Texas A&M from 1924 to 1971, achieving every academic rank on the faculty and serving as President, Chancellor and President Emeritus. Texas A&M University's development through dedication to excellence in education is the result of Dr. Harrington's vision and leadership.

LANGFORD ARCHITECTURE CENTER

Modernistic and unique is the style of the Langford Architecture Center, located on the east side of the Texas A&M campus. The energy-efficient complex is named in honor of Ernest Langford, who served as head of the Architecture Department for 27 years and was mayor and civic leader of College Station for 23 years.

Graduates of Texas A&M College of Architecture have achieved a reputation for excellence throughout the world. Remembrances of the origin of their quest for excellence are renewed by many as they fondly recall the hours spent in the Langford Architecture Center.

OCEANOGRAPHY AND METEOROLOGY BUILDING

Fifteen stories of the finest classrooms and laboratories, dedicated to the sciences of Oceanography and Meteorology, tower above the Texas A&M campus. Dedicated in 1973 by international dignitaries including undersea explorer and environmental scientist, Jacques Cousteau, the Oceanography and Meteorology Building has been heralded as the best geosciences facility in the nation.

The finest laboratories provide students with the latest techonology advancements for studies of ocean dynamics, hydromechanics, air pollution meteorology, laser radar and infrared radiation. A prominent meteorological radar platform sits distinctively atop the building.

AGGIE TRADITIONS

BONFIRE

What began as a casual custom of gathering scrap wood in the 1920's has turned into the tradition of building and burning the world's largest bonfire. This custom also emerged as a symbol of the undying Aggie Spirit and the flaming desire "to beat the hell out of t.u."

The entire student body puts in its spare time and muscle in the few weeks it has to build and guard the bonfire. The bonfire is held the week of Thanksgiving prior to the Aggie-Longhorn game, on the intramural field south of Duncan Dining Hall. Yell practice that accompanies burning of the bonfire begins with the entrance of the yell leaders and the band playing the "Aggie War Hymn."

THE TWELFTH MAN

In Dallas on New Year's Day in 1922, Texas A&M played national champion Centre College in the Dixie Classic Football game. In this hard played game an underdog Aggie team (SWC Champs that year) was slowly but surely whipping a team which boasted three All-Americans. Unfortunately, the first half produced so many injuries for Texas A&M that Coach Dana X. Bible feared he wouldn't have enough men to finish the game. At that moment he called into the stands for King Gill, a reserve who had left the football team after the regular season to play basketball. Gill, who was spotting players and wasn't in uniform, willingly volunteered and donned the uniform of injured player Heine Weir. Gill never actually played, but he was the only man left on the bench when the game ended. Texas A&M won by an eight point margin: 22-14. Gill's readiness to play symbolized the willingness of the Aggie fans to support their team to the point of actually entering the scrimmage. This spirit has continued and even today the Aggie student body, known as the Twelfth Man, remains standing as a gesture of its loyalty and readiness for duty.

YELL PRACTICE

The purpose of any Aggie yell practice is to build enthusiasm and spirit for an upcoming athletic contest. Under the direction of yell leaders, Aggies show their support for the team by shouting Aggie yells with spirit and singing Aggie songs with pride.

The first Midnight Yell Practice was conceived as a lark by a small group of Aggies in 1932. Just before the t.u. game that year a handful of Aggies congregated in Puryear Hall. One of the group suggested having the Fish in the nearby dorms fall out and snake around the campus, ending with a yell practice in front of the YMCA Building at midnight. The small band of tradition-makers planted flares around the building and rousted the Corps. Even the band showed up and the Midnight Yell Practice was born.

After every home game, a yell practice is held to get ready for the next game. If the Aggie team was victorious, freshman students escort the yell leaders to the Fish Pond across from All Faiths Chapel and hold yell practice in that area. If, unfortunately, the team was outscored, the fans remain in the stands and the yell practice is held there. Aggie yell practice creates a strong sense of pride in all who participate.

REVEILLE

Since 1931 there has always been at least one female member of the Corps of Cadets. Her name has been respected and her honor held high. The lady's name is — Reveille.

Texas A&M's mascots have not always been registered Collies; Reveille I was a stray. A carload of Aggies was returning to the campus after a football game in 1931. On the highway a small black and white dog appeared suddenly in the car's headlights. The driver was unable to stop before he hit the dog. They bundled her into the car and took her to campus with them, where she slept in one of the dorms.

The dog was dubbed Reveille by her newfound friends after she yelped repeatedly as the bugler played Reveille the next morning. In a short time her friends included every cadet in the Corps. When the band took the field at halftime of her first football game, Reveille headed the march and performed as if she were the featured entertainer. She won the hearts of the crowd, just as she had the students, and her performance earned her the title of Official Mascot of Texas A&M.

When Reveille died on January 18, 1944, she was given a formal military funeral in the center of the gridiron on Kyle Field. She now lies at the entrance to Kyle Field. Two other Texas A&M mascots, Reveille

II and III, are buried beside her. Reveille IV currently serves Texas A&M with the dignity and spirit of her predecessors.

Today, Reveille is maintained by one Corps unit, Company E-2, with one sophomore cadet being responsible for her care during the year. Reveille spends the summer with her new master for the upcoming year, so that both may become better acquainted.

SILVER TAPS

The ceremony of Silver Taps is dedicated to the deceased Aggie and is a solemn and serious event. In 1898 the first Silver Taps was held for Lawrence Sullivan Ross with three rifle volleys in front of Old Main. Silver Taps was held there until Old Main burned in 1912; then it was moved to Goodwin Hall. In 1918 the ceremony was moved to the Academic Building, built on the site of Old Main. Over the years, new traditions were added; in the 1920's the flag was put at half-mast through the day of Silver Taps. During the 30's the special music "Silver Taps" was arranged and played by two buglers. The three volley salute was added, and now six buglers play. Today, the MSC chimes ring out prior to Silver Taps to announce this ceremony of loyalty and respect.

Today, just as in 1898, Aggies attend Silver Taps willingly to honor the Aggie and say good-bye as only Aggies do. On the day of Silver Taps, the flag in front of the Academic Building is at half-mast and notices are posted on the doors of the library, Rudder Tower Complex, and the Memorial Student Center. The Ross Volunteer Firing Squad marches in a slow cadence to the statue of Sul Ross and fires three volleys with seven rifles. After the salute, "Silver Taps" is played three times. This concludes the ceremony but not the feelings of respect and honor.

ELEPHANT WALK

Just before the annual clash between Texas A&M and t.u., seniors gather between the flagpole and the Academic Building, form a single line and wander about the campus like dying elephants seeking a secluded spot to end their days. By this day the bonfire is already built, and the seniors are no longer of any use to the Twelfth Man. What is more appropriate for a totally useless Aggie to end his days than in this pachydermatous promenade?

FINAL REVIEW

To mark the end of each year for the Corps of Cadets, a special review is held on the Parade Grounds across from the Memorial Student Center. On the day of spring commencement and commissioning, two parades are held for Final Review. The first parade includes every cadet. For seniors, this occasion marks the last time they are members of the Corps of Cadets. For the second parade, the seniors turn over the "reign" to the juniors and watch as the new officers assume command.

As Final Review ends, so ends the Corps of Cadets for that academic year. The Corps does not operate as a unit during the summer months but begins again with the start of the fall semester.

TEXAS A&M SENIOR CLASS RING

Design of the class ring at A&M is as deep in symbolism as it is in tradition. The shield on the top of the ring symbolizes protection of the good reputation of the alma mater. The 13 stripes in the shield refer to the 13 original states and symbolize the intense patriotism of graduates and undergraduates of A&M. The five stars in the shield refer to phases of development of the student; mind or intellect, body, spiritual attainment, emotional poise and integrity of character. The eagle is symbolic of agility and power, and ability to reach great heights as ambitions.

One side of the ring symbolizes the seal of the State of Texas authorized by the constitution in 1845. The five-pointed star is encircled with a wreath of olive or laurel leaves symbolizing achievement and a desire for peace and live oak leaves symbolizing the strength to fight. They are joined at the bottom by a circled ribbon to show the necessity of joining these two traits to accomplish one's ambition to serve.

The other side with its ancient cannon, saber, and rifle symbolizes that the men of Texas fought for their land and are determined to defend their homeland. The saber stands for valor and confidence. The rifle and cannon are symbols of preparedness and defense. The crossed flags of the United States and Texas recognize the dual allegiance to nation and state.

Reprinted from *The Texas Aggie*
October 1969

An undergraduate wears the ring with the class number toward him until the annual Ring Dance. At that time the ring is turned around so that it no longer faces the wearer - it faces the world.

ASSOCIATION OF FORMER STUDENTS

Since its founding in 1879, the Association of Former Students of Texas A&M University has dedicated itself to serve the University, its students, faculty, staff, and former students. Its objectives are to promote the interests and welfare of Texas A&M, to perpetuate the ties of friendship formed during college days and to strengthen the programs of the Association.

Everyone receiving a degree from Texas A&M is automatically a member of the Association, which has more than 100,000 Aggies and is one of the strongest alumni associations in the world. Anyone who has ever attended Texas A&M may become a member upon request, as may any friend of the University and the Association. Many permanent facilities on campus have been made possible through Association support, including the Memorial Student Center, Cain Olympic swimming pool, All Faiths Chapel, the campus golf course, the Forsyth Alumni Center, Cain Hall, University Library expansion and the Visitors' Information Center.

PARENTS' DAY

Each year in April, one couple receives the honor of being named Aggie Parents of the year. This award is presented at the ceremony on Parents' Day. This special event is sponsored by Student Government and is shared by Corps members, non-Corps students and their parents. Other activities of the day include ceremonies to announce the Gathright Academic Awards, the Corps of Cadets awards, the Buck Weirus Spirit Awards, various sports events, a traditions and yell practice program, concerts, a chapel service and a reception for visiting parents.

THE MUSTER TRADITION

Muster was first held in 1883 when Aggies met on June 26 to "live over again our college days, the victories and defeats won and lost upon drill ground and classroom. Let every alumni answer a roll call," wrote the former students, then known as ex-cadets. These early meetings were usually parties and banquets held during the annual commencement activities. The tradition was soon to be held on a permanent date.

During the late 1890's, the Corps made annual visits to the San Jacinto battlefield near Houston to participate in sham battles and maneuvers followed by a parade down Houston's Main Street on April 21.

In the early 1900's, a Track and Field Day, a series of competitive athletic events similar to intramurals, was held every April 21. When the events were called off in 1903, a "determined student body, 300 strong, marched in orderly military precision to the home of President David F. Houston to insist upon some observance of the anniversary of the battle that won Texas' Independence." April 21 marks the day Sam Houston's small band of volunteers defeated Santa Anna's troops, freeing Texas from Mexican rule in 1836.

It was also agreed that, in addition to honoring the freedom of Texas, April 21 would be a time to pay homage to all students and former students who have passed on, and that some living comrade would answer "Here" when the roll call for the absent was read.

During World War I, groups of Aggies met in foxholes all over Europe and at Army posts in America, but no Musters were held on campus.

In 1923, the former students provided Aggies with an opportunity to "meet old friends again and live over the days at College Station" by planning a state and nationwide rally of former students. "If there is an A&M man in one hundred miles of you, you are expected to get together, eat a little and live over the days you spent at the A&M College of Texas," urged the March, 1923, *Texas Aggie*. By 1929 meetings had become international.

In 1942, A&M Muster gained national recognition when it was held at Corregidor Island in the Philippines. Fifteen days before the fall of the island, 25 men, led by General George Moore '08, "mustered in the dim recesses of the Rock and answered 'Here' for their dead classmates." Wartime brought Aggies together in almost every area of the world, and two men were reported to have held Muster in a submarine.

And so it has been over the years, since that small group started what has come to be one of our greatest traditions. The Muster is symbolic of the great loyalty which binds Aggies to their school and to each other.

The Muster is more than a ceremony. It represents a pledge and responsibility of A&M men and women which has been handed down from generation to generation from year to year.

It is a way for each of us to renew each year our loyalty and unity which constitute the basic foundation of our friendship for each other and love and devotion for our school.

Reprinted from the book entitled,
*"The Centennial History of the
Association of Former Students
of Texas A&M"*

Celebrities & Friends

CELEBRITIES AND FRIENDS

Achievements and generous spirit which make a person very special identify the celebrities and friends who have graciously shared their favorite recipes with us. Each contributor has star status, whether known worldwide or recognized locally. Join with these celebrities and friends as they show us how they make "Hullabaloo in *Their* Kitchens."

RONALD REAGAN,
PRESIDENT OF THE UNITED STATES

 President Ronald Reagan's favorite recipe would be delicious served with his wife's favorite chicken recipe. The President sent this entry.

President Reagan's
Favorite Macaroni and Cheese

½	pound macaroni	1	teaspoon dry mustard
1	teaspoon butter	3	cups grated sharp cheese
1	egg, beaten	1	cup milk
1	teaspoon salt	1	tablespoon hot water

Boil macaroni in water until tender and drain thoroughly. Stir in butter and egg. Mix mustard and salt with hot water and add to milk. Add cheese leaving enough to sprinkle on top. Pour into buttered casserole, add milk, sprinkle with remaining cheese. Bake at 350° for about 45 minutes or until custard is set and top is crusty.

NANCY REAGAN

First Lady of the United States, Nancy Reagan, sent us this favorite recipe with her best wishes.

Baja California Chicken

8 boned chicken breasts	4 tablespoons olive oil
Seasoning salt and pepper, to taste	4 tablespoons tarragon vinegar
2 cloves garlic, crushed	⅔ cup dry sherry

Sprinkle chicken with seasoning salt and pepper. Crush garlic into oil and vinegar in skillet. Sauté chicken pieces until golden brown, turning frequently. Remove; place in baking dish. Pour sherry over pieces and place in 350° oven for 10 minutes. Serves 8.

GEORGE BUSH

Vice President George Bush shares one of his favorites, which he borrowed from a dear friend, Antoinette Hatfield, wife of Senator Mark O. Hatfield.

Lemon Bars

For Lemon Lovers of America!

1 cup margarine	2 cups flour
2 cups powdered sugar	

Mix ingredients (batter will be stiff) and spread in jelly roll pan. Bake 15 minutes at 350° until pale tan. Cool.

FROSTING:

4 teaspoons lemon juice	1 teaspoon baking powder
Rind of 2 lemons, grated	4 tablespoons flour
4 eggs, well beaten	1 cup shredded coconut, optional
2 cups sugar	

Mix all ingredients and pour over baked crust. Bake another 25 minutes at 350°. Cool and cut in squares.

MRS. LYNDON B. JOHNSON

Former First Lady of the United States, Mrs. Lyndon B. (Lady Bird) Johnson is another native Texan who wanted to share a favorite recipe enjoyed from the Pedernales River to the Potomac.

Shrimp Squash Casserole

1½ pounds yellow squash, about 3 cups
¾ cup raw shrimp
2 tablespoons butter
2 tablespoons flour
½ teaspoon salt
⅛ teaspoon pepper
1 cup chicken broth (use bouillon cube)

½ cup whipping cream or 1 small (5.33 ounces) can chilled evaporated milk
1 tablespoon instant minced onion
½ cup coarse bread crumbs
¼ cup grated Parmesan cheese
1 tablespoon butter, melted

Wash and dry squash; cut crosswise into ¼ inch slices. Thoroughly rinse shrimp under cold water and drain. Heat 2 tablespoons butter in saucepan. Blend in flour, salt and pepper. Cook until it bubbles. Remove from heat and add chicken broth gradually, stirring constantly. Bring to boil for 1 or 2 minutes. Blend in cream and minced onion. Add raw shrimp. Put layer of squash in bottom of 1½ quart casserole; spoon half shrimp sauce over squash. Repeat layers. Cover tightly and set in 400° oven for 30 minutes. Meanwhile, toss crumbs and Parmesan cheese with melted butter. After 30 minutes baking time, remove casserole from oven; reduce heat to 350°; remove cover and top with bread crumbs. Bake another 15 minutes or until crumbs are golden brown.

TEXAS A&M UNIVERSITY
CORPS OF CADETS

Spirit, comradeship and dedication to excellence have formed the traditions surrounding the Texas A&M University Corps of Cadets. Men excelling in military leadership and in personal endeavors have credited discipline and precision qualities acquired as members of the Corps. Aggie families and friends of all ages stand taller with pride as the Corps passes in review.

Still the centerpiece of traditions at Texas A&M University, the Corps continues to provide superb leadership skills and development as it molds boys into men of character. The familiar drumbeat cadence and the ruffle of unfurled flags increase the pulse of the thousands of members and former students who cherish the private memories of challenge and achievement as members of the Corps of Cadets.

BILL CLEMENTS

Rita Clements offers former Texas Governor Bill Clements' favorite, served frequently in the Governor's Mansion in Austin.

First Lady of Texas Chicken Enchiladas

3 large chicken breasts	1 teaspoon ground cumin
1 cup chopped onion	½ teaspoon salt
1 clove garlic, minced	½ teaspoon dried oregano,
2 tablespoons margarine	crushed
1 can (16 ounces) tomatoes, cut up	½ teaspoon dried basil, crushed
1 can (8 ounces) tomato sauce	12 corn tortillas
¼ cup chopped green chilies	2½ cups shredded Monterey Jack cheese
1 teaspoon sugar	¾ cup sour cream

In saucepan, simmer chicken breasts in water to cover until tender. Drain and carefully remove skin and bones. Sprinkle chicken with a little salt. Cut into 12 strips and set aside. In saucepan, cook onion and garlic in margarine until tender; add tomatoes, tomato sauce, chilies, sugar, cumin, salt, oregano and basil. Bring to boil and reduce heat. Simmer covered for 20 minutes. Remove from heat. Dip each tortilla in tomato mixture to soften. Place one piece of chicken and about 2 tablespoons of cheese on each tortilla, roll up and place seam down in long baking dish. Blend sour cream into remaining sauce mixture, pour over tortillas, sprinkle with remaining cheese. Cover and bake at 350° until heated thoroughly.

PHIL GRAMM

 United States Representative Phil Gramm, a former Professor of Economics at Texas A&M University, submitted this recipe, which he claims is the best cheesecake he's ever tasted!

Cheesecake - Bon Appetit

CRUST:
¾ cup coarsely ground walnuts
¾ cup finely crushed graham crackers

3 tablespoons melted unsalted butter

FILLING:
4 packages (8 ounces each) cream cheese, room temperature
4 eggs

1¼ cups sugar
1 tablespoon fresh lemon juice
2 teaspoons vanilla

TOPPING:
2 cups sour cream
¼ cup sugar

1 teaspoon vanilla

GLAZE:
1 quart medium strawberries
1 jar (12 ounces) red raspberry jelly

1 tablespoon cornstarch
¼ cup Cointreau
¼ cup water

Position rack in center of oven; preheat to 350°. Lightly butter 9 or 10 inch spring form pan.

CRUST: Combine walnuts, graham cracker crumbs and butter. Press compactly onto bottom of pan.

FILLING: Beat cream cheese in large bowl until smooth. Add eggs, sugar, lemon juice and vanilla. Beat all thoroughly and spoon over crust. Set pan over baking sheet to catch dripping, if any. Bake 10 inch cake 40 to 45 minutes, or 9 inch cake 50 to 55 minutes. Remove from oven and let stand at room temperature for 15 minutes. Retain oven temperature at 350°.

TOPPING: Combine sour cream, sugar and vanilla and blend well. Cover and refrigerate. When cake has finished baking, spoon topping over starting at center and extending to ½ inch of edge. Return to oven and bake 5 minutes longer. Let cool, then refrigerate for at least 24 hours, preferably 2 to 3 days.

GLAZE: Several hours before serving, wash and hull berries and let dry on paper towel. Combine a little jelly with cornstarch in saucepan and mix well. Add remaining jelly, Cointreau and water. Cook over medium heat stirring frequently until thickened and clear, about 5 minutes. Cool to lukewarm, stirring occasionally. Using knife, loosen cake from pan, remove spring form. Arrange berries over top and spoon glaze over berries. Refrigerate until glaze is set.

OLIN "TIGER" TEAGUE

Revered friend of Texas A&M, the late Congressman Olin "Tiger" Teague '32, enjoyed a favorite salad, as prepared by his wife, Freddie, who shares it with us.

Avocado Salad

1   package (3 ounces) lime or
   lemon Jell-O
1   cup hot water
1   cup minced celery
1   package (8 ounces) cream
   cheese

½   cup mayonnaise
1   carton (6 ounces) frozen
   avocado guacamole
Salt and pepper to taste

Mix Jell-O and boiling water, cool slightly and add celery. Mix cheese, mayonnaise and thawed avocado. Add salt and pepper to taste. Blend with Jell-O mixture. Pour into oiled dish. Cover and chill.

PHYLLIS GEORGE

 From the Kentucky Governor's Mansion, former Miss Texas and Miss America, and now First Lady of Kentucky, Phyllis George Brown sends this Southern recipe.

Grits Souffle

1   cup medium white sauce
(bring to boil and remove
from heat)

5   tablespoons grated
Parmesan cheese

4   tablespoons grated
Cheddar cheese

1   cup cooked grits

4   egg whites, beaten stiff
(not dry)

Butter a 7 inch souffle dish and coat with Parmesan cheese. Mix prepared white sauce, cheeses and grits. Fold in beaten egg whites. Pour mixture into prepared souffle dish and bake for 40 minutes at 325°. Serves 4. *ENJOY!*

C.E. "PAT" OLSEN

 C.E. "Pat" Olsen '23, for whom the 5,000 seat TAMU baseball stadium, Olsen Field, is named, pitches a no-hitter with his favorite cookie recipe.

Oatmeal Cookies

1   cup sugar

½ cup Crisco

½ cup butter

2   eggs, beaten

2   cups flour

1   teaspoon soda

1   teaspoon cinnamon

⅛ teaspoon salt

2   cups dry oatmeal

1   cup chopped pecans

1   cup raisins or currants

Cream sugar, Crisco and butter in large bowl. Add eggs, flour, soda, cinnamon and salt. Beat until mixed well. Fold in oatmeal, pecans and raisins by hand. Chill 2 to 4 hours. Drop by teaspoonsful on slightly greased cookie sheet. Bake at 375° for 12 to 15 minutes. As soon as cookies cool on cake racks, put in jar or tins that can be tightly closed. Yields 9 dozen.

BILL CLAYTON

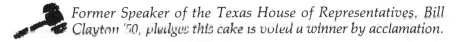

Former Speaker of the Texas House of Representatives, Bill Clayton '50, pledges this cake is voted a winner by acclamation.

Coconut Pound Cake

CAKE:

2 cups sugar	6 eggs
1 cup shortening	2 cups flour, sifted
1 teaspoon vanilla	1 can (3½ ounces) coconut
1 teaspoon butter flavoring	Dash salt

SAUCE:

1 cup sugar	½ cup water
2 teaspoons coconut flavoring	

CAKE: Preheat oven to 325°. Cream shortening and sugar. Add vanilla and butter flavoring. Add eggs 1 at a time. Mix well using high speed of electric mixer. Sift in flour and salt, adding slowly. Fold in coconut. Pour into 10 inch tube pan that has been well greased and dusted with flour. Bake 1 hour and 20 minutes, until toothpick inserted into center comes out clean.

COCONUT SAUCE: While cake is in its last baking minutes, bring sauce ingredients to boil for about 1 minute.

FOR HARD GLAZE CRUST: Remove cake from oven and brush or pour sauce over hot cake in pan. Put back in oven for not over 5 minutes. Remove cake from pan at once.

FOR SOFT GLAZE CRUST: When cake is done, remove from pan immediately. Brush on sauce with pastry brush while cake is still warm. *Remove large air bubbles from batter before baking by tapping pan lightly on work surface or by cutting gently through the batter with a knife.*

SUSAN GURLEY McBEE

Susan Gurley McBee '69, Texas House of Representatives, District 70, proclaims this recipe has been featured at everything, ranging from church suppers to ladies' luncheons, to large political gatherings — always tops in the polls!

Del Rio Chicken Spaghetti

2   cans (3 pounds, 4 ounces each) whole chicken in broth
1   package (1 pound) spaghetti, broken in thirds
¼   cup margarine
3   bell peppers, diced
3   onions, diced
3   cups diced celery

2   jars (4 ounces each) pimientos, diced
1   can (8 ounces) mushrooms, sliced
4   cans (10¾ ounces each) cream of mushroom soup
1   pound Kraft American cheese, grated
Salt and pepper to taste

Drain chicken, saving broth. Cook spaghetti in broth until pasta is al dente. There should be some broth left in the pot after cooking. Sauté diced vegetables in margarine until soft. Skin and bone chicken and chop into pieces. Mix all ingredients together in large bowl or pot. If mixture seems too dry, add a little extra chicken broth. Pour into dishes and bake at 350° for 30 to 45 minutes.

This recipe fills two 3 quart and one 2 quart Pyrex dishes, or 1 oven roaster. It freezes beautifully. It's lovely to have in your freezer for quick and easy entertaining.

This recipe may be doubled or tripled for a large gathering. Serve with curried peach halves, garlic bread and a green salad.

H. R. "BUM" BRIGHT

H. R. "Bum" Bright '43, Chairman of the Texas A&M Board of Regents, has a sweet tooth! His wife, Peggy, dedicated supporter of A&M Mothers' Clubs, submitted his favorite dessert recipes.

Peppermint Ice Cream

1 cup sugar	1 cup half-and-half
¼ teaspoon salt	2 cups whipping cream
1½ cups milk	8 ounces peppermint sticks,
4 egg yolks	crushed
1 tablespoon vanilla	

Measure sugar and salt into heavy saucepan. Lightly beat egg yolks and milk and add to sugar mixture. Cook over low heat stirring constantly until mixture just begins to bubble. Remove from heat and add vanilla and half the peppermint, finely crushed. Stir until melted. Let cool. Add half-and-half, whipping cream and other half of peppermint candy, coarsely crushed. Pour into can of electric freezer. Makes ½ gallon ice cream.

Cream Cheese Pound Cake

1 package (8 ounces) cream cheese	1½ teaspoons vanilla
¾ cup margarine or butter	4 eggs
1½ cups sugar	2 cups cake flour
	1½ teaspoons baking powder

Combine softened cream cheese and margarine. Add sugar and vanilla. Beat until very smooth and fluffy. Add eggs one at a time. Sift flour and baking powder and add to creamed mixture gradually. Pour into greased and floured Bundt pan or 9x5 inch loaf pan. Bake at 325° for 1 hour and 20 minutes. Cool about 5 minutes and then remove from pan. *This converts to a marvelous holiday fruit cake.* Increase butter to 1 cup. Toss about 1 cup candied fruit or raisins with an additional ¼ cup flour and add ½ cup chopped pecans.

JOE C. RICHARDSON, JR.

Joe C. Richardson, Jr. '49, Board of Regents, Texas A&M, sends this recipe, which all should love.

Sour Cream Pralines

½ cup butter	1 cup whipping cream
1 pound light brown sugar	2 teaspoons vanilla
2 cups sugar	1 pound pecan halves
1 cup dairy sour cream	Dash salt

Melt butter over low heat, add brown sugar, stir until dissolved and well blended. Add sugar. Stir to blend. Add sour cream and whipping cream. Blend well and add salt. When well blended, increase to medium heat, stirring constantly to avoid scorching. Cook to soft ball stage (238° on candy thermometer), then remove from heat, cool briefly. Add vanilla and pecans. Beat until creamy. Drop by teaspoons on waxed paper. When firm, remove from waxed paper and store in a tightly closed container.

NORMAN MOSER

Norman Moser '37, Board of Regents, sent this recipe from his home in DeKalb, Texas.

Marinated Tomatoes

⅓ cup wine vinegar	1 teaspoon salt
1 cup Wesson oil	½ teaspoon pepper
1 green pepper, chopped	Tomatoes, skinned and sliced

Mix vinegar and oil with green pepper and seasonings; pour over skinned, sliced tomatoes and refrigerate for several hours before serving.

JOHN B. COLEMAN

John B. Coleman, M.D., Board of Regents, says this is a different main dish you'll enjoy.

Sassy Zucchini

1	pound ground beef	1	teaspoon salt
1	medium onion, chopped	¾	cup water
1	can (16 ounces) tomatoes, cut up	1	cup packaged, precooked rice
1	envelope (1.5 ounces) spaghetti sauce mix	4	cups zucchini, cut in 1 inch strips

In large skillet, cook ground beef and onion until meat is browned and onion is tender. Mix in undrained tomatoes, water, spaghetti sauce mix, salt, and bring to boil. Stir in rice and zucchini pieces. Cover pan tightly and simmer 15 to 20 minutes or until zucchini is tender, stirring occasionally. Serves 6.

ROBERT G. CHERRY

Executive Secretary to the Board of Regents, Robert G. Cherry, submits the following colorful (maroon) dish, full of Fightin' Texas Aggie Spirit!

Gig 'Em Chili

Put 3 pounds of ground beef in a pot. Coarse ground is better. Add salt, barely cover with water and simmer for 2 hours and then add chili powder until it's Aggie maroon, at least 1 ounce. Add a few dashes of cumin. Put in a number 2 can of tomatoes, or small can of tomato paste, and a chopped onion. Simmer for another hour. It's better on the second day, best on the third day if it lasts that long. Go light on skimming — greasy is good! Serve with crisp crackers and Tabasco sauce as you like it.

WILLIAM A. McKENZIE

William A. McKenzie '44, Board of Regents, offers his favorite chili recipe, which has conveniences galore.

Snowbird Chili

3 pounds ground beef
2 tablespoons flour
3 teaspoons cumin seeds
3 tablespoons chili powder
2 or 3 pods of garlic, place on toothpicks for easy removal after cooking

1 package (1.25 ounces) French's chili mix
1 can (46 ounces) tomato juice
Salt and pepper to taste

Brown meat. Add other ingredients, mixing flour with a little tomato juice to dissolve. Simmer all for 2 hours. *This recipe may be cooked ahead.* Freezes well. May be used as a dip, too.

GARRY MAURO

Garry Mauro '70, Commissioner of General Land Office, says of this recipe, "I got the following recipe where every good Aggie gets his favorite recipes - from my mother!"

Beer Bread

3 cups self-rising flour
1 teaspoon baking soda
½ cup sugar

1 can regular beer
1 stick butter or margarine

Combine flour, soda, sugar and beer. Mix well. Divide dough into 3 small or 2 medium pans. Let set for 10 minutes. Melt butter and pour over dough. Bake at 350° for 45 minutes.

Variation: For cheese or onion bread, add 1 cup grated Cheddar cheese or ½ envelope Lipton's onion soup mix.

REVEILLE

This is Reveille's all-time favorite recipe! (Translated from Reveille's barks and wags by John T. White '76, Assistant Area Coordinator-Corps and Advisor to Company E-2 and Reveille.)

Reveille's Favorite Dish

Preheat bonfire at 400°

1 pound ground steer meat, using Longhorn type if possible	2 ounces cat meat
	2 ounces frog legs, chopped
2 ounces ground horse meat, Red Raider and Mustang type	1 cup Gravy Train chunks, crushed
	1 owl's egg
	½ cup flour
2 ounces bear meat	2 12 ounce hog chops

Mix the first 7 ingredients in a large bowl. Make sure that all the ingredients are mixed well. Trim any excess fat off the chops and make a diagonal cut along the side of each chop. Stuff the meat mixture into each chop, filling each cavity well. Dredge the chops in flour and broil for 45 minutes over a roaring bonfire, basting the chops with butter. *Serve immediately on a bed of 'COTTON', preferably on New Year's Day.*

TOM LANDRY

Coach Tom Landry, Dallas Cowboys' famous mentor, says these popover-type corn bread muffins are his favorite, and should "score" at your home, too!

Tom Landry's Corn Bread Muffins

1¼ cups cornmeal	½ tablespoon sugar
1 teaspoon salt	2 cups milk
2 tablespoons baking powder	2 small eggs
¾ cup flour	2 tablespoons shortening

Sift dry ingredients. Beat eggs well. Add a little more than half of the milk to the eggs and beat well. Add egg mixture to flour mixture and beat well. Stir in rest of milk and melted shortening. Fill hot, well greased muffin tins about half full. Bake at 500° for about 15 minutes. Makes 12 muffins. *500° is the correct temperature!!*

DR. ARTHUR G. HANSEN

Dr. Arthur G. Hansen, Chancellor of Texas A&M University System, and an avid fisherman, submits one of his all-time favorites from Door County, Wisconsin.

Fish Boil

2 gallons water
1 pound salt
12 new potatoes, scrubbed, one tip off each
6 large carrot chunks or 6 medium carrots, scraped

12 small white onions
6 pieces fresh corn
12 whitefish steaks, each cut about 3 to 4 inches thick
Partially clarified butter
Chopped parsley

Using a large stockpot with a wire basket inside, pour in water and half the salt. Bring to boil over high heat. Keep to slow to medium boil and add potatoes. After potatoes have cooked 10 minutes, add carrots. Test potatoes. They should take 20 to 25 minutes in all. When carrots have cooked for 5 minutes, add onions and corn. When the potatoes and carrots are about 8 minutes away from being done (vegetables should have a little resistance when pierced with a knife), add remaining salt and the fish. Ladle corn into one large or 6 small tureens. Top with carrots, onions and potatoes. Place fish on top to serve, with partially clarified butter and sprinkling of chopped parsley. Serves 6.

FRANK E. VANDIVER

Renée Vandiver, wife of Texas A&M University President, Frank E. Vandiver, sends their favorite recipe, which she says may be made ahead of time and frozen before it is baked. Serve with French bread and a big green salad.

Renée's Tamale Pie

MEAT FILLING:

2 pounds top ground round or extra lean ground beef
1 large onion, chopped fine
1 can (8 ounces) tomato sauce

1 chicken bouillon cube
4 tablespoons chili powder (more if desired)
½ cup water
Tabasco sauce to taste

MUSH:

3 cups water
1 beef or chicken bouillon cube

1 teaspoon salt
1 cup cold water
1 cup cornmeal

MEAT FILLING: Brown meat with onion; add remaining ingredients. Cook 10 to 15 minutes. This mixture should be moist enough to spread.

MUSH: Heat 3 cups water with bouillon cube and salt. Mix 1 cup cold water with cornmeal. Pour cornmeal and water into boiling water, stirring constantly with whisk. This lumps if you do not stir *as it is added.* Cook until thick. Pour *half* of mush into 2 quart casserole dish; let cool until firm. Add meat filling and pour remaining mush over top. Sprinkle with paprika and bake 30 minutes at 350°. Serves 6. *This may be made ahead and frozen before it is baked.*

DR. FRANK HUBERT

Dr. Frank W. R. Hubert, former Chancellor of Texas A&M University, generously shares his favorite recipe, as prepared by wife, Mary Julia.

Chicken Salad

2 whole chickens	2 cans (4¼ ounces each)
1 medium onion	pitted black olives, diced
1 full stalk celery	1 rib celery, diced
Salt and pepper to taste	1½ cups mayonnaise
6 hard cooked eggs, diced	

Cut up chickens and boil covered in water, together with onion and stems from stalk of celery. Salt and pepper to taste. Cook about 2 hours until chicken is done. Remove celery and onion and discard. Debone chicken and dice into large mixing bowl. Kitchen scissors help. Add eggs, olives and celery. Stir in mayonnaise, mixing thoroughly. Serves 10 to 12.

M. T. HARRINGTON

President Emeritus of Texas A&M University, M. T. Harrington '22, affirms these cookies are his favorite between-meal nibbles.

Cream Cheese Cookies

½ cup butter or margarine, softened	1 cup sugar
	1 cup flour
1 package (3 ounces) cream cheese, softened	½ cup chopped pecans
	1 teaspoon vanilla

Blend butter with cream cheese. Mix in flour and sugar. Add nuts and vanilla. Drop from teaspoon onto ungreased cookie sheets. Bake in 350° oven for 10 to 12 minutes or until edges of cookies are brown. *Makes about 5 dozen chewy cookies.*

MARGARET RUDDER

Margaret Rudder, wife of the Past President of A&M University, the late Earl Rudder '32, submitted a favorite recipe which serves many guests. (Margaret says it may be divided into portions and frozen, if you don't have a houseful of Aggies around to devour it immediately.)

Chicken Rice Casserole

3 whole chickens, cooked; reserve broth
2 boxes (6¼ ounces each) long grain and wild rice with herbs
3 cans (10¾ ounces each) cream of chicken soup
1 can (10¾ ounces) cream of mushroom soup

1 pint half-and-half or 1 can (13 ounces) condensed milk
2 cups grated Cheddar cheese
2 cups chopped onion
2 cups chopped celery
2 cups chopped green peppers
½ cup margarine

Boil chickens, debone and cut meat into chunks. Prepare rice in chicken broth. Drain excess liquid. Stir in soups, half-and-half and 1 cup of cheese. Sauté onion, celery and green peppers in margarine. Stir into chicken mixture. Pour into large baking pan. Top with remaining cheese and bake until cheese melts in a 350° oven. Serves 25.

DR. JARVIS E. MILLER

 Past President of Texas A&M University, Dr. Jarvis E. Miller '50, sent this recipe — a favorite of Aggies, always.

Strawberry Shortcake

1	cup butter (or margarine-butter mixed)	2	teaspoons baking powder
2	cups sugar	½	teaspoon salt
2	eggs	2	teaspoons vanilla
1	cup sweet milk		Fresh strawberries
3	cups sifted flour		Whipped cream

Stir butter to soften. Gradually add sugar, and cream until light and fluffy. Add eggs, one at a time, beating well after each. Sift dry ingredients and add alternately with milk to creamed mixture beginning and ending with flour. Beat well after each addition. Add vanilla and stir until well blended. Pour into three greased, floured 9 inch layer pans. Bake at 350° for about 20 minutes. Cool on cake rack for 10 minutes. Loosen around edges and remove from pans. At dessert time, slice a generous portion of cake and top with fresh strawberries and whipped cream. *Enjoy a treat!*

DR. ROBERT L. WALKER

 Dr. Robert L. Walker '58, Vice President for Development, Texas A&M, submits this master plan for his favorite recipe.

Cheesy Chivy Potato Casserole

6	potatoes, cooked and cooled	1	teaspoon salt
½	cup butter	¼	teaspoon pepper
2	cups grated Cheddar cheese	2	cups sour cream
		⅓	cup chopped green onions

Butter a 2 quart casserole. Grate potatoes or cut in chunks. In pan over low heat, combine butter and cheese, stirring until cheese melts. Remove from heat and stir in salt, pepper, sour cream and onions. Pour over potatoes; stir lightly and turn into prepared casserole. Dot with butter and bake at 350° for 30 minutes.

DR. JOHN KOLDUS

Dr. John Koldus, Vice President for Student Services, Texas A&M University, shares a tasty recipe from his Hungarian heritage.

Hungarian Stuffed Cabbage

1 to 1½ pounds ground beef or mixture of half ground beef, half ground pork	¾ cup white rice
	1 head cabbage
	1 can (28 ounces) whole tomatoes
¼ cup chopped onion	½ can water
Salt and pepper to taste	

Brown meat and onions. Salt and pepper to taste. Precook rice and drain; mix with meat and onions. Core cabbage and steam in covered saucepan about 15 minutes until leaves are pliable. Drain. Separate each leaf of cabbage and slice bulk off back veins so leaf can be manipulated. Place 2 tablespoons of meat stuffing mixture on 12 to 14 cabbage leaves; roll up each and tuck in ends. Place any remaining cabbage leaves in bottom of saucepan. Arrange all cabbage rolls on top of bed of cabbage leaves. Pour tomatoes on top. Add water and, if desired, more salt and pepper. Cover saucepan and cook on low heat on top of stove until cabbage is tender, about 45 minutes.

J. WAYNE STARK

Special Assistant to the President for Cultural Development, J. Wayne Stark '39, sends a "definitely-Texas" recipe, which is served at the San Jacinto Inn near the Houston ship channel.

San Jacinto Biscuits

4 cups flour	3 teaspoons baking powder
1 teaspoon salt	¾ cup Crisco
1 teaspoon sugar	1¾ cups milk

Mix dry ingredients together and cut in Crisco with pastry blender. Add milk and stir with wooden spoon until blended. Form ball and roll out one inch thick. Cut with biscuit cutter and bake for 15 minutes in 425° oven until golden brown. Biscuits will be very flaky and tasty, and are excellent when rewarmed in the oven.

DR. CHARLES H. SAMSON

Dr. Charles H. Samson, Civil Engineering Department, and Acting President of TAMU, 1981-82, submits his favorite main course dish from his wife's kitchen.

Meatballs and Sauce for Spaghetti

1½ pounds ground beef
½ pound lean ground pork
(have meats ground
together twice)
½ green pepper, diced
1 small onion, diced
1 medium apple, grated or
½ cup applesauce

1 cup bread crumbs
1 egg
Salt and pepper to taste
1 large can (46 ounces)
tomato juice
1 can (6 ounces) tomato
paste
1 clove garlic

Sauté diced green pepper and onion. Mix well with other meatball ingredients. Form meatballs. Brown outsides quickly in hot shortening. Place tomato juice, tomato paste and clove of garlic in saucepan. Add meatballs to sauce mixture and allow to simmer, adding additional tomato juice if required for right consistency. While sauce is cooking, stir gently and scrape sides of kettle to loosen thickened portion. Before serving, crush 1 meatball into mixture to thicken sauce.

MRS. FRED R. BRISON

Mrs. Fred R. Brison, widow of the late Professor Fred Brison of the Department of Horticulture, has used the following recipe as a trademark on her table for hundreds of receptions for friends and visitors from near and far since the 1920's when Professor Brison came to Texas A&M University.

Toasted Pecans

1 tablespoon butter
1 cup pecans

Salt

Melt butter in flat pan and stir in pecans. Salt to taste. Place in 400° oven for 10 minutes. Stir every 4 minutes.

RON BLATCHLEY

A Saturday lunch favorite of Ron Blatchley, Director of Student Affairs, is this hearty soup.

Potato Soup

3 cups peeled and diced
   potatoes
½ cup diced celery
½ cup diced onion
½ cup sliced carrots, optional
2 chicken bouillon cubes

½ teaspoon salt
2 cups milk
1 cup (8 ounces) sour cream
2 tablespoons flour
1 tablespoon chopped chives

In large saucepan, combine vegetables, water, salt and bouillon. Cover and cook until vegetables are tender, about 20 minutes. Add one cup milk and heat. In a bowl, combine sour cream, flour, chives and remaining cup of milk. Gradually stir this mixture into hot soup. Cook over low heat, stirring until thickened. Serves 4 to 6.

BOB LACEY

Bob Lacey '60, Office of Administration and Records Registrar, encouraged his wife, Jinx, to submit this recipe, guaranteed to make your guests happy and hollerin' for more, and for days afterwards.

Weird Beans

1 large can Ranch Style
   beans
1 large can pork and beans
1 large can stewed tomatoes
6 to 8 strips fried bacon,
   chopped (including
   drippings)

1 chopped green pepper
6 chopped green onions
   (tops and all)
½ cup brown sugar
½ cup mustard
½ cup catsup

Mix well. Place in baking dish and cover with more strips of bacon. Bake at 350° until bubbly and bacon is cooked.

DR. CAROLYN ADAIR

Dr. Carolyn Adair '69, Director of Student Activities, says she is delighted to share her favorite recipe. To preserve all the original flavor, we are writing it exactly as it was passed on to us.

Gumbo

(Shrimp, Chicken or Pork)

Cover the bottom of a large pot with oil. Sauté 1 cup chopped onion and 1 cup chopped celery until soft. Add 2 small cans of tomato sauce, 1 clove of garlic chopped and filé gumbo to taste (about 2 to 3 tablespoons), salt, pepper and 1 tablespoon sugar. Last, add 1 cup or box of sliced okra. If you fry it in oil first, it won't be slimy. Simmer until it's a nice thick, soupy consistency. Now! If using chicken, brown pieces while sauce is cooking and throw it in the sauce and simmer long enough to take up the sauce (30 to 40 minutes). Chicken may be precooked, boned and added to the sauce at any point. If using pork strips, brown them in first pot and make sauce on top. If using shrimp, first clean them and add to sauce 10 to 15 minutes before serving. Serves 8.

Also, here is Carolyn's favorite punch recipe Aggies seem to love!

Aggie Punch

Mix together 1 large can pineapple juice, 1 small can frozen orange juice, 3 to 4 bottles Ginger Ale, Sprite or 7-Up and lots of crushed ice. Serves a multitude. Bon appetit!

CLINTON A. PHILLIPS

Texas A&M University Dean of Faculties, Clinton A. Phillips, says he is an "outdoor cook", who shares one of his backyard secrets with us.

Grilled Chicken Breasts

Mix ½ cup beer, ¼ cup oil, 1 teaspoon oregano, 2 teaspoons salt, and a dash of Tabasco. Brush over 8 halves skinned chicken breasts. Grill for one hour, repeating brushings with sauce a couple of times during cooking.

DR. CHARLES McCANDLESS

Dr. Charles McCandless '56, Associate Vice President for Academic Affairs, Texas A&M University, submits his favorite cake recipe.

Poor Man's Cake

2	cups raisins	1	tablespoon soda
2	cups sugar	1	teaspoon cinnamon
3	cups water	1	teaspoon nutmeg
½	cup Crisco	1	teaspoon cloves
4	cups flour	1	teaspoon ginger
Pinch salt		1	cup chopped nuts

ICING:
¼	cup butter	1	teaspoon vanilla
2	cups powdered sugar	Milk or cream	

Put raisins and 2 cups of water on to boil for 15 minutes. Take off heat and add Crisco, sugar and 1 cup of cold water. Sift flour, salt, soda and spices 2 or 3 times and add to above mixture. Add nuts. Pour into greased, floured tube pan and bake at 325° to 350° for one hour or until done.

ICING: Cream butter. Add powdered sugar, vanilla and milk or cream to make spreading consistency. Spread over top of cake.

J. MALON SOUTHERLAND

J. Malon Southerland '65, Acting Director and Assistant Vice President for Student Services, Texas A&M University, says this dip is a favorite after football games. Be sure you serve something cool to drink!

Malon's Dip

1   jar (8 ounces) Pace's picante sauce, medium hot
1   package (8 ounces) Philadelphia cream cheese

1   cup cooked small shrimp or crabmeat

Pinch cream cheese in hunks and place in blender, pour in picante sauce and blend 5 to 10 seconds or less. Should not be runny. Add shrimp or crab meat. Serve with Tostitos or Doritos.

COL. JOE T. HANEY

Col. Joe T. Haney '48, who directs the 'Fightin' Texas Aggie Band, says this recipe is a winner with Aggies of all ages.

Bevo Burger Filets

2   pounds lean ground beef
1   onion, chopped
1   can (6 ounces) ripe olives, chopped
1   green pepper, chopped

1   can (8 ounces) mushrooms, chopped
Fresh grated Parmesan cheese
8   slices of bacon

Flatten ground beef in oblong shape on foil and top with remaining ingredients. Roll up long side as a jelly roll, and cut in 1½ inch filets. Wrap each slice with bacon and skewer with a toothpick. Grill over coals 8 minutes on each side.

COL. JAMES R. WOODALL

Col. James R. Woodall '50, former Commandant of the Texas A&M University Corps of Cadets, says hungry Aggie cadets can consume a lot of lasagna, and this is a tried-and-true recipe.

Corps Lasagna

¼ cup oil
2 cups chopped onion
1 cup tomato paste
1 teaspoon sugar
½ teaspoon basil
2 cloves garlic
2 cans (28 ounces each) tomatoes
2 teaspoons salt
1 teaspoon oregano
½ cup water
1 pound ground beef
1 egg

¼ teaspoon garlic salt
½ teaspoon salt
¼ teaspoon pepper
½ teaspoon basil
2 teaspoons parsley
Enough oil to brown
1 carton (16 ounces) cottage cheese
1 pound Mozzarella cheese, shredded or sliced
Parmesan cheese
Lasagna noodles cooked as directed

Mix first 10 ingredients in saucepan and let simmer for 1½ hours. Meanwhile, mix together meat, egg and seasonings and brown in skillet that is just coated with oil. In large lasagna pan, layer cooked lasagna noodles, then tomato mixture, then meat mixture, then all of cottage cheese, then Mozzarella cheese and sprinkle with Parmesan cheese. Repeat layers except for cottage cheese until pan is full. Bake 30 to 45 minutes in 350° oven. Serves 8 to 10.

JIM REYNOLDS

Jim Reynolds, Director of Memorial Student Center at Texas A&M University, shares this concoction, straight from a Big Thicket campfire. Note the disclaimer!

Hunter's Chili

(Alias: Jayhawk Chili, Killer Chili)

2 pounds ground beef
2 large onions
2 large bell peppers (1 green and 1 red if available)
5 cans of beans (2 red kidney, 2 dark red kidney, 1 brown)
3 cans (2 pounds each) whole tomatoes, drained
2 cans (8 ounces each) tomato sauce
1 can (10 ounces) Rotel tomatoes
1 can Snappy Tom tomato juice
2 packages Williams chili seasoning
2 tablespoons garlic salt
1 teaspoon red pepper (add a second if cold weather!)
Anything else lying on the cabinet which looks edible, but non-explosive
1 pound coon or sharp Cheddar cheese, grated
1 large bag of Fritos

Slowly brown ground beef in large skillet. Coarsely chop onion and bell peppers, adding to ground beef as it begins to turn gray. Onion and pepper should cook about 5 minutes. Drain. Note: Don't remove the bottom of the onion until last and it won't make you cry. Drain beans and whole tomatoes, and dump into a 1½ gallon heavy pot. Dump in the ground beef and beans, tomatoes, juice and seasonings. Stir it, but don't use your best serving spoon, since the mixture has a tendency to tarnish anything with which it comes in contact. Simmer for three hours minimum. The longer the better. (The mixture expands by approximately 20% when heated.)

It's okay for the cook to eat a little of the cheese and a few Fritos just before serving.

SERVING: Place a small handful of Fritos in the bottom of each bowl. Scoop on chili. Sprinkle liberally with grated cheese and toss on a few more Fritos. (The cheese and Fritos hold in the heat.) Pray. Eat. *A large (2 cup minimum) high walled regulation chili bowl is best for serving - keeps the stuff warm even for slow eaters.*

ANTIDOTE: Carbonated beverages in substantial quantities should be made available. Pineapple sherbet and shortbread cookies can help if served approximately ½ hour after ingestion. Victim should refrain from any strenuous activities, except hunting or fishing, for 24 hours.

DISCLAIMER: No warranties expressed or implied. Eat at your own risk. Preparation may be hazardous to your kitchen. The Surgeon General has determined that preparing and/or consuming Hunter's Chili may destroy brain cells.

COL. DONALD L. BURTON

Col. Donald L. Burton '56, Commandant of the Corps, says this specialty has been prepared in the Burton household every 3rd of July for years.

Big Mama's Special Pitman's Sauce

In an 8 quart pot, the heavier the better, add the following in the order given; stir, cover and let simmer at the lowest heat possible for 2 hours. Makes about 1 gallon.

4	quarts of heavy tomato puree	1	teaspoon black pepper
2	bottles beer (pour one in now, save one for thinning the mix later)	2	teaspoons dry mustard
		1	teaspoon thyme
		1	teaspoon sweet basil
1	cup dark brown sugar (packed)	8	dashes soy sauce
		4	beef bouillon cubes
¼	cup butter	1	tablespoon lemon juice or tarragon vinegar
2	tablespoons chili powder		
1	tablespoon red pepper flakes (hot)	¼	teaspoon fennel
		1	teaspoon parsley flakes
1	tablespoon salt	1	teaspoon cumin
		¼	teaspoon rosemary

Dress the beef, ribs, chicken or other meat after it has been "Qued," never while cooking.

JOHN T. WHITE

This recipe is submitted by John T. White '76, Assistant Area Coordinator-Corps, Advisor to Company E-2 and Reveille.

Squash Squares

3 cups of grated zucchini squash
1 cup Bisquick
4 eggs, well beaten
½ cup grated Parmesan cheese
1 medium onion, diced well

1 teaspoon oregano
1 teaspoon seasoned salt
1 teaspoon salt
Dash pepper
2 cloves garlic
½ cup cooking oil

Mix all ingredients in a large bowl. Grease a 9x12 inch baking dish and pour mixture into the pan. Bake at 400° for 35 minutes or until brown on top. Allow to cool and cut into squares. Before serving, heat at 325° for 15 minutes.

DR. WILLIAM V. MUSE

Dr. William V. Muse, Dean of College of Business Administration, Texas A&M University, contributed this recipe, which he says is delicious the first day and even better reheated the next day.

Ratatouille

2 yellow onions, chopped
2 cloves garlic
Olive oil
1 eggplant
4 or 5 small zucchini

1 pound tomatoes, fresh or canned
Salt and pepper
¼ cup minced parsley

Sauté chopped onion and garlic in a few tablespoons of olive oil in a heavy skillet. Peel eggplant, cut into cubes and add to skillet. Slice zucchini and add it to skillet. Cook for 15 minutes, adding more oil if necessary. Add chopped tomatoes, parsley, salt and pepper. Cover and simmer 1 hour. Serves 6 to 8.

DR. J. BENTON STOREY

Dr. J. Benton Storey '49, Professor of Horticulture of Texas A&M University, has shared the pie recipe which won First Place in a Brazos County Pecan Baking Contest over about 40 other pecan pie entrants. It has been published in The Pecan Quarterly and is a favorite of the Horticulture 418 students who participate in the pecan product evaluation laboratory each spring.

Ritzy Pecan Pie

3 egg whites	1 teaspoon vanilla
1 cup sugar	½ pint whipping cream
1 cup chopped pecans	2 tablespoons sugar
1 cup rolled Ritz crackers	½ cup pecans (additional)

Beat egg whites until stiff, gradually adding 1 cup sugar. Fold in pecans, Ritz crackers and vanilla. Place in slightly greased pie plate with sides slightly higher than center. Bake in 325° oven about 30 minutes. When cool, whip the cream, adding 2 tablespoons sugar and top cooled pie with it. Sprinkle top with additional pecans and refrigerate. May be served immediately.

Variation: Dream Whip may be substituted for whipping cream.

GREG DAVIS

Patsy Davis, wife of Quarterback Coach Greg Davis, calls the signals for this "power up the middle" special recipe.

Mexican Hot Sauce

½ onion, chopped	1 can (4 ounces) chopped green chilies
1 can (16 ounces) whole tomatoes, drained	1 jalapeño pepper, chopped
1 can (10 ounces) Rotel tomatoes, drained	

Mix together in order given, adding salt, pepper, red pepper and garlic to taste, if you like. Serve with Mexican chips.

GORDON P. EATON

Gordon P. Eaton, Provost and Vice President for Academic Affairs, is pleased to have us include this colorful recipe with a Continental flair.

Crepes d' Aggie*

12 flour tortillas
1   pound Monterey Jack
    cheese
12 thin slices of trimmed lean
    ham

1   can (4 ounces) chopped
    green chili peppers (cool
    to moderate rather than
    hot chilies)

CHEESE SAUCE:
½   cup margarine
½   cup flour
1⅓ cups milk
⅔   cup chicken stock
¾   cup grated Cheddar cheese
1   teaspoon mustard

½   teaspoon salt
½   teaspoon MSG
Dash pepper

Paprika

Spread out tortillas. Cut Monterey Jack cheese into ½" x ½" wide sticks, 2 to 3 inches long. Roll ham slices and place one on each tortilla, along with 2 sticks of cheese. Spoon on chopped chilies. Roll up each tortilla and place side by side on greased baking pan.

SAUCE: Mix ingredients and cook over low heat, stirring regularly until the consistency is that of a very thick cream. Pour this over the tortillas and sprinkle all with paprika. Bake at 350° for 30 to 35 minutes. Serves 6.

In purest French form, "d'Aggie" is pronounced "da-zheé."

DR. KEITH L. BRYANT, JR.

 Dr. Keith L. Bryant, Jr., Dean of Liberal Arts, reports that one of his chores at home is cooking breakfast. He shares with us his favorite popovers, which are great served with a platter of fresh fruit, butter, and homemade jams and jellies.

Cinnamon Popovers

3 eggs	1 teaspoon ground
1 cup milk	cinnamon
1 cup flour	¼ teaspoon salt
3 tablespoons melted butter	
or margarine	

Preheat oven to 400°. In blender, combine ingredients. Cover and blend 30 seconds. Fill 6 to 8 *well greased* custard cups half full. Bake in 400° oven 40 minutes. Remove from cups and serve hot. (2½ inch muffin pans can be used instead of custard cups.) The popovers will rise 4 to 5 inches. If you prefer crispy popovers, prick the tops with a fork to let the steam escape before removing popovers from the oven.

DR. ROBERT S. STONE

 Dr. Robert S. Stone, M.D., Dean of the College of Medicine, writes up this prescription as his favorite cake recipe and you can take that to the bank!

$500 Cake

1 cup sugar	¼ teaspoon salt
2 cups flour	1 cup cold water
4 tablespoons cocoa	1 cup mayonnaise
1 teaspoon baking powder	1 teaspoon vanilla
1 teaspoon baking soda	

Stir together sugar, flour, cocoa, baking powder, soda and salt. Add water gradually. Mix together mayonnaise and vanilla; stir into rest of batter. Bake in greased, floured pan at 350° for 45 minutes. Cake does well in a Bundt pan or ring. It is moist enough to dust with powdered sugar only instead of icing.

J. B. BECKHAM

Dean J. B. Beckham '50, College of Science, submits from his wife's kitchen, his choice recipe.

Quiche

½ cup of margarine, melted
3 eggs, slightly beaten
½ cup Bisquick

Salt and pepper to taste
1 cup grated Swiss cheese or other white cheese

Mix margarine with eggs, Bisquick, salt and pepper. Blend with whisk to remove lumps. Add Swiss cheese. Then add, as you like, precooked bacon, ham, sausage or seafood; sliced mushrooms, zucchini, or French cut green beans. Combinations are great! Chopped onion may be added if desired. Pour into quiche pan. Be sure all cheese is under the sauce. Bake 30 to 40 minutes, until browned on top, in 350° oven. Don't worry - it will be a success!

DR. GEORGE C. SHELTON

Dean of the College of Veterinary Medicine, Dr. George C. Shelton '48, has appropriately submitted a dairy product recipe.

English Cheddar Cheese Delight

1 cup grated Cheddar cheese, sharp
1 cup mayonnaise
1 cup chopped ripe olives
1 chopped onion

1 teaspoon curry powder
1 teaspoon salt
1 teaspoon pepper
6 English muffins, split

Combine cheese, mayonnaise, olives, onion, curry powder, salt and pepper. Spread on English muffin halves and cut each into four quarters. Bake in 350° oven for 10 to 15 minutes. Sufficient for 48 appetizers or 12 sandwiches. *This spread saves well. May be stored in covered container in refrigerator and used as desired.*

DR. EDWARD BURNS

Dr. Edward Burns of the Department of Horticultural Sciences, TAMU, says this recipe is one many American pioneers enjoyed.

Old Settler's Boiled Pudding

½ cup brown sugar
1 cup sour cream
1 cup chopped fruit (plums, peaches, etc.)

2 cups flour
1 teaspoon baking soda

Mix all ingredients into a dough and steam in a double boiler for 2 hours. (The early settlers cooked the pudding by placing the dough in a cloth bag and dropping it in a kettle of boiling water. Apple dumplings were made the same way.)

Dr. Burns submits this recipe as "the Winner" from the chili capital of the world.

Terlingua Chili

3 pounds beef, cut into ½ inch pieces
¼ cup olive oil
1 quart water
2 bay leaves (optional) to be removed after first simmer
8 pods or 6 tablespoons chili powder
3 teaspoons salt
10 cloves garlic, finely chopped (or substitute 2 small chopped onions, plus 5 garlic cloves; or 1 teaspoon garlic powder)
3 teaspoons paprika

1 teaspoon cumin
1 teaspoon oregano or marjoram
1 teaspoon red pepper
½ teaspoon pepper
1 tablespoon sugar
¼ cup catsup
¼ teaspoon monosodium glutamate
1 can (15 ounces) tomato sauce
3 teaspoons flour plus 6 tablespoons corn meal, or 5 tablespoons Masa Harina

Sear the meat in oil until gray. Add water and simmer for 1½ hours. Add all ingredients except flour and meal and cook 30 minutes. Then add flour and meal mixed in small amount of cold water. Cook for 5 minutes. Add more water as needed to reach desired consistency.

DR. SAM GILLESPIE

Dr. Sam Gillespie, Assistant Dean of the College of Business, submits this recipe for casual dining, and he warns that you'd better have plenty of napkins on hand. Peeling shrimp, baked in rich, spicy butter sauce can get very messy, but it is well worth the time spent wiping hands! The second recipe is an excellent dish for special guests.

Louisiana Shrimp

3 pounds of shrimp in shells (36 to 42 per pound or 43 to 50 okay also)	½ teaspoon thyme
½ cup butter	1 teaspoon oregano
2 tablespoons salt	2 bay leaves
2 teaspoons pepper	1 tablespoon Worcestershire sauce
2 teaspoons red pepper	1 teaspoon Tabasco

Melt butter and add all spices. Put shrimp, still in shells, in a 10x15 inch pan. Pour sauce over shrimp and bake at 350° for 20 minutes (or until shrimp turn carrotine color and transluscent), turning 3 or 4 times. *Fantastic finger-food! Don't be afraid to use all the seasoning; it's wonderfully good tasting.*

Flounder with Crab Stuffing

6 pan-dressed flounder, ¾ pound each or one 3 pound flounder	3 eggs, beaten
1 pound blue crab meat	1 tablespoon chopped parsley
½ cup chopped onion	2 teaspoons salt
⅓ cup chopped celery	½ teaspoon pepper
⅓ cup chopped green pepper	¼ pound butter or margarine
2 cloves garlic, finely chopped	¼ cup lemon juice
⅓ cup oil	2 teaspoons salt
2 cups soft bread cubes	2 teaspoons water
	Paprika

Rinse flounder and pat dry. To make pocket for stuffing, lay fish flat on cutting board, light side down. With sharp knife, cut down center of fish along backbone from tail to 1 inch from head. Turn knife flat and cut flesh along both sides of backbone to tail, allowing knife to run over rib bones. Set aside. Check crabmeat for any remaining shell or cartilage. Sauté onion, celery, green pepper and garlic in oil until tender. Combine with bread, eggs, parsley, salt and pepper. Mix thoroughly. Stuff flounder loosely. Combine butter, lemon juice, salt and water. Place fish in well oiled baking dish. Pour butter mixture over fish. Sprinkle with paprika. Bake at 350° for 30 to 40 minutes, or until fish flakes easily when tested with fork. Makes 6 servings. *If you don't care to make pocket and stuff flounder, fillet the flounder, or purchase 12 fillets. Make sandwich of fillets, placing stuffing between. Stuffing makes 6 cups.*

DR. ROD O'CONNOR

 Who else but Dr. Rod O'Connor, Professor and former Director of First Year Chemistry Programs, could send his no-fail instructions when he is the cook.

Cheese Sandwich à la Chemist

2 bread slices (any type, not necessarily fresh)	2 smears oleo
1 cheese slice, plastic-wrapped	1 6 inch square aluminum foil

Set oven for BROIL. Remove cheese from plastic wrapping (otherwise it tastes funny). Smear oleo on one side of the first bread slice. Place this on the aluminum foil, oleo side down. Layer on the cheese and cover it with the second bread slice. Smear oleo on top of bread. Place under broiler until top is light brown. Remove and turn entire sandwich over. (Caution: Use tongs to save fingers.) Replace sandwich under broiler until the second bread slice is lightly browned. Remove and allow to cool slightly. (Don't forget to turn off the stove or the wife will make funny noises.) For extra special occasions, serve with a pickle and a paper towel (for wiping fingers to avoid telltale spots on the chair arm). *When cooled, the aluminum foil makes a fine dining plate and there are no dishes to wash, unless you forget to use a paper bathroom cup for your milk.*

ROBERT L. BOONE

Robert L. Boone, Director of the Singing Cadets, says he is a transplanted Chesapeake Bay boy, and therefore, seafoods are his favorite. He submits the following gumbo, which he says is great served with a tossed salad and warmed, crusty French bread.

Shrimp and Crab Gumbo

1   pound fresh okra
4   tablespoons cooking oil
    (bacon drippings add
    flavor)
1   medium white onion,
    diced
1   medium bell pepper, diced

4   pods garlic, diced or
    crushed
1   quart boiling water
Salt and pepper to taste
1   pound cleaned and
    deveined shrimp
½   to 1 pound crab claw
    meat

ROUX:
2   tablespoons margarine

4   tablespoons flour

½   to 1 pound cooked rice
    (keep warm)

Wash, dry and slice okra into ¼ to ½ inch pieces. Fry in 4 tablespoons of cooking oil. Cook 20 minutes over medium heat, stirring frequently. Add diced onion, pepper and garlic. Continue cooking until all vegetables are browned. Add boiling water. Salt and pepper to taste. Cook 30 to 45 minutes over medium heat. During this time, clean and devein shrimp. Add to vegetables, cooking about 20 minutes more. Clean crabmeat, removing bits of claw and membrane. Add about 10 minutes before serving.

ROUX: Use separate skillet. Melt margarine and sprinkle in flour, stirring constantly until dark brown. Be careful not to burn. Stir into gumbo. Add more water, depending on how soupy you like your gumbo. If water is added, allow enough time for all the wonderful flavors to spread! Serve in a bowl over cooked, warm rice.

DR. A. J. TURGEON

Dr. A. J. Turgeon, immediate past Professor and former Resident Director of TAMU Research and Extension Center, shares a special recipe whose ingredients fulfill the promise of its name.

Cantonese Smorgasbord

2 tablespoons peanut or vegetable oil
½ pound ground pork
1 chicken breast, skinned, boned and cut into ¾ inch pieces
2 cloves garlic, minced
1 pound shrimp, cleaned
1 pound scallops
3 green onions with tops, cut into 1 inch pieces

1 can (13¾ ounces) chicken broth
2 tablespoons cornstarch
2 tablespoons sherry
1 tablespoon soy sauce
½ teaspoon salt
½ teaspoon sugar
1 egg, slightly beaten
Hot cooked rice

Add oil to electric wok. Set heat control at 350°. When light goes out add ground pork. Stir fry until nearly done. Place on paper towel and set aside. Add chicken and garlic. Stir fry until chicken turns white, about one minute. Add shrimp, scallops and green onions. Cook until shrimp turns pink, about 2 minutes. Add broth and pork. In cup, mix cornstarch, sherry, soy sauce, salt and sugar. Add to shrimp mixture and cook, stirring constantly, until mixture boils for 1 minute. Turn off heat. Stir in egg. Serve immediately over cooked rice. Serves 4.

JUDY EDWARDS

Judy Edwards, District Extension Director, Texas Agricultural Extension Service, shared her all-time favorite recipe for a Texas favorite. (Judy says their friends from north of the Red River like this one, too!)

Oven Barbecued Brisket

3	to 4 pound beef brisket with moderate fat		Celery salt
3	tablespoons liquid smoke		Onion salt
3	tablespoons Worcestershire sauce		Garlic salt
			Salt and pepper to taste
		1	bottle barbecue sauce

Pour liquid smoke and Worcestershire sauce over meat. Generously sprinkle all surfaces with celery, onion and garlic salts, salt and pepper. Cover and refrigerate overnight in heavy roaster. Bake covered at 250° for 5 hours. Pour barbecue sauce over meat. Bake uncovered 1 more hour. Let cool for about 20 minutes, and slice crosswise.

JACKIE SHERRILL

Jackie Sherrill, Athletic Director and Head Football Coach, likes the spirit of this genuine Twelfth-Man Specialty recipe, as made by wife, Daryle.

Aggie Fruitcake

2	cups flour	1	can (1 pound, 4 ounces) crushed pineapple, with juice
2	cups sugar		
2	teaspoons soda		
2	eggs, beaten	1	cup nuts

FROSTING:

1	box powdered sugar	1	package (3 ounces) cream cheese, softened
½	cup margarine, softened		
		1	teaspoon vanilla

Sift together flour, sugar, and soda. Add eggs and pineapple, including juice. Stir in nuts. Pour into a greased 9x13 inch pan. Bake at 350° for 40 to 50 minutes. Mix frosting ingredients and ice when cake is cool.

JEAN CARLTON

Jean Carlton, Extension Agent for Dallas TAMU, offers a sauce made with new Texas A&M mild jalapeno peppers.

Picante Sauce

12 large red ripe tomatoes,
   peeled if desired
2 cups TAM mild jalapeño
   peppers, caps and seeds
   removed
2 medium sweet onions, cut
   into chunks

2 cups red wine vinegar
1½ teaspoons salt
2 teaspoons brown sugar
2 ribs celery, cut into
   chunks, optional

Place ingredients in blender and process to a point where small pieces of pepper and onion remain. Simmer in heavy saucepan, stirring frequently, until desired thickness is attained, 45 minutes to 1 hour. Pour boiling sauce into hot canning jars. Wipe edge carefully. Seal one jar at a time and place in boiling water bath canner and process for 35 minutes. Makes approximately 4 pints. This recipe may be halved or quartered and refrigerated until used.

DAN LaGRASTA

From the kitchen of Barbara LaGrasta, wife of the On-Campus Recruiting Coordinator, Dan, we have the "blue-chipper."

Leu's Quick Orange Rolls

2 cans (10 each) biscuits
½ cup butter or margarine,
   melted

Grated peel from 1 orange,
   mixed with
1½ cups sugar

Dip individual biscuits into melted butter, then into orange-sugar mix. Arrange in a ring mold and bake at 375° about 30 minutes. Serve hot.

JERRY PETTIBONE

Administrative Aide, Recruiting Coordinator, and Wide Receivers Coach, Jerry Pettibone, says wife Susy's cake is as good as a Bowl bid at the end of a winning season.

Chocolate Chip Cake

1 box (18.25 ounces) Deluxe II yellow cake mix	¾ cup water
1 box (3⅝ ounces) chocolate instant pudding	½ cup sugar
	4 whole eggs
¾ cup Crisco oil	1 cup sour cream
	1 cup chocolate chips

Combine cake mix and pudding. Add Crisco oil. Mix together water and sugar and stir into cake mix. Add eggs, 1 at a time; then sour cream. Stir in chips. Bake in greased and floured tube pan at 350° for 1 hour, 5 minutes.

FROSTING:

½ cup butter, melted	1 pound powdered sugar
4 tablespoons cocoa	1 teaspoon vanilla
7 tablespoons milk	

Combine all ingredients and beat well. Pour over baked cake while hot.

R. C. SLOCUM

Defensive Coordinator, Linebackers, R.C. Slocum, tackles with gusto this recipe as served by wife, Janet.

Aggie Artichokes

2 cans (8 ounces each) artichokes, drained and mashed	1 cup Parmesan cheese
	1 tablespoon garlic powder
	Few drops Tabasco sauce
1 cup mayonnaise	Paprika

Mix together and bake at 350° for 30 minutes. Sprinkle with paprika. *1 can crabmeat may be added.*

JIM HELMS

Jim Helms, leader of offensive backs, says wife, Dabney, does a fine job with this main course dish.

Chicken and Dumplings

1   whole chicken, cut up   Salt and pepper
3   cups flour

Boil chicken pieces in enough lightly salted water to cover. When done, remove from heat, and take chicken pieces out of broth. Mix enough of the boiling chicken fat with flour to make stiff dough. Knead dough while still hot and roll out into medium thin layer. Cut into strips and spread on floured board. Let dry about 15 minutes. Add coarse black pepper to remaining broth and let come to boil. Then add dumplings slowly, taking care not to shake off all loose flour. Stir and let boil hard 5 minutes. When done, dumplings will go to bottom of pan. Let stand before serving so broth can thicken. Add salt to taste, if necessary. Chicken meat may be removed from bone and added back into dumpling/broth mix.

CHARLES THORNTON

Former Associate Athletic Director, Charles Thornton, says this recipe prepared by his wife, Doris, will provide a championship meal.

Ham Spaghetti

1   cup (one large slice,   1   can (16 ounces) tomatoes
    cubed) ham   1   can (10¾ ounces) cream
3   ribs celery, diced   of mushroom soup
1   onion, diced   1   small package (12 ounces)
2   tablespoons fat   spaghetti

Brown ham, celery and onion in fat. Add tomatoes and simmer covered 30 to 40 minutes. Then add mushroom soup and simmer slowly 8 to 10 minutes more. Meanwhile, cook spaghetti according to package directions, drain and add to sauce mixture. *Cheese may be added to thicken, if desired.* Serves 4 to 6.

PAT RUEL

Offensive Linemen Coordinator, Pat Ruel, known as the Desert Fox, furnished this fondue recipe, which wife, Marti, says gets praises like a well-protected quarterback.

Fondue Bourguignonne

1   quart peanut oil
16 large shrimp, cooked and
    shelled

4   chicken breasts, skinned,
    boned and cut in 1 inch
    pieces
2   pounds top round, cut in
    1 inch cubes

Heat oil until bubbly and pour into a 2 quart metal fondue pot. Place prepared shrimp, chicken and beef on platter with fondue forks. Let each guest cook his own to taste. Serve with Hollandaise, Bernaise, seafood cocktail or barbecue sauces. Serves 8 to 10 persons.

PAUL REGISTER

Defensive Tackle Coach, Paul Register, says his favorite recipe is this man-handler meat loaf prepared by his wife, Martha.

Meat Loaf and Piquant Sauce

1   pound ground beef
¼   cup chopped green pepper
2   tablespoons chopped
    onion
1   egg

⅔   cup condensed milk or one
    small can
1   teaspoon salt
¼   teaspoon pepper
½   cup fine bread crumbs or
    cracker crumbs

SAUCE:
3   tablespoons brown sugar
¼   cup catsup

¼   teaspoon nutmeg
1   teaspoon dry mustard

Combine all meat loaf ingredients and mix well. Place in buttered baking dish and top with piquant sauce. Bake at 350° 45 minutes to 1 hour.

CURLEY HALLMAN

 Secondary Coach Curley Hallman '69, likes his wife's special dips almost as much as intercepting a t u pass.

Dale Hallman's Hot Cheese Dip

1 pound Velveeta cheese, grated fine
1 pint mayonnaise
1 teaspoon garlic powder

1 small onion, grated fine
7 hot peppers, or small jar hot chili peppers

Mix all ingredients well. Serve heated. May be served cold after standing in refrigerator overnight. *Delicious either way!*

GEORGE PUGH

 Tight End Coach George Pugh says wife Deborah's dessert brings a smile like a third-and-ten conversion.

7-Up Cake

1 box (18.25 ounces) lemon supreme cake mix
1 box (3¾ ounces) instant pineapple pudding

¾ cup Wesson oil
4 eggs
1 bottle (10 ounces) 7-Up

Grease and flour four layer pans. Preheat oven to 350°. Beat together cake ingredients and 7-Up. Distribute into prepared pans and bake about 30 minutes. Cool.

FILLING:
1½ cups sugar
1 tablespoon flour
3 eggs
½ cup butter

1 can (15¼ ounces) crushed pineapple
1 can (6 ounces) coconut

Combine ingredients in top of double boiler and stir until thickened. Cool slightly and put between layers of the 7-Up cake.

JERRY C. COOPER

Jerry C. Cooper '63, Editor of The Texas Aggie, *tells us that he once won a blue ribbon for this recipe. This was originally called Red Velvet Cake, but careful attention when mixing the food coloring and the cocoa can result in a beautiful Aggie Maroon. The recipe was also called the $1 Million Cake, because a woman who first tasted it at New York's Waldorf Astoria Hotel asked for the recipe and later received a bill for $1 Million.*

Maroon Velvet Cake

2 ounces red food coloring	2¼ cups cake flour
3 tablespoons cocoa	1 teaspoon salt
½ cup shortening	1 teaspoon vanilla
1½ cups sugar	1 tablespoon vinegar
2 eggs, beaten	1 teaspoon soda
1 cup buttermilk	

ICING:

½ cup soft butter	⅔ cup milk, room
½ cup shortening	temperature
1 cup powdered sugar	1 teaspoon vanilla
3 tablespoons flour	

CAKE: Mix red food coloring with cocoa and set aside. Cream shortening and sugar; add beaten eggs, then coloring paste. Beat well. Sift cake flour and salt 3 times; add to creamed mixture along with buttermilk. Add vanilla and beat well again. Remove from mixer and add mixture of vinegar and soda; mix by hand until blended. Bake in 2 layers at 350° for 30-35 minutes.

ICING: Cream butter and shortening with sugar. Add flour 1 spoonful at a time. Add milk and vanilla. Beat a long time with mixer until icing is light and fluffy. *Aggies call this the "Maroon and White Cake." Many a cake has been cut with a Senior's saber!*

RANDY MATSON

Executive Director of The Association of Former Students, Randy Matson '67, who also holds the distinguished gold and silver medals of the Olympics, sends his favorite healthful and tasty cookies, guaranteed to take top honors.

Whole Wheat Chocolate Chip Cookies

1   cup Crisco
1½ cups packed brown sugar
2   eggs
1   teaspoon vanilla
2¼ cups whole wheat flour
     (sift 3 times, then
     measure)

1   teaspoon baking soda
½   teaspoon salt
2   cups chopped pecans
1   cup (6 ounces) Hershey's
     semisweet chocolate chips

Cream Crisco, brown sugar, eggs and vanilla. Sift flour several times; then sift together with baking soda and salt. Add to creamed mixture. Stir in pecans and chocolate chips. Drop by large rounded teaspoonsful onto ungreased cookie sheet. Bake at 375° approximately 8 to 10 minutes, until light brown.

A. W. DAVIS

President of the Association of Former Students, A. W. Davis '45, vouches for this favorite that is super for Aggie parties.

Pimiento Cheese Spread

Miracle Whip
2   pounds soft, diced
     Velveeta cheese
½   pound sharp, diced
     Cheddar cheese

½   jar (8 ounces) sweet pickle
     relish
2   cans (8 ounces each) diced
     pimientos
½   teaspoon garlic salt,
     optional

Use enough Miracle Whip to start mixing cheese, and keep adding the cheeses until mixture is consistency you desire. Beat with electric mixer until fluffy. Add pickle relish and pimientos and mix thoroughly. *This mix is good as a dip or as sandwich spread. Keeps indefinitely when covered in refrigerator.*

DR. SHELBY METCALF

Dr. Shelby Metcalf '74, Texas A&M University's basketball coach for twenty years, guarantees your team will "fast-break" back for more of his favorite cake recipe.

Apple Cake

1 cup oil	2 heaping teaspoons cinnamon
2 heaping cups of sugar	3 cups chopped peeled apples (about 3 Delicious apples)
2 beaten eggs	
2 teaspoons vanilla	
3 cups flour	1½ cups chopped pecans
1 teaspoon soda	
½ teaspoon salt	

Combine oil, sugar, eggs and vanilla. Mix dry ingredients together and add to first mixture. This is a *stiff* dough - may need to be mixed by hand. Add apples and nuts. Spread into a greased and floured 9x13 inch pan. Bake approximately 55 minutes at 300°. Turn out immediately and let cool. Serve with Cool Whip as topping. This cake may also be baked in a tube pan. Bake about 60 minutes at 350°.

PAUL W. "BEAR" BRYANT

The late Coach Paul W. "Bear" Bryant, who directed championship teams at Alabama and Texas A&M, sent his favorite recipe shortly before his untimely passing.

Baked Eggs

Butter a shallow baking dish and break the number of eggs needed to fill it. Sprinkle with salt and pour milk around the eggs until the yellow tops are peeping out. Dot with butter. Grate cheese over the top. Bake in slow oven 300° until cheese is bubbly and eggs are of desired doneness. Serve in nest of grits or on crisp toast.

TOM CHANDLER

 Tom Chandler, Head Baseball Coach at Texas A&M nearly three decades, tells wife, Willowdeen that she can't serve this recipe too often to suit him!

Green Chili Squash

10 to 14 yellow squash
1 medium onion, chopped
1 can (7 ounces) green chilies or 1 can (10 ounces) Rotel tomatoes with green chilies, drained

½ pound American cheese
2 or 3 dashes of garlic powder
Salt and pepper to taste

Wash squash well and slice ½ inch thick. Boil squash with chopped onion in covered pan with small amount of water until tender. Drain *well.* Add cheese cut in chunks, mashed green chilies, salt and pepper. Stir until cheese is melted. Let simmer over low heat a few minutes to evaporate all extra moisture. It may be served right away or may be placed in a baking dish and baked in oven until bubbles appear. This recipe freezes well.

PAT JOHNSTON

 Pat Johnston, President of the Federation of Texas A&M University Mothers' Clubs, 1982-83, says the following recipe is great to serve to the masses that show up for football weekends and may be served for breakfast, lunch or dinner!

Crustless Spinach Quiche

2 packages (10 ounces each) frozen spinach
2 tablespoons butter
1 bunch green onions, chopped

10 eggs
2 packages (10 ounces each) Muenster cheese, grated
Salt and pepper to taste

Cook spinach. Drain and put in skillet containing butter and onions. Cook until all water is absorbed. In large bowl, beat eggs and add cheese, salt and pepper. Mix all ingredients together. Pour or spoon into 9x13 inch greased baking dish. Bake 1 hour at 350° or until knife comes out clean. Serves 10 to 12.

MRS. REX ROBINSON

Mrs. Rex (Beth) Robinson, Federation of Texas A&M University Mothers' Clubs Recording Secretary, 1982-83, says Aggies, and their friends particularly enjoy this South-of-the-Border variation.

Mexican Corn Bread

1 cup yellow cornmeal	½ pound ground beef
½ teaspoon soda	1 large onion
¾ teaspoon salt	3 Jalapeño peppers
2 eggs, well beaten	½ pound grated Cheddar cheese
1 cup sweet milk	
1 can (16 ounces) cream style corn	

Mix cornmeal, soda, salt, eggs and milk and blend in corn. Sauté beef. Chop onions and peppers. Set aside. Grease skillet and heat. Sprinkle sides and bottom with cornmeal. Brown meal slightly. Pour half batter mix in skillet and sprinkle cheese over the batter, then meat, onion and peppers. Pour remaining batter over top. Bake at 350° for 45 to 50 minutes. *This can be stored in the refrigerator for several days. It also freezes well.*

JIM JETER

Jim Jeter '70, Associate Executive Director of Former Students, shares one of his favorite recipes - guaranteed to enhance any meal.

Glazed Fruit Salad

1 can (20 ounces) chunk pineapple (in its own juice)	1 package (4 ounces) pineapple or lemon instant pudding
1 can (16 ounces) mandarin oranges	4 or 5 bananas, sliced
	1 pint fresh strawberries, sliced

Drain pineapple and oranges. Reserve liquids. Add pudding mix to liquid. Stir until blended. Fold in bananas, strawberries, pineapple and oranges. Stir until well coated. *This salad keeps well and is refreshing as a salad or dessert.*

SHIRLEY WINTERROWD

Shirley Winterrowd, Fifth Vice President of the Federation of Texas A&M University Mothers' Clubs, 1982-83, sends an unusual dip which is baked in the oven.

Taco Dip

1   can (15½ ounces) refried beans
½ cup chopped green onions; tops, too
1   pound lean hamburger, cooked and drained, seasoned with garlic salt

1   jar (8 ounces) mild or hot picante sauce
8   ounces Monterey Jack cheese, grated
8   ounces sour cream
Guacamole salad made from 2 avocados (your own favorite recipe)

Spread refried beans in 8x11 inch casserole. Add chopped onions, hamburger, picante sauce and grated cheese. Bake for 15 to 20 minutes at 350°. Remove from oven and cool for about 5 minutes. Spread sour cream and top with guacamole salad. Serve immediately with chips. *My family prefers El Galindo chips.*

BUCK WEIRUS

Buck Weirus '42, Executive Director Emeritus of the Association of Former Students and Spirit Award commemorant, shares his favorite for breakfast enjoyment.

Waffles

4   eggs, separated
1   cup All-Bran
1   cup flour
2   cups buttermilk

2   tablespoons cooking oil
1   teaspoon baking soda
½ teaspoon salt

After separating eggs, stir the yolks and add All-Bran, flour, buttermilk, oil, soda and salt. Beat egg whites until fluffy. Fold into batter. Bake in hot waffle iron.

JANET SINGER

Janet Singer, Corresponding Secretary for the Federation of Texas A&M University Mothers' Clubs, 1982-83, shares the following recipe which she says is great for New Year's Eve parties - especially for those who like hot dips!

Black-Eyed Pea Dip

¼ bell pepper, chopped
8 jalapeño peppers, chopped
2 ribs celery, chopped
1 large onion, chopped
1 teaspoon coarse black pepper
2 tablespoons Tabasco sauce
½ cup catsup
1 teaspoon salt
3 chicken bouillon cubes

¼ teaspoon nutmeg
¼ teaspoon cinnamon
2 cans (20 ounces each) black-eyed peas (approximately 4 cups)
1¼ cups tomatoes
1 teaspoon garlic powder
½ cup bacon drippings
3 tablespoons flour

Chop peppers, celery and onion very fine. Add pepper, Tabasco, catsup, salt, bouillon cubes, nutmeg and cinnamon. Bring to a slow simmer. Add peas, tomatoes and garlic powder. Cook 30 minutes on medium heat. Add bacon drippings blended with flour. Cook another 10 minutes, stirring occasionally to avoid sticking. Serve hot with tortilla chips.

CAROL GREANEY

Carol Greaney, Parliamentarian, Federation of Texas A&M University Mothers' Clubs, 1982-83, sends us a favorite appetizer recipe.

Broccoli Dip

1 package (10 ounces) frozen chopped broccoli
¼ cup chopped onion
1 can (10¾ ounces) cream of mushroom soup

½ cup chopped celery
1 tablespoon butter
1 roll (6 ounces) Kraft garlic cheese, cubed
¼ cup slivered almonds

Cook and drain broccoli; sauté celery and onion in butter. Add broccoli, undiluted soup, cheese and almonds. Heat until cheese melts. Serve hot.

BOBBY ROPER

Bobby Roper, Aggie Defensive End Coach, likes this speedy recipe of wife, Sue, like a quick-opener that goes for a TD.

Shrimp Hurry Curry

1½ pounds raw peeled cleaned shrimp, fresh or frozen
1 can (10½ ounces) frozen cream of shrimp soup
2 tablespoons butter
1 can (10¾ ounces) cream of mushroom soup

¾ cup sour cream
1½ teaspoons curry powder
2 tablespoons chopped parsley
Rice, toast points or patty shells

Thaw frozen shrimp and soup. Melt butter in 10 inch fry pan. Add shrimp and cook over low heat for 3 to 5 minutes, stirring frequently. Add soups and stir until thoroughly blended. Stir in sour cream, curry powder and parsley. Heat and serve over fluffy rice, toast points or patty shells. Serves 6.

MAGGIE JAHN

From Maggie Jahn, who served as 2nd Vice President, Federation Texas A&M University Mothers' Clubs, 1982-83, comes the following pretty, as well as delicious, recipe.

Strawberry Mousse

1 pint strawberries, frozen
1 package (3 ounces) strawberry gelatin

¼ cup sugar
2 cups whipping cream

Mash thawed strawberries; drain, reserving liquid. Add enough water to juice to make 1½ cups liquid. Bring juice mixture to a boil. Add gelatin and stir until dissolved; chill until consistency of unbeaten egg whites. Combine strawberry pulp and sugar, mix well; stir into gelatin mixture. Beat cream until soft peaks form; fold into strawberry mixture. Spoon into lightly oiled 7 cup mold. Chill until set. Serve slices garnished with whipped cream and fresh strawberries. *Very pretty!*

RACHEL GONZALES

Rachel Gonzales, First Vice President of the Federation of Texas A&M University Mothers' Clubs, 1982-83, submits this recipe from her home in San Antonio.

Spicy Round Steak

1 beef round steak, cut ¾ inch thick (approximately 2 to 2½ pounds)
1 can (8 ounces) tomato sauce
2 tablespoons brown sugar
2 tablespoons Worcestershire sauce
1 tablespoon lemon juice
1 clove garlic, minced
1 teaspoon chili powder
½ teaspoon ground cumin
½ teaspoon salt
⅛ teaspoon pepper
1 tablespoon cooking fat
½ cup water
1 onion, sliced into ¼ inch slices

Combine tomato sauce, brown sugar, Worcestershire sauce, lemon juice, garlic, chili powder, cumin, salt and pepper in a saucepan. Cook slowly 10 minutes, stirring occasionally. Cool. Place steak in utility dish or plastic bag; add marinade and turn to coat. Cover or tie bag securely and marinate in refrigerator 6 to 8 hours, or overnight, turning at least once. Pour off and reserve marinade. Brown steak in cooking fat in large frying pan. Pour off drippings. Add reserved marinade and ½ cup water. Cover tightly and cook slowly 45 minutes. Add onions and continue cooking, covered, 30 to 45 minutes, or until steak is tender. Remove steak to warm platter. Serve cooking liquid thickened with flour, if desired, with steak. Makes 6 servings. *This marinade can be used with venison very successfully.*

ANITA M. DAVIDSON

Anita M. Davidson, Manager and Dietician for Cain Athletic Dining Hall, says the following recipe is a favorite of Aggies of all ages.

Saucy Apple Dumplings

¼ cup sugar	4 medium baking apples,
½ teaspoon ground	pared and cored
cinnamon	Milk
¼ teaspoon ground nutmeg	Pie crust

Mix sugar, cinnamon and nutmeg. Roll apples in sugar mixture. Reserve leftover sugar mixture. Roll out a pie crust into a 14 inch square. Cut into four 7 inch squares. Cover pastry to prevent drying. Place one apple in center of each pastry square. Moisten edges of square; join corners on top of apple and press together. Pinch edges; brush with milk. Place in 9 inch square ungreased baking dish. Sprinkle with remaining sugar mixture. Bake at 425° until tender, about 35 minutes. Serve with Fluffy Swiss Sauce.

FLUFFY SWISS SAUCE:

2 tablespoons butter or	½ teaspoon vanilla
margarine, softened	½ cup shredded Swiss cheese
½ cup powdered sugar	(about 2 ounces)
1 egg yolk	

Beat butter, sugar, egg yolk and vanilla until light and fluffy. Stir in cheese. Serve over warm apple dumplings.

SHIRLEY NEAL

Shirley Neal, Seventh Vice President, Federation of Texas A&M University Mothers' Clubs, 1982-83, shares the following pie favorite of family and guests, alike.

Raspberry Pie

CRUST:

3 cups flour	1 egg, well beaten
1 teaspoon salt	6 tablespoons water
1¼ cups shortening	1 teaspoon vinegar

Sift together flour and salt. Add shortening and mix with fork until crumbly. Add egg, water and vinegar. Mix well and form into 5 balls and chill. Each ball makes one 9 inch crust. Bake crust at 400° for about 8 minutes, until brown. Roll out remaining crust and refrigerate or freeze until needed.

FILLING:

2 packages (10 ounces each) frozen raspberries	⅛ teaspoon salt
1¼ cups raspberry juice	¼ teaspoon vanilla
2½ tablespoons sugar	½ cup chopped walnuts
5 tablespoons cornstarch	Whipped cream

Defrost frozen raspberries according to label. Drain off and measure liquid; add water if necessary to make 1¼ cups. Combine in saucepan sugar, cornstarch and salt. Stir in liquid, cook over low heat stirring until mixture clears and thickens. Add drained raspberries, vanilla and walnuts. Cool with pan set in bowl of ice water, stirring often. Pour into baked cooled pie shell. Chill until set. Serve with whipped cream.

BARBARA McDOUGAL

 Barbara McDougal of Tyler, Texas, Treasurer of the Federation of A&M University Mothers' Clubs, 1982-83, says this recipe is simple to put together, and always a hit! It will serve a bunch of Aggies.

Four Layer Dessert

1ST LAYER:

1 cup flour
½ cup margarine

1 cup chopped pecans

Mix together and press into a 9x13 inch pan. Bake at 350° for 20 to 25 minutes. Let cool.

2ND LAYER:

1½ cups powdered sugar
1 package (8 ounces) cream cheese

1 cup Cool Whip

Mix ingredients thoroughly and spread over crust.

3RD LAYER:

2 cups milk
1 package (3⅝ ounces) instant chocolate pudding

1 package (3⅝ ounces) instant vanilla pudding

Mix milk with puddings and beat until thick. Spread over second layer.

4TH LAYER:

1 cup Cool Whip

Chopped pecans

Top with Cool Whip and sprinkle with pecans. *Cherries or chocolate slivers may be used as garnish.*

LOIS WALTON

 Lois Walton, Federation of Texas A&M University Mothers' Clubs, 1982-83, Social Chairman, submits this casserole creation.

Shrimp Casserole

2½ pounds raw shrimp,
    shelled and deveined
1 tablespoon fresh lemon
    juice
3 tablespoons salad oil
1 cup precooked rice or
    ¾ cup regular rice
2 tablespoons butter
¼ cup minced green pepper
¼ cup minced onion
1 teaspoon salt

⅛ teaspoon pepper
⅛ teaspoon mace
Dash red pepper
1 can (10½ ounces)
    condensed tomato soup,
    undiluted
1 cup whipping cream
½ cup sherry
¾ cup slivered blanched
    almonds

Cook shrimp in boiling water and drain; place in 2 quart casserole, sprinkle with lemon juice and oil and refrigerate. Cook rice as directed, drain and refrigerate. One hour and fifteen minutes before serving, preheat oven to 350° and set aside about 8 shapely shrimp for garnish. Sauté green pepper and onion in butter. Add rice, salt, pepper, mace, red pepper, soup, cream, sherry and ½ cup almonds. Mix with shrimp and toss well. Bake uncovered 35 minutes at 350°. Top with 8 reserved shrimp and ¼ cup almonds. Bake another 20 minutes, until bubbly and slightly brown. Serves 6 to 8.

SHIRLEY LOWERY

This recipe has been tried and tested on incoming Aggie Moms and new students with rave reviews. It originally came from a Louisiana friend of our Federation of Texas A&M University Mothers' Clubs Historian, 1982-83, Shirley Lowery.

Chocolate Pecan Ice Cream

3 well beaten eggs	2 cans Milnot evaporated
1½ cups sugar	milk
3 squares unsweetened	3 cups whipping cream
chocolate, melted	1½ cups pecans
1¼ teaspoons vanilla	5 tablespoons butter

Gradually add sugar to eggs. Add chocolate, vanilla, evaporated milk and whipping cream. Put mixture into freezer and churn until mushy, about 20 minutes. Sauté pecans in butter and add to ice cream mixture. Continue to churn until frozen, about 40 minutes in all.

Variation: 2½ cups white Karo may be substituted for sugar. Whipping cream may be substituted for evaporated milk.

BOBBY JOE CONRAD

Bobby Joe Conrad '58, twelve year veteran with the NFL Cardinals, says this is his favorite chicken recipe. It is a sure-winner when served over long grain rice.

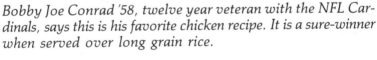

Chicken in Wine

½ cup butter or margarine,	Onion slices
melted	Garlic and paprika
2 chicken breasts, halved	1 cup white cooking wine
4 tomatoes	

After butter has melted, brown chicken breasts. Remove chicken from pan and add onion slices and garlic. Cook a little while, then return chicken to pan. Peel and quarter tomatoes and add to chicken. Sprinkle with paprika. Pour white wine over chicken and simmer about 45 minutes.

JANE BOEHM

From Angleton, Texas, comes the following family favorite recipe from Sixth Vice President Federation of Texas A&M University Mothers' Clubs, 1982-83, Jane Boehm.

PAN BROILED SHRIMP IN BUTTER

½ cup butter or margarine
2 cloves of garlic, minced
1 cup finely chopped onion
1 pound cleaned, deveined shrimp

2 tablespoons chopped fresh parsley or 1 tablespoon dried parsley
Juice of 1 small lemon

Melt butter in frying pan. Add garlic and onion, sauté until soft but not brown. Add shrimp and cook for about 8 minutes or until shrimp turn pink, stirring frequently. Add parsley and lemon juice. Cook 2 or 3 minutes longer.

For a more tart taste, cut up lemon and cook with shrimp; concentrated lemon juice works well, too. Use about ⅓ cup. Put lid on pan during last 2 or 3 minutes of cooking.

MRS. WILLIAM D. COX, JR.

Mrs. William D. Cox, Jr. (Mary Lee), President of Dallas Federation of Women's Clubs, declares this recipe's title says it all! The motion carries!

Pie Delicious

24 creme-filled chocolate cookies
¼ cup melted margarine
2 cups whipping cream, whipped

1 jar (7 ounces) marshmallow creme
¼ cup half-and-half

Roll cookies into crumbs, reserving ½ cup. Mix with melted margarine. Pat into glass pie plate. Add half-and-half to marshmallow creme using electric mixer. Fold in whipped cream. Pour into pie crust. Sprinkle with remaining crumbs. Freeze. Optional: Strawberries may be served over individual slices of pie.

TOM ARRINGTON

Tom Arrington, Creamery Manager, offered this recipe from the Creamery, to make 100 pounds, if the football team is on the way over.

Jalapeño Cheese Formula

50 pounds mild Cheddar
   cheese
25 pounds aged Cheddar
   cheese
9.5 pounds 38 to 40% fat
   cream
3 pounds sodium citrate
1 pound salt

10 pounds water
1 pound dry milk
1 or 1½ cans (10 ounces)
   jalapeño peppers
Cheese color, if desired
7.5 ml. smoked flavor, if
   desired

The cheese should be chopped or grated before starting process. Dissolve the dry milk in the water. Put the chopped cheese, cream, sodium citrate, salt and reconstituted milk in a container and heat to 160°. The cheese must be stirred during the heating process and it will become a smooth, flowing mass. After cheese is melted, add jalapeño peppers which have been chopped or ground, and mix into cheese. Finally, pour the melted product into containers and cool in refrigerator.

Mr. Arrington has scaled down his 100 pound jalapeño cheese formula to a one pound yield.

Jalapeño Cheese Spread

½ pound mild Cheddar
   cheese
¼ pound aged Cheddar
   cheese
3 tablespoons whipping
   cream

1 tablespoon sodium citrate
1 teaspoon salt
3 tablespoons water
1 teaspoon dry milk
2 to 4 tablespoons chopped
   jalapeños

Grate the cheeses; add cream, sodium citrate, salt, water, dry milk and heat to 160°, stirring until the cheese is melted and smooth. Add chopped peppers and pour into container to cool in refrigerator.

Mr. Arrington suggests eliminating the use of cheese color and smoked flavor. The cheese has enough color without additional color and the smoked flavor really does not add to the cheese.

JACK G. FRITTS

Past President of the Former Students Association, Jack G. Fritts '53, boasts of the prowess of favorite cook, Gaye, with this winner.

Peanut Butter - Chocolate Chip Bars

These bars freeze or travel well, but disappear rapidly.

2 eggs	1 package (18.5 ounces) yellow cake mix
⅓ cup water	1 package (12 ounces)
¼ cup butter or margaine, softened	semisweet chocolate pieces, use real chocolate
1 cup crunchy peanut butter	

Preheat oven to 350°. Grease and flour a 10x15 inch jelly roll pan. Beat eggs, water, butter, peanut butter and half cake mix until smooth. Stir in remaining cake mix and chocolate pieces. Dough will be stiff. Spread in pan and bake 20 minutes until lightly browned. Cool and cut into bars. *To keep bar cookies from crumbling, score about half way through when pan first comes out of oven.*

ROBERT SMITH, III

Robert Smith, III, '61, Past President of Former Students Association, says you can bank on his favorite candy recipe.

Chocolate Fudge

⅔ cup evaporated milk	2 squares (1 ounce each) unsweetened chocolate
1 cup sugar	1 tablespoon butter
1 cup light brown sugar	1 teaspoon vanilla
2 tablespoons light corn syrup	⅛ teaspoon salt
	1½ cups chopped pecans

In saucepan, combine milk, sugars, corn syrup and chocolate; cook, stirring constantly until dissolved; then cook to 230° on a candy thermometer, or until it forms a soft ball when dropped into cold water. Remove from heat; add butter and let stand to cool. Stir in vanilla and salt. Beat until thickened and creamy. Make quickly into small balls and roll in chopped nuts. Yields 2 dozen small balls.

JIM MOORE

Jim Moore '52, Past President of the Former Students Association, claims this real hit as one of his favorite dishes, as prepared by wife, Phyllis.

Wild Rice Casserole

½ cup *real* wild rice
1½ cups chicken broth
1 tablespoon butter
2 tablespoons minced onion
⅛ teaspoon marjoram
Dash dried basil
Dash tarragon

1 can (4 ounces) sliced mushrooms or equal amount fresh sautéed
1 can (10¾ ounces) cream of mushroom soup
1 carton (8 ounces) sour cream

Rinse rice well. Cook in chicken broth until tender. Meanwhile, sauté minced onion in butter and add other seasonings, mushrooms and soup. Simmer to blend flavors. Add cooked rice and sour cream heating thoroughly, but do not boil. Serves 6. *To make this a main dish, add chicken breasts (cooked and cut up) and green peppers. May be doubled or even quadrupled successfully. Wild rice has to be cooked for a very long time.*

SUSAN HOPKINS

Susan M. Hopkins, Receptionist for the Former Students Association, vows you can get that gravy and potatoes taste for only 100 calories - a waistline battling idea that is tasty.

Diet Potato

1 medium potato
1 bouillon cube (beef or chicken)

Dash salt and pepper
Aluminum foil

Wash potato well and wrap in foil. Bake in preheated oven at 450° for 45 minutes. Unwrap foil and slice potato lengthwise down the middle. "Stir" in bouillon cube. Re-wrap potato with foil and bake another 7 to 10 minutes. *It will taste great without adding butter or sour cream!*

DON R. WILLIS

Don R. Willis '58, President of the Dallas A&M Club 1982, claims this could become another tradition, it's so good!

Mammaw's Potato Soup
(With an addition or two)

4 medium potatoes, sliced	1 tablespoon flour
¼ cup chopped onion	¼ teaspoon cumin
¼ cup chopped celery	Pinch oregano
2 tablespoons butter	Salt and pepper
2 cups milk	

Mix potatoes, onion and celery in pot and cover with water. Boil until most of water is gone. Add more water. Boil until that's gone. Add butter. Add milk mixed with flour, cumin, oregano, salt and pepper to taste. Simmer for at least one hour. *I sometimes add a little chopped ham and a slice of jalapeño.* Serves 4 adults or 2 teenagers.

ROGER STAUBACH

Former outstanding Dallas Cowboy quarterback, Roger Staubach, shares with us his favorite salad, a guaranteed winner!

Roger Staubach's Spinach Salad

1 bag fresh spinach	¼ teaspoon paprika
4 ounces Bleu cheese	1 can (10¾ ounces) tomato
1 can (2.8 ounces) French	soup
fried onion rings	¾ cup oil
¾ cup sugar	¾ cup vinegar
½ teaspoon salt	1 onion, quartered
1 teaspoon dry mustard	

Wash and remove stems from spinach. Tear in bite size pieces. Crumble Bleu cheese and onion rings over spinach. In a tall bottle, mix dry seasoning ingredients first. Add liquid ingredients (soup, oil, vinegar) and shake well. Put onion in for flavor, but remove before serving. The dressing will be enough for 2 bags of spinach.

JOHN A. ARNOLD

Aggie stalwart, John A. Arnold '47, sends this family recipe which he says even precedes many of the oldest Aggie traditions. This recipe has been in our family since the teens that I know of, is almost failure proof, and I might add is laripin' good.

Aunt Ada's Pecan Pie

½ cup sugar
1 tablespoon flour
3 eggs

1 cup light Karo
1 cup pecan pieces
½ teaspoon vanilla

Blend together sugar and flour. Add eggs and mix well. Stir in Karo, pecan pieces and vanilla. Mix well and pour into unbaked pie shell. Bake at no more than 350° for about 45 minutes.

Mr. Arnold would also like to share the following recipe which was printed in "Holland's Cook Book" as published by the Texas Farm and Ranch Publishing Company of Dallas, Texas, in October 1923.

Ox Tail Soup

Cut from a ham bone the small bits that cannot be saved in slices, put in a pan with an onion and a carrot, sliced fine, and a lump of butter the size of an egg and let brown. Put in the pan 4 tablespoonsful of flour and let brown again; add 2 quarts of good stock and boil 40 minutes. Cut an ox tail in short lengths, put in a frying pan with a lump of butter and a very little water, cover close and let it boil until the water is all gone, let the ox tail fry to a nice even brown all around, strain the stock and pour over the ox tail; add a cupful of boiled barley or rice, season with pepper and salt, let come to a boil and serve.

J. L. HUFFINES, JR.

J. L. Huffines, Jr. '44, Past President of the Aggie Club, and Cotton Bowl Council leader, sends this sweet tooth indulgence - and an Aggie Favorite!

Dentist's Delight

1 package (14 ounces) caramels	¾ cup margarine, softened
⅔ cup evaporated milk, divided	1 cup chopped nuts
1 package (18½ ounces) German chocolate cake mix	1 package (6 ounces) semisweet chocolate morsels

Combine caramels and ⅓ cup evaporated milk in top of double boiler. Cook until caramels are melted. Remove from heat. Combine cake mix, remaining ⅓ cup milk and margarine. Mix with electric mixer until dough holds together. Stir in nuts. Press ½ of dough into a greased 9x13 inch baking pan. Bake 6 minutes at 350°. Sprinkle chocolate morsels over cooked crust. Pour caramel mixture over chocolate morsels. Put remaining dough on top. Bake 15 to 18 minutes at 350°. Cool. Chill 30 minutes. Cut into small squares. Serve with ice cream or whipped cream.

MARY MARTIN

Actress Mary Martin, of "Peter Pan" and "South Pacific" fame, is a native Texan who sings the praises of her quick and delicious cold summer soup.

Creme Senegalese

1 can (10¾ ounces) Campbell's tomato soup	16 ounces sour cream
1 can (10¾ ounces) Campbell's pea soup	1 very healthy teaspoon curry powder

Place ingredients in blender or mixer and thoroughly mix and CHILL. If too thick, thin out with half-and-half at serving time - but it should be served thick. *This is delicious served hot as well.*

BOB FRYMIRE

Bob Frymire '45, President of The Aggie Club and Frymire Engineering Company, aggrees this meets his engineering standards for good eating.

Spinach Casserole

3 packages (10 ounces each) frozen chopped spinach	¼ cup margarine
4 ounces cream cheese, softened	½ pint sour cream
Medium onion, chopped	1 can (7 ounces) artichoke hearts
	Paprika to garnish

Cook spinach as directed. Drain well and add cream cheese to hot spinach, blending well. Sauté onion in margarine (don't brown), add sour cream and put into spinach mixture. Pour into medium casserole dish. Drain artichokes and put on top of casserole, pushing artichokes down until only the tops show. Sprinkle with paprika and bake in moderate oven 25 to 30 minutes.

EDDIE DOMINGUEZ

Restaurateur and avid Basketball supporter Eddie Dominguez '66, sends this recipe which is a traditional favorite and well-practiced on his court!

Spanish Rice

½ cup cooking oil	2 chicken flavor bouillon cubes
1 cup long grain rice	
2 cups water	2 teaspoons salt
1 medium white onion, chopped	½ teaspoon garlic salt
	1 teaspoon pepper
2 medium tomatoes, chopped	

Heat oil and brown rice, stirring to prevent burning. Drain oil. Add water, onion, tomatoes, bouillon cubes, salt, pepper and garlic salt. Cook until water has boiled down to top of rice. Turn heat to low and cover. Keep covered until water has completely evaporated. Stir and serve.

H. B. ZACHRY

H. B. Zachry '22, Chairman of the Board of H. B. Zachry Company, and Distinguished Alumnus, thinks the pioneer spirit should make all Texans appreciate this recipe.

Venison Roast

Remove frozen roast from freezer and soak in water for 24 hours. Drain and cover again with water. Add 2 tablespoons vinegar to each 4 cups of water. Soak another 24 hours. Drain. Wipe meat and score entire roast about 1 inch deep. Season with generous amounts of salt and pepper. Completely cover with butter, pushing down into cuts. Top with brown sugar. Pour red wine over meat to make an inch of liquid in pan. Cook at 325° until black. Baste every 15 minutes for the first 2 or 3 hours of cooking.

Zucchini Soup

4　pounds zucchini
6　slices bacon
1　beef bouillon cube
4　cups water

1　can (10½ ounces) beef bouillon
Salt, pepper and garlic salt to taste
Grated Parmesan cheese

In a large pan, heat 1 cup water and dissolve bouillon cube. Add zucchini which has been washed and cut up, to this water. Cook until tender. Fry bacon until crisp; crumble and add to cooked zucchini. In blender, puree zucchini, bacon and 3 additional cups of water. Return to large pan, add canned bouillon and heat. Add salt, pepper and garlic salt to taste. Serve topped with 1 or 2 tablespoons Parmesan cheese. *This soup may be frozen for later usage.*

Mrs. H. B. Zachry (Polly)
San Antonio, Texas

BONFIRE

No singular tradition symbolizes the burning Spirit of Aggieland as the bonfire. An exacting combination of engineering skills, extended hard work and, finally, teamwork in assembly, the bonfire yields an intensity of radiance and energy to provide an awesome setting for yell practice prior to the t.u. game on Thanksgiving Day.

All who have experienced the electrified air of anticipation recall the rush of genuine Texas A&M excitement as the Fightin' Texas Aggie Band, led by torch-bearing Aggie Yell Leaders, approaches the bonfire. Experience again this epoch of tradition as Dallas Aggie Moms revitalize the Spirit of Aggieland through their *Hullabaloo in the Kitchen.*

JOHN DAVID CROW

John David Crow '58, All-American Halfback, 1957 Heisman Trophy winner, and NFL player for the St. Louis Cardinals, says he and wife, Carolyn, survived on this recipe during their A&M days.

Carolyn's Vegetable Soup

3   tablespoons oil
1½ pounds lean stew meat, cubed
2   tablespoons flour
1   quart water
1   tablespoon salt
1   teaspoon pepper
1   large onion, chopped
3   ribs celery, chopped
3   carrots, chopped
1   can (8½ ounces) small lima beans
1   can (16 ounces) cream corn
1   can (16 ounces) tomatoes, quartered
1   can (8 ounces) tomato sauce
1   potato, chopped, or ¼ cup rice, uncooked
1   bay leaf
1   tablespoon sugar
1   small box (10 ounces) frozen okra, optional

In large Dutch oven, brown meat in oil and remove. Brown flour in drippings, stirring until dark brown. Add water, tomatoes, tomato sauce and seasonings. Let simmer 5 minutes. Add meat and vegetables, except okra. Let simmer until vegetables are done, several hours for full flavor. Add okra the last 30 minutes.

"RED" CASHION

"Red" Cashion '53, popular NFL Referee, and Vice Chairman of Board, ARCO in Bryan, calls this one a touchdown every time.

Texas Jambalaya

8   tablespoons bacon
    drippings
2   large onions, chopped
2   large garlic cloves, minced
8   ribs celery, chopped
2   green peppers, chopped
1   teaspoon thyme
½   teaspoon pepper
1   teaspoon paprika
2   whole bay leaves
4   tablespoons chopped
    parsley
4   teaspoons salt

2   tablespoons Worcestershire
    sauce
1   can (1 pound, 4 ounces)
    tomato juice
1   can (1 pound, 4 ounces)
    tomatoes
4   tablespoons flour
4   tablespoons cold water
4   pounds cleaned, raw
    shrimp
2   packages frozen lump crab
    meat
2   cans (10 ounces each)
    clams

Melt drippings in skillet, add vegetables and seasonings. Cook about 10 minutes, until tender. Blend flour and water and add to gravy to hasten thickening. Add shrimp, crab meat and clams. Simmer 20 minutes and serve over hot rice with hot French bread. *You may add cooked, boned, chopped chicken after seafood is cooked.*

SHERI RYMAN

Sheri Ryman '83, Texas A&M's own Miss Texas 1981, sends this favorite of Aggies for use as "study aid."

Kiss Cookies

½ cup butter
½ cup peanut butter
½ cup sugar
½ cup firmly packed brown sugar
1 unbeaten egg

1 teaspoon vanilla
1¾ cups sifted flour
1 teaspoon baking soda
½ teaspoon salt
Small bag Hershey's kisses

Cream together butter and peanut butter. Gradually add sugars, egg and vanilla. Beat well. Blend in flour, soda and salt. Shape into balls, using a rounded teaspoon for each. Roll balls in sugar and place on ungreased cookie sheet. Bake at 375° for 8 minutes. Remove from oven and place Hershey's kiss on top of each cookie, pressing down firmly so that cookie brown. Tester suggests do not return cookie to oven if firm candy kiss is desired.

JOHN AND SHEILA MABRY

Clothiers John and Sheila Mabry affirm that this secret recipe for English soup suits the most discriminating taste.

Sheila's Soup

2 cans (10½ ounces each) Old Fashioned Vegetable Soup
1 can water
1 level teaspoon thyme
1 level teaspoon oregano

1 level teaspoon basil
9 drops Tabasco
Salt
Pepper
¼ cup butter

Blend the soup in blender for 15 seconds or until pureed. Add water and spices and heat. *Serve in appetizer cups - an excellent appetizer soup.*

CINDY HENDERSON

Cheerful Cindy Henderson '76, familiar Dallas-Fort Worth area gardening advisor is an Aggie, and proud of it! Cindy submits this recipe, which she says came as a package deal with her husband, Curt.

Mother-In-Law Spaghetti Sauce

1½ pounds ground beef
¼ cup olive oil
2 cloves finely minced garlic
1 large onion, chopped
2 or 3 ribs celery, chopped
1 green pepper, chopped
1 pepperoni sausage, thinly sliced
1 can (4 ounces) mushrooms, stems and pieces, with juice

4 cans (8 ounces each) tomato sauce
4 cans (6 ounces each) tomato paste
2 or 3 tablespoons spaghetti sauce seasoning
1 tablespoon sugar
Salt and pepper to taste
Parmesan cheese

Brown ground beef in olive oil; add garlic, onion, celery, green pepper and pepperoni. Simmer a few minutes. Add mushrooms, tomato sauce and tomato paste. Season with spaghetti sauce seasoning, sugar, salt and pepper. Stir in a generous amount of Parmesan cheese and add water if too thick. Simmer for at least an hour - longer is better. *And it's always better the next day.* You may freeze in proper containers. Serves 6 to 8.

GENE STALLINGS

Gene Stallings '57, former A&M Head Football coach, came home from Dallas Cowboy Training Camp raving about this dish. He taught his wife how to perpare it. This is a man pleaser!

Gene's Baked Potatoes

10 large new potatoes	1½ cups grated Colby cheese
¾ cup butter	Bacon bits
5 fresh chopped onions	1 pint sour cream
Salt and pepper to taste	

Boil potatoes until a fork easily punctures them. Pour off water and peel while hot. Mash by hand, leaving in medium size chunks while mixing in butter, salt, pepper, onions, bacon bits and half the cheese. Stir in sour cream and pour into a baking dish. Top with remaining cheese and bake until bubbly at 325°.

JIM MYERS

Coach Jim Myers, of Dallas Cowboys and Texas A&M coaching fame, sent in his choice recipe by his favorite team-mate, Carolyn.

Viva La Chicken

4 whole chicken breasts	1 large onion, chopped or grated fine
1 dozen corn tortillas	
2 cans (10¾ ounces each) cream of chicken soup	4 ounces green chili salsa (mild or hot)
1 can (10¾ ounces) cream of mushroom soup	1 pound grated Cheddar cheese (medium or sharp)
¼ cup milk	

Wrap chicken breasts in foil and bake at 400° for 1 hour. Cool and bone. Cut in large pieces. Mix soups, milk, onion and salsa. Cut tortillas in 1 inch squares or strips. Butter large shallow baking dish. Put 2 table-spoons of juice from chicken in bottom of casserole. Place a layer of tortillas, chicken, soup mixture and cheese; repeat. Let stand in refrigerator 24 hours. Bake at 300° for 1 to 1½ hours.

DANNY WHITE

 Dallas Cowboy's quarterback Danny White "passed" us this recipe, which, during holidays is delicious especially when served in a "Super Bowl."

Cherry Holiday Cake

1 cup sugar	Dash salt
1 cup flour	½ cup chopped walnuts
1 teaspoon soda	1 egg, beaten
1 teaspoon cinnamon	2 cups sour pitted cherries
1 tablespoon melted butter	(save juice!)

SAUCE:
Cherry juice	½ cup sugar
1 tablespoon melted butter	1 tablespoon cornstarch

Combine all ingredients and blend. Pour into greased and floured 8 inch square pan and bake for 40 minutes at 350°.

SAUCE: Blend ingredients and cook over medium heat until thick. Pour warm on top of cake when serving.

BOB HOPE

 Comedian Bob Hope, everyone's favorite personality and friend of Texas A&M University, declares the server of this favorite will be "Thanked for the Memories."

Bob Hope's Favorite Chicken Hash

2 chicken breasts, broiled	½ teaspoon lemon juice
2 strips of bacon, cooked crisp	Salt and pepper
½ onion, chopped	2 tablespoons sour cream
2 tablespoons butter	1 teaspoon dry sherry wine

Cut broiled chicken breasts into thin strips and crumble bacon. Sauté onion in butter and add lemon juice and seasonings. Stir in chicken and bacon. Heat thoroughly. Shortly before serving time, stir in sour cream and sherry. Do not cook after adding last two ingredients; just heat thoroughly.

ANN LANDERS

ANN LANDERS

Advice columnist Ann Landers contributed this recipe, which she tested in her own oven. It was sent to her by a Washington, D.C. reader. She declares it is a winner, even for the lovelorn.

Best Ever Lemon Pie

1   baked (9 inch) deep pie shell

FILLING:

1¼ cups sugar	3 egg yolks
6 tablespoons cornstarch	3 tablespoons butter
2 cups water	1½ teaspoons lemon extract
⅓ cup lemon juice	2 teaspoons vinegar

NEVER FAIL MERINGUE:

1 tablespoon cornstarch	6 tablespoons sugar
2 tablespoons cold water	1 teaspoon vanilla
½ cup boiling water	Pinch of salt
3 egg whites	

FILLING: Mix sugar and cornstarch together in top of double boiler; add water. Combine egg yolks with juice and beat. Add to above mixture and cook until thick over boiling water, about 25 minutes. This does away with starchy taste. Now add butter, lemon extract and vinegar, stirring thoroughly. Pour into pie shell and let cool.

MERINGUE: Blend cornstarch and cold water in saucepan. Add boiling water and cook, stirring until clear and thickened. Let stand until completely cold.

Beat egg whites at high speed until foamy. Gradually add sugar and beat until stiff but not dry. Turn mixer to low speed, add salt and vanilla. Gradually beat in cold cornstarch mixture; turn mixer to high speed and beat well. Spread meringue over cooled pie filling. Bake at 350° about 10 minutes. *This meringue cuts beautifully and never gets sticky!*

DAVID WADE

Internationally recognized as "The Gourmet" on radio and television, David Wade presents this variation of an Aggie favorite, sure to win gold medals at your table!

Festive Potato Salad

3   cups boiled potatoes, diced
2   tablespoons oil
1   tablespoon vinegar
1   teaspoon salt
½   cup ripe olives
1½ cups finely shredded
    cabbage
¼   cup chopped dill pickle
½   cup coarsely grated carrot

2   tablespoons diced pimiento
2   tablespoons diced green
    pepper
⅔   cup mayonnaise
2   teaspoons grated onion
1   teaspoon prepared
    mustard
Pepper to taste

Dice hot, freshly boiled potatoes to make 3 cups. Blend oil, vinegar and salt and sprinkle over potatoes. Mix lightly and let stand until cold. Cut olives into large pieces. Combine olives, potatoes, cabbage, pickle, carrot, pimiento and green pepper. Blend mayonnaise, onion, mustard and pepper; pour over salad mixture and blend lightly. Serve well chilled. Serves 6.

MRS. FRANK RASOR

Mrs. Frank Rasor, Fourth Vice President of the Federation of Texas A&M University Mothers' Clubs, 1982-83, shares this tasty favorite.

Hash Brown Casserole

1   package (32 ounces) frozen
    hash brown potatoes
¼   cup margarine
1   carton (8 ounces) sour
    cream

1   can (10¾ ounces) cream
    of mushroom soup
Chopped onion
Bacon bits
Grated Cheddar cheese

Place frozen hash brown potatoes in greased dish or pan. Melt margarine and pour over potatoes. Salt and pepper as desired. Sprinkle chopped onion over casserole. Spread sour cream, cream of mushroom soup, bacon bits and top with grated cheese. Bake at 375° for one hour. *This recipe may be increased or decreased depending on the number of hungry Aggies you have on hand.*

PAUL HARVEY

Paul Harvey, radio commentator and motivational speaker, sends this favorite appetite motivator, guaranteed to announce good news to your dining audience.

Lemon Ice Box Cake

1 tablespoon gelatin	1 teaspoon grated lemon rind
¼ cup cold water	
½ cup sugar	4 egg whites
½ cup lemon juice	½ cup sugar
½ teaspoon salt	1½ dozen lady fingers
4 egg yolks	½ pint whipped cream, optional

Soak gelatin in cold water. Combine first ½ cup sugar, lemon juice, salt and egg yolks. Stir and cook in double boiler until consistency of custard. Stir in gelatin and grated lemon rind and cool. Whip egg whites until stiff and slowly beat in ½ cup sugar. When custard begins to thicken, beat with spoon until fluffy and fold in egg whites. Line a pan with wax paper and lady fingers. Pour in lemon mixture and cover top with lady fingers. Refrigerate 12 hours. Serve with whipped cream. Serves 8. *Vanilla wafer crumbs may be substituted for lady fingers.*

RUBY CARPENTER

Ruby Carpenter, Auditing Committee, Federation of Texas A&M University Mothers' Clubs, 1982-83, sends this recipe for scrumptious munching.

Butter Cookies

4 cups sifted flour	½ cup cornstarch
1 cup powdered sugar	1 pound butter

Blend all ingredients together in mixer. Make 4 or more rolls of cookie dough. Wrap in wax paper and refrigerate until cold and firm. Slice thin and bake on cookie sheet at 350° for 6 to 8 minutes, just until lightly brown. Cookies will be about 1 inch in diameter and about ¼ inch thick. Makes 10 dozen. *These cookies are great for teas. Will keep indefinitely, cooked or uncooked. Will freeze.*

RICK COOK

Rick Cook, interior and floral decorator, designer, caterer, contributing editor for Dallas-Fort Worth Home and Garden Magazine, creative talent personified from Arkansas to New York to Texas shares some of his culinary successes with Hullabaloo.

Curried Chicken Salad

5 cups chunked cooked chicken
3 Granny Smith apples, diced
¾ cup diced pineapple

½ cup currants
1 cup diced celery
¼ cup coarsely chopped walnuts

DRESSING:
¾ cup enriched chicken broth
2 teaspoons curry powder
1 teaspoon lemon juice

¾ cup mayonnaise
¾ cup sour cream

Combine salad ingredients. Set aside. Combine chicken broth and curry. Simmer 2 to 3 minutes. Cool. Add lemon juice, mayonnaise and sour cream. Blend well. Pour over chicken mixture. Allow flavors to blend 1 hour. Serve stuffed in tomatoes or between sliced and buttered croissants. Serves 10 to 12.

Summer Pasta Salad

1 pound fresh pasta, cooked
1 cup green olives, chopped or sliced
1 cup ripe olives, chopped or sliced
½ cup chopped sweet red pepper

1¼ cups sliced celery
1½ cups grated zucchini
⅓ cup chopped parsley
2 tablespoons cilantro
¾ pound asparagus tips

DRESSING:
4 cloves garlic
¼ cup red wine vinegar
¼ cup raspberry vinegar
1 teaspoon salt

½ cup cooking oil
½ cup olive oil
Coarse ground pepper

Combine warm pasta with remaining salad ingredients. Blend dressing ingredients and pour over salad. Allow flavors to blend before serving. Serves 10 to 12.

ROSANNE GREENE

Rosanne Greene, food stylist and proprietress of Rosanne Greene's School of Cooking - Dallas, graciously shares a recipe from one of her classes. She is the first Dallasite to become a Certified Member of the International Association of Cooking Schools.

Potage Veloute Aux Champignons
Cream of Mushroom Soup

¼ cup minced onions	⅓ bay leaf
5 tablespoons butter	⅛ teaspoon thyme
5 tablespoons flour	Salt and pepper to taste
6 cups chicken stock	Chopped stems from 1 pound
2 parsley sprigs	fresh mushrooms

Sauté the yellow onions until tender, add the flour, stir in the hot stock, parsley, bay leaf, thyme and salt and pepper to taste. Add stems of mushrooms. Simmer partially covered for 20 minutes or more, skimming occasionally. Strain, pressing juices out of stems. Return soup to pan.

2 tablespoons butter	Thinly sliced mushroom caps
1 teaspoon lemon juice	Salt

Melt butter. Add mushrooms, lemon juice and salt. Cover and cook slowly for about 5 minutes. Add to soup base. Simmer for 10 minutes.

2 egg yolks	1 to 3 tablespoons butter
½ to ¾ cup whipping cream	

To enrich the sauce, beat the egg yolks and cream together. Add some soup to egg and cream mixture. Gradually add to soup base. Correct seasoning. Add butter. Decorate with fluted mushrooms (cooked in butter and lemon juice) and/or minced chervil or parsley. Serve hot.

DON JANUARY

Don January, legendary Dallas pro-golfer, claims this salad, as made by wife, Pat, takes top prize at any tournament.

Day Ahead Green Salad

2   cups iceberg lettuce (in small pieces)
2   cups fresh spinach (in small pieces)
2   bunches green onions, sliced
8   pieces crisp bacon, crumbled
5   hard cooked eggs, sliced

1   cup sliced mushrooms
1   can (5 ounces) sliced water chestnuts
1   can (7 ounces) hearts of palm or artichoke hearts, optional
1   package (10 ounces) frozen green peas, uncooked

DRESSING:
2   cups sour cream
1   cup mayonnaise

2   packages (7 ounces each) Good Seasons Italian Salad Dressing

In a clear glass bowl, layer half of lettuce, spinach, onions, bacon, eggs, mushrooms, water chestnuts, and hearts of palm or artichoke hearts, ending with half of uncooked peas.

DRESSING: Mix sour cream, mayonnaise and Good Seasons. Layer ½ of this dressing on top of peas. Layer rest of ingredients in same order, ending with remaining dressing. Seal and refrigerate for 24 hours. Serves 12.

Appetizers & Beverages

APPETIZERS

Webster's Dictionary defines an "appetizer" as something that stimulates the appetite; "a small portion of tasty food or a drink at the beginning of a meal to stimulate the appetite."

In France appetizers are called *"hors d'oeuvres"* or *"canapes"*; in Sweden that something before a meal is called *"smörgasbord"*; in Denmark it is *"smörrebord"*; in Norway, *"kaltibord"*; and in Itally, *"antipasto."* Whatever the country, appetizers can be served either hot or cold. They can be a variety of flavors and a variety of foods. The basic components are usually meat, fish, cheese, eggs and vegetables in various flavorful combinations.

Color and attractiveness of food are an important part of appetizers, since they are intended to appeal to and entice your indulgence.

Appetizers are a beginning to a meal or an accompaniment to a beverage at a festive party, so the choice of appetizers should complement the main course and not be a repetition of what is to come.

The Dallas A&M Mothers have collected the following appetizer recipes and would like to offer them to you to please your palate and tantalize your taste.

Artichoke Dip

2 cans (14 ounces each) artichoke hearts
1 cup Hellmann's mayonnaise
¼ cup Spice Islands dehydrated bacon and chives

Drain artichoke hearts in colander. Cut with kitchen scissors or chop medium fine. Add mayonnaise and bacon and chives. Beat with mixer on slow speed. Serve with Melba toast rounds. Serves 6 to 8.

Mrs. Jack McAuliff (Betty)

Black-Eyed Pea Dip

4 cups cooked black-eyed
  peas, drained
3 small jalapeño peppers,
  chopped
1 tablespoon juice from
  jalapeños
1 can (4 ounces) chopped
  green chilies

¼ cup chopped onion
½ teaspoon garlic powder
½ pound sharp cheese,
  grated
1 cup butter or margarine,
  softened

Mash peas, add remaining ingredients and mix thoroughly. Serve with corn chips or tortilla chips.

Mrs. Robert E. Clark (Sylvia)

Broccoli Cheese Dip

1 roll (6 ounces) garlic
  cheese, or substitute 6
  ounces pasteurized
  American cheese and ½
  teaspoon garlic powder
1 can (4 ounces)
  mushrooms, drained

1 can (10¾ ounces) cream
  of mushroom soup,
  undiluted
1 package (10 ounces) frozen
  broccoli, cooked and
  drained
3 ribs celery, diced
¼ to ½ cup chopped onion

Sauté mushrooms, celery and onions. Melt cheese and add sautéed vegetables. Add mushroom soup and broccoli. Bake at 325° for 15 minutes. Serve in chafing dish with rye bread cut into thin slices.

Mrs. Terry Dwyer (Tori)

Variation: May substitute one roll (6 ounces) jalapeño cheese and dash Tabasco.

QUICKIE: Hollow out cherry tomatoes and fill with well seasoned guacamole. Pretty and tasty!

Clam Shrimp Dip
Easy

1 package (8 ounces) cream cheese, softened	1 teaspoon chopped parsley
	1 teaspoon horseradish
1 can (10 ounces) Campbell's cream of shrimp soup	1 can (7½ ounces) minced clams, drained

Beat cream cheese until fluffy, then add other ingredients. Serve with chips or crackers.

Mrs. Jack McAuliff (Betty)

Confetti Dip

3 egg yolks, beaten	½ cup finely chopped onions
3 tablespoons sugar	½ cup finely chopped green
3 tablespoons white vinegar	pepper
½ teaspoon salt	1 jar (2 ounces) pimientos
2 tablespoons margarine	Dash Tabasco sauce
1 package (8 ounces) cream cheese, softened	Dash Worcestershire sauce

Cook beaten egg yolks, sugar, vinegar, salt and margarine in double boiler. Stir until thickened. Blend with cream cheese. Fold in remaining ingredients. Serve with chips or vegetable sticks. *Sugar may be adjusted to taste.*

Mrs. Tom Graham (Norma)

DIP FOR FRUIT

1 jar (8 ounces) marshmallow cream	Grated orange rind
	Orange juice to make right
1 package (8 ounces) cream cheese	consistency for dipping

Combine all ingredients.

Aggie Mom

QUICKIE: Combine 2 packages (3 ounces each) cream cheese with mayonnaise, 1 can (4½ ounces) black olives and dill weed to taste. Serve with crackers.

Low-Cal Dip

1 package (6 ounces) Ranch Green Goddess dry mix

1 carton (16 ounces) low fat cottage cheese

Mix in blender for 3 minutes. Serve with raw vegetables: yellow squash, carrots, cauliflower, broccoli and celery.

Mrs. Richard Hatch (Arlene)

Nacho Appetizer
Easy, fast to fix and quickly consumed!

1 can (10½ ounces) bean dip

1 can (4 ounces) chopped green chilies, drained

1 carton (8 ounces) frozen avocado dip

1 can (4½ ounces) chopped ripe olives

2 or 3 hard cooked eggs, chopped

1 cup shredded Cheddar cheese

1 medium sized tomato, chopped

Tortilla chips

Spread bean dip in a 7" circle on serving plate. Top with layers of chilies, thawed avocado dip, olives, eggs and cheese. Invert a bowl over top to shape. Refrigerate until ready to serve. Remove bowl. Top with tomatoes. Serve with chips.

Mrs. William D. Leavitt (Joni)

Variation: On top of avocado dip add a layer of 1 cup sour cream, 1 package Taco seasoning mix combined with ½ cup Hellmann's mayonnaise; layer 1 bunch green onions, chopped on top of olives.

Aggie Mom

Raw Vegetable Dip

1 cup mayonnaise

1 cup sour cream

1 teaspoon anchovy paste

2 cloves garlic, crushed

2 teaspoons lemon juice

2 teaspoons paprika

Salt and pepper to taste

Blend all ingredients together. Fold in ¼ cup Parmesan cheese and ¼ teaspoon sugar. Chill. Serve with raw vegetables.

Mrs. George Kardell (Roe)

Raw Vegetable Spinach Dip

1 package Knorr's vegetable soup mix	1 cup sour cream
1 cup mayonnaise	1 package (10 ounces) frozen chopped spinach

Thaw spinach and drain well. Pat with paper towels. Mix all ingredients. Serve with vegetables or chips.

Mrs. James Doyle (Barbara)

Variation: Add 2 green onions with tops, chopped fine and 1 can (8 ounces) chopped water chestnuts.

Mrs. Joy Anderson

Vegetable Dip

2 cups sour cream	1 package (7 ounces) Good Seasons Italian dressing mix

Mix ingredients 6 to 8 hours before serving. Store covered in refrigerator.

Mrs. James E. Keeling (Betty)

Roquefort Cheese Dip

1 package (8 ounces) cream cheese	1 teaspoon Lawry's seasoned salt
2 tablespoons grated onion	2 tablespoons mayonnaise
1 ounce Roquefort cheese	⅓ cup milk

Assemble all ingredients in blender and process until smooth. Serve with carrot, celery, red cabbage, cauliflower, green pepper and cucumber sticks.

Mrs. Harry Holmes (Lillian)

Fill celery ribs with a mixture of cream cheese and caraway seeds.

Celery salt and thyme blended in melted process cheese makes nice cheese spread.

Shrimp Bayou Dip

2 pounds cooked shrimp	3 tablespoons lemon juice
⅔ cup chopped celery	2 tablespoons horseradish
¼ cup chopped green onion	1 tablespoon mustard
1 package (8 ounces) cream cheese	½ teaspoon paprika
	½ teaspoon salt
½ cup chili sauce	¼ teaspoon Tabasco sauce

Combine coarsely chopped shrimp, celery and green onions. Add softened cream cheese. Combine remaining ingredients with shrimp and cheese mixture. Refrigerate 12 hours and serve with crackers.

Mrs. James R. Jones (Bobbie)

Texas Crabgrass

1 cup butter	1 or 2 cans (7 ounces each) crabmeat
1 medium onion, finely chopped	1½ cups Parmesan cheese
2 packages (10 ounces each) frozen spinach, cooked and drained well	

Sauté onion in butter until soft. Add spinach and Parmesan cheese; heat. Add crabmeat and serve hot with tortilla chips. Yields 1½ quarts.

Aggie Mom

Mary's Crab Spread

1 package (8 ounces) cream cheese, softened	Dash Tabasco sauce
	Dash Worcestershire sauce
1 jar (5 ounces) Old English cheese spread	8 to 10 ounces crabmeat, flaked
¼ cup mayonnaise	½ teaspoon lemon juice

Combine all ingredients and serve with crackers.
Variation: For a dip add 2 to 4 tablespoons cream until the right consistency. Serve with chips.

Mrs. Arthur Collins (Mary)

French Ham and Cheese Fondue

3 cups cubed French bread
3 cups cubed cooked ham
½ pound mild Cheddar
cheese, 1 inch cubes
3 tablespoons flour
1 tablespoon dry mustard

3 tablespoons melted butter
or margarine
4 eggs
3 cups milk
Tabasco sauce

Make a layer of one third of bread, ham and cheese cubes in a buttered, straight side 2 quart baking dish. Mix flour and mustard; sprinkle about 1 tablespoon over layer; drizzle 1 tablespoon melted butter over layer. Repeat with remaining bread, ham, cheese, flour mixture, and butter to make two more layers. Beat eggs with milk and Tabasco sauce in medium size bowl until fluffy. Pour over layers in baking dish. Cover and refrigerate at least 4 hours or overnight. Bake uncovered in moderate oven at 350° for 1 hour or until puffed and golden. Serve at once. Serves 6.

Mrs. Robert W. Loewe (Patricia)

Bacon Cheese Spread

¼ cup roasted, unblanched
almond slices
2 strips crisp bacon
1 cup grated American
cheese

1 tablespoon chopped green
onion
½ cup mayonnaise
Dash Tabasco sauce

Chop almonds, crumble bacon and blend with remaining ingredients. Serve with party crackers.

Mrs. Kenneth D. Cheairs (Dorothy)

Curry Spread

1 cup chopped black olives
1 cup grated sharp Cheddar
cheese
¼ cup chopped green onions
and tops

¼ teaspoon curry powder
4 tablespoons mayonnaise
Salt and pepper to taste

Mix and spread on party size rye or pumpernickle bread. Heat under broiler until bubbly.

Aggie Mom

Beef Spread

1 package (8 ounces) cream
   cheese
½ cup sour cream
2 tablespoons milk
¼ cup chopped green pepper
2 tablespoons onion flakes

¼ teaspoon garlic powder
½ package (2.5 ounces)
   chipped beef, diced
½ cup chopped pecans
2 tablespoons melted butter

Blend cream cheese, sour cream and milk. Add green pepper, onion flakes, garlic powder and diced beef. Blend together and place in 8 inch pie plate. Brown pecans in melted butter. Sprinkle over top of mixture in pie plate. Bake at 350° for 20 minutes. Serve with Ritz crackers. *Leftovers are good cold or reheated. Cover when reheating.*

Marilyn Manning

Holiday Cheese Ball

1 package (6 ounces) Kraft
   Blue Chip cheese
2 jars (5 ounces each) Kraft
   Old English cheese
2 packages (8 ounces each)
   cream cheese
1 or 2 tablespoons grated
   onion

1 tablespoon Worcestershire
   sauce
1 cup chopped pecans
½ cup chopped parsley
½ teaspoon Accent
Dash Tabasco sauce

Let cheeses stand at room temperature and cream together. Reserve ½ cup pecans and ¼ cup parsley. Add remaining ingredients. Mix together thoroughly. Line bowls or molds with waxed paper or foil and fill with cheese mixture, pressing down firmly. Fold excess paper over cheese and refrigerate from 8 to 10 hours or overnight. Let stand at room temperature before using. Roll in remaining parsley and nuts.

Variation: Cheese ball may be rolled in chili powder or chopped stuffed olives.

Mrs. James E. Keeling (Betty)

Variation: Reduce nuts to ½ cup. Add ¼ cup chopped chives. Roll in ¼ cup pecans and ¼ cup chives.

Mrs. Rodney W. Kelly (Pat)

Cheese Ball
Ideal for the food processor

2 packages (8 ounces each) cream cheese, softened
1 can (8½ ounces) crushed pineapple, drained
¼ cup finely chopped green pepper
2 tablespoons finely chopped onion
1 teaspoon seasoned salt
2 cups chopped pecans
Parsley

Combine cream cheese, pineapple, green pepper, onion, seasoned salt and 1 cup of pecans. Blend well and shape into a ball. Coat outside of ball in remaining pecans and chill. Garnish with parsley. Serve with chips and crackers. Yields one (7 inch) ball.

Mrs. John J. Jones III (Geraine)
Mrs. W. C. Marks (Belle)

Holiday Cheese Log

1 pound sharp cheese, grated
1 package (3 ounces) cream cheese, softened
1 teaspoon garlic powder
2 tablespoons mayonnaise
3 dashes Tabasco sauce
½ cup chopped pecans
Chili powder
60 Ritz crackers
20 stuffed olives, sliced for garnish

Have sharp cheese and cream cheese at room temperature. Mix cheeses well. Add garlic powder, mayonnaise, Tabasco and pecans. Form into two logs and roll in chili powder to cover. Wrap logs in plastic wrap or foil and chill about two hours or until firm. When ready to use, slice and place on Ritz crackers. Top each with an olive slice. Yields 60 servings. *The logs can be made the day before a party.*

Mrs. Sam C. Laden, Jr. (Mary Lou)

Deep Fried Mushrooms

1 pound fresh mushrooms
2 eggs, slightly beaten
Flour
Bread crumbs

Wash and clean mushrooms. Cut large ones in half. Dip in flour, eggs and bread crumbs. Deep fry in oil. Serve with mustard dip.

Mrs. Glinn White (Bettyeann)

Mustard Dip for Vegetables and Fried Mushrooms

1 cup sour cream
1 cup Miracle Whip salad dressing
3 tablespoons Dijon mustard
¼ cup chopped onion
1 clove garlic
Dash salt
3 dashes Worcestershire sauce
Paprika

Combine all ingredients. Sprinkle paprika on top. Serve with raw vegetables. *Delicious with fried mushrooms.*

Mrs. Glinn White (Bettyeann)

Mushroom and Olive Rolls

1 can (10¾ ounces) mushroom soup, undiluted
½ cup chopped ripe olives
1 green onion, chopped
1 teaspoon Worcestershire sauce
1 large loaf thinly sliced sandwich bread
Melted butter

Mix soup, olives, onion and Worcestershire sauce. Cut crusts from bread. Spread slices with above mixture, roll and fasten with toothpicks. Cut in half after rolled. Place in buttered pan and brush with melted butter. Bake at 450° for 10 minutes. Serve hot.

Mrs. H. Smith (Alyne)

Mushrooms with Stuffing

1 pound large fresh mushrooms
2 tablespoons chopped shallots
6 tablespoons butter or margarine
1 cup Pepperidge Farm herb-seasoned stuffing mix
½ cup chicken broth
¼ teaspoon garlic salt

Clean mushrooms and remove stems. Sauté chopped stems and shallots in 4 tablespoons butter. Stir in stuffing, chicken broth and garlic salt. Stuff mushrooms with mixture and place in oven tempered pie pan with 2 tablespoons butter. Bake in 350° oven for 20 minutes or until done. Appetizers may be prepared ahead and refrigerated or frozen. Serves 4 to 6.

Mrs. Frank E. Ducotey (Ruth)

Crab Puffs

1 package (8 ounces) cream cheese	2 drops sesame oil
2 tablespoons bread crumbs	1 can (7 ounces) crabmeat
½ teaspoon monosodium glutamate	1 package (16 ounces) wonton skins
	Planters Peanut oil for frying

Mix first 5 ingredients and place 1 teaspoon on each wonton skin. Fold skins over from each corner, seal with a drop of water. Deep fry in oil until brown, about 2 minutes. Drain. Serve plain or with hot mustard dip.

Variation: Fill with preserves, fry, drain and sprinkle with powdered sugar.

Mrs. Jack Starry (Dorothy)

Clam Puffs

PASTRY:

1 cup clam broth	1 cup flour
½ cup butter	4 eggs, room temperature

FILLING:

3 cans (10½ ounces each) minced clams, reserve juice	Tabasco to taste
	1 teaspoon pepper
6 packages (3 ounces each) chive cream cheese, softened	1 teaspoon Lawry's seasoned salt

If necessary, add water to clam broth to equal 1 cup. Heat broth and bring to boil. Add flour all at once and stir vigorously with wooden spoon over low heat until mixture leaves sides of pan and forms a smooth ball. Transfer to mixing bowl. Add eggs, one at a time, beating thoroughly after each addition until thick dough is formed. Place level teaspoons of dough on ungreased baking sheet about 1 inch apart. Bake at 400° for 10 minutes. Reduce heat to 300° without opening door for 20 to 25 minutes. Cool puffs, cut in half and fill with clam filling. Replace tops and serve.

FILLING: Drain clams and combine with cream cheese. Add seasonings. Mix well.

Puffs may be frozen on flat tray and stored in plastic bags when frozen. On serving day, heat at 400° for 15 minutes.

Mrs. Frank E. Ducotey (Ruth)

Sue's Marinated Sprouts

1 package (10 ounces)
  Brussels sprouts
½ cup Italian dressing

½ teaspoon dill weed,
  optional
1 tablespoon sliced green
  onion

Cook Brussels sprouts as directed; drain. Mix Italian dressing, dill weed and green onions. Pour over sprouts. Chill several hours. Drain off excess dressing before serving. Serves 4.

Mrs. George D. Neal (Carolyn)

New Orleans Shrimp

36 medium sized whole
  cooked, peeled shrimp
1 medium onion, finely
  chopped
1 clove garlic
½ cup Kraft's French
  Dressing

1 tablespoon finely chopped
  parsley
1 ounce horseradish
2 tablespoons hot prepared
  mustard
Pinch thyme

Mix all ingredients well. Chill overnight. Remove whole garlic clove. Serve with crackers as an appetizer or on lettuce leaf as a salad. *This is a tried and true recipe. Very good as an appetizer and can be made ahead of time.*

Mrs. Jack McAuliff (Betty)

Shrimp Mold

1 can (10¾ ounces) tomato
  soup
1 package (16 ounces) cream
  cheese
1 tablespoon Knox gelatin
¼ cup cold water

1 cup mayonnaise
¾ cup chopped celery
¼ cup chopped onion
¼ cup chopped green pepper
2 medium cans (4¼ ounces
  each) shrimp, drained

Heat mixture of soup and cream cheese to boiling. Dissolve gelatin in cold water. Add gelatin and mayonnaise to hot soup mixture. Blend thoroughly. Add celery, onion, green pepper and shrimp. Stir well. Pour into mold and refrigerate five or more hours. Serve on crackers.

Mrs. Frank E. Ducotey (Ruth)

Smoked Oyster Roll

1 package (8 ounces) cream
cheese
1½ tablespoons Hellmann's
mayonnaise
1 teaspoon Worcestershire
sauce
Dash garlic powder

Dash onion powder
Dash salt
Dash Tabasco
6 jalapeño peppers
1 can (3.75 ounces) smoked
oysters, drained well

Mix cream cheese, mayonnaise, Worcestershire sauce, garlic powder, onion powder and salt. Add Tabasco until mixture is pink. Spread mixture about ¼ inch thick on waxed paper. Spread chopped jalapeño peppers over cream cheese. Add smoked oysters cut into small pieces over jalapeños. Roll mixture and chill 30 minutes. Roll in parsley and serve with crackers.

Mrs. Jack Starry (Dorothy)

Ham Crisps

1 package (8 ounces) cream
cheese, softened
1 can (4½ ounces) deviled
ham
¼ cup mayonnaise
2 teaspoons prepared
mustard
⅛ teaspoon salt

Dash pepper
2 tablespoons sweet pickle
relish
30 small round crackers
1 small cucumber, thinly
sliced
Parsley

Combine cream cheese and deviled ham and beat with mayonnaise, mustard, salt, pepper and pickle relish. Chill for several hours or overnight. Just before serving spread ½ teaspoon ham mixture on each cracker. Top with cucumber slice, then a heaping teaspoon of ham mixture. Garnish each cracker with a sprig of parsley. *The day before, make ham topping; place sliced cucumbers in plastic bag. Chill. Put together just before serving so that they will be crisp.*

Mrs. John Eric.

Sausage Balls

1 pound sharp Cheddar cheese, shredded	1 pound uncooked Owens sausage
	3 cups dry biscuit mix

Heat sausage and pour off grease. Add cheese and stir with wooden spoon in large saucepan until cheese is melted. Stir in dry biscuit mix until smooth. Cool and chill for one hour, then form into small balls. Place on ungreased cookie sheet. Bake at 400° for 8 to 10 minutes. Remove and place on paper towel to drain. *Can be frozen and reheated when needed.*

Mrs. Homer Green (Wilma)

Sweet and Sour Cocktail Weiners

1 jar (6 ounces) prepared mustard	1 pound weiners or Vienna sausages
1 jar (10 ounces) currant jelly	

Steam weiners for 15 minutes; drain and cool. Slice weiners diagonally in bite sized pieces. Mix mustard and jelly in chafing dish or double boiler and simmer until blended. Add sliced weiners and simmer 15 minutes. Serve hot. *Makes enough sauce for 2 pounds of weiners. May substitute cocktail sausages. Any leftover sauce may be refrigerated for several days.*

Mrs. H. Smith (Alyne)

Bacon Rolls

Bacon slices, cut in half crosswise	Bread slices, crust removed and cut in half
	Parmesan cheese

Place slice of bread on top of slice of bacon. Sprinkle with Parmesan cheese. Roll up and fasten with toothpick. Bake at 400° for 20 to 25 minutes. *May be frozen before baking. Defrost at room temperature for 15 to 20 minutes, then bake.*

Variation: Grated sharp Cheddar cheese may be substituted for Parmesan cheese.

Mrs. Bob Hamblen (Jan)

Meatball Appetizers

1	pound ground beef	2	tablespoons butter
1	teaspoon Accent	3	tablespoons molasses
¾	teaspoon salt	3	tablespoons prepared
1	tablespoon chopped onion		mustard
½	cup soft bread crumbs	3	tablespoons vinegar
¼	cup milk	¼	cup catsup
1	tablespoon flour	¼	teaspoon thyme

Break up meat with a fork. Sprinkle with Accent, salt and onion. Mash together crumbs and milk. Add to meat mixture and toss lightly until all ingredients are combined. Form into fifty ¾ inch balls and roll in flour. Brown in butter in skillet. Combine remaining ingredients and blend until smooth. Add to meatballs. Simmer 8 to 10 minutes. Stir occasionally until sauce thickens and meatballs are glazed. Bake at 300° for 1 hour. Serve in chafing dish. *Meatballs may be made several days in advance and frozen.*

Mrs. Bobby M. Greenwood (Judy)

Asparagus Ham Appetizers

1	package (8 ounces) cream cheese, softened		Salt and pepper to taste
1	can (4 ounces) deviled ham		Worcestershire sauce to taste, optional
4	tablespoons chopped onion	1	can (15 ounces) asparagus spears
½	teaspoon dry mustard	8	to 10 very thin slices boiled ham

Combine cream cheese and deviled ham. Add onion, mustard, salt, pepper and Worcestershire sauce and spread on slices of boiled ham. Place 1 spear of asparagus on each slice of ham and roll up. Wrap and place in freezer or refrigerator for at least two hours. Just before serving, slice each ham roll into 5 pieces and serve on round crackers.

Variations: Deviled ham in filling may be omitted. For an elegant dish, roll asparagus in ham slices and serve whole.

Aggie Mom

Cheese Wafers

½ pound sharp Cheddar
   cheese, grated
½ cup butter or margarine

½ teaspoon salt
Pinch red pepper to taste
1½ cups sifted flour

Combine cheese, butter, salt and pepper. Let stand until mixture comes to room temperature. Cream well. Add flour and mix. Form mixture into roll about 1 inch in diameter. Wrap in wax paper. Chill. Slice into thin wafers and bake at 350° for 10 minutes. *May be kept in refrigerator 1 week before baking or may be frozen, baked or unbaked.*

Mrs. G. Gross (Jean)

Cheese Petite Sixes

1 pound butter, softened
4 jars (5 ounces each) Kraft
   Old English cheese spread,
   softened
1½ teaspoons Worcestershire
   sauce
1 teaspoon Tabasco sauce

1 teaspoon garlic salt
Dash red pepper
3 loaves thinly sliced
   sandwich bread
Dill weed
Paprika

Mix first 6 ingredients in mixer or blender. Spread a portion of mixture on 3 slices of bread and stack. Repeat with remaining bread. Remove crusts and cut into sixes, first half and then cut each half into 3 pieces. With remaining mixture, ice slices on top and all sides except bottom. Sprinkle top with dill weed and paprika. May be frozen up to 3 weeks before using. After taking out of freezer, place in 350° oven for 15 to 20 minutes until slightly brown on top. Serve hot. Yields 150 cheese petites.

Mrs. Robert Stauch (Janet)

Chili Cheese Squares

1 pound Cheddar cheese,
   grated
1 can (4 ounces) chopped
   green chilies

6 eggs, beaten
Salt, pepper and paprika to
   taste

Sprinkle one half cheese in greased 8 inch square baking dish. Sprinkle with drained chilies, then rest of cheese. Add eggs, salt and pepper. Sprinkle with paprika. Bake at 350° for 35 minutes. Cut into small squares. May be frozen and reheated.

Mrs. R.E. Spurling (Margaret)

Chili Relleno

2 cans (7 ounces each) chopped green chilies
¾ pound Monterey Jack cheese, grated

¾ pound sharp Cheddar cheese, grated
1 carton (8 ounces) sour cream
10 eggs, beaten

Grease 9x12 inch baking dish. Cover bottom with green chilies. Layer with cheeses. Pour sour cream and beaten eggs over mixture. Bake at 350° for 45 minutes. Cut into squares. Serves 12.

Mrs. Leroy Rowlett (Jo)

Kuchen Bremerhaven (German Crustless Quiche)

3 tablespoons finely diced shallots
⅓ stick butter
2 ounces frozen baby shrimp, thawed and squeezed dry
½ cup boiled ham, thinly sliced and diced

3 tablespoons scallions, sliced
6 ounces Swiss cheese, shredded
5 eggs, beaten
1 cup whipping cream
Nutmeg to taste
Salt and pepper to taste

Sauté shallots in half of butter. Grease 10 inch pie pan with remaining butter. Evenly distribute shallots, shrimp, ham, scallions and cheese in pan. Blend eggs, cream and seasonings with wire whisk. Pour egg mixture over other ingredients. Bake 30 minutes at 350° until brown on top. Cut into bite size pieces. Bake a day ahead and refrigerate. Serves 6 to 8.

Mrs. Thomas F. Samson (Judi)

QUICKIE: Canned jalapeños seeded and stuffed with tuna fish and Hellmann's mayonnaise. Or, jalapeños stuffed with bean dip, topped with grated cheese then heated in oven just before serving.

QUICKIE: Cover 1 block (8 ounces) cream cheese with Pickapeppa Sauce and serve with crackers.

BEVERAGES

From the earliest of days, man has needed liquids to keep his body healthy and refreshed, but man has also drunk beverages for their soothing or stimulating properties. From early man first sipping water from a babbling brook, we've come full circle to modern man buying especially bottled water for its purity. In between these two points in time are coffee, tea, wine, mild and other assorted beverages and their mixtures. In ancient history, the Biblical book of Genesis tells us that Noah drank some wine. Later, Confucius mentions tea in 500 B.C. and we are introduced to coffee in 800 A.D.

Tea originated in China, spreading across continents, reaching Europe in the Seventeenth Century, until today it is the national drink of China, Japan, England and Russia. One half of the world's population drinks tea, making it the second most popular beverage in consumption to first place coffee.

The history of coffee is steeped in an Ethiopian legend about shepherds allowing their herds to eat coffee leaves and berries and noticing the effect on their animals. Not only were they frisky but they stayed awake all night. We now know that the caffeine in the coffee produced those stimulating results. The one third of the world that drinks coffee consumes it in quantities large enough to make it the most popular beverage.

Tea and coffee made their way to America where we drink copious quantities of both - plain, sweetened or iced. Adding the ice is a strictly American innovation.

Cocoa, from which we derive our chocolate, is South American in origin. The Aztec, Maya and Toltec Indians cultivated the cacao tree long before Columbus graced these shores. They used the cacao bean for money as well as food. When Cortez took cocoa to Spain in the year 1528, sugar was added to it to make a sweet beverage. Today, who could live without hot chocolate, not to mention chocolate pie or cake?

So, we have varied backgrounds for beverages. Whether you are preparing for a party, reception or a family picnic, we offer the following recipes for your use and enjoyment.

Hot Almond Tea

3 small tea bags	½ cup lemon juice
6 cups water	1 teaspoon vanilla
1 cup sugar	1 tablespoon almond extract

Bring to boil 2 cups water. Add tea bags. Bring to boil 4 cups water. Add sugar and stir until dissolved. Add tea to water and sugar mixture. Add lemon juice, vanilla and almond extract. Serve hot.

Mrs. Charles D. Price, Jr. (Joyce)

Almond Lemonade Tea
A refreshing summertime drink

4 cups strong tea	3 cans water
1 cup water	1 cup sugar
1 can (6 ounces) frozen lemonade	1 teaspoon almond extract

Mix all ingredients together in a large pitcher. Serve over ice. Yields 8 (8 ounce) servings. *If preferred, artificial sweetner may be used instead of sugar.*

Mrs. Lee Radford (Betty)

Pink Tea Refresher

3 cups boiling water	6 tablespoons sugar
1 family size tea bag	1 tablespoon lemon juice
1 cup cranberry juice cocktail	

In teapot pour water over tea bag and brew for 4 minutes. Remove teabag and stir in cranberry juice, sugar and lemon juice. Serve over ice in tall glasses. Serves 6. *This is also delicious served hot.*

Mrs. Bob Hamblen (Jan)

Spiced Percolator Punch

9 cups unsweetened
  pineapple juice
9 cups cranberry juice
  cocktail
4½ cups water

1 cup firmly packed brown
  sugar
4½ teaspoons whole cloves
4 sticks cinnamon, broken in
  pieces
¼ teaspoon salt

Combine pineapple juice, cranberry juice cocktail, water and brown sugar in 30 cup automatic coffeemaker. Place cloves, cinnamon stick pieces and salt in coffeemaker basket. Perk and serve piping hot. Yields 23 (8 ounce) servings.

Mrs. Conrad Leissler (Bonnie)

Variation: Increase pineapple juice to 2 cans (46 ounces each). Decrease cloves to 2 tablespoons. Add water to fill line on coffeemaker if necessary.

Mrs. Durwood Pickle (Elizabeth)

Variation: Use only pineapple juice, cranberry juice, whole cloves and cinnamon sticks.

Mrs. Thomas Samson (Judi)

Wassail Bowl

1 gallon apple cider
1 cup firmly packed light
  brown sugar
1 can (12 ounces) frozen
  lemonade, undiluted
1 can (6 ounces) frozen
  orange juice, undiluted

½ teaspoon nutmeg
3 sticks cinnamon, broken in
  halves
10 whole allspice
1 tablespoon whole cloves

Combine apple cider, brown sugar, lemonade, orange juice and nutmeg in large covered pan. Tie cinnamon sticks, allspice and cloves in a cheese cloth bag and drop into pan. Simmer 20 minutes. Discard bag and serve hot. Yields 24 (4 ounce) servings. *A tiny peppermint candy cane may be placed to the side of each cup of punch at Christmastime for a nice holiday touch.*

Mrs. Frank S. Covaro (Genie)

Hot Cranberry Punch

1	pound fresh cranberries	12	whole cloves
2	quarts water	4	cups orange juice
2	tablespoons grated orange peel	1	cup lemon juice
6	sticks cinnamon	1½	cups sugar

Combine in a large saucepan, cranberries, water, orange peel, cinnamon sticks and cloves. Cook until cranberries are soft. Strain and add orange juice, lemon juice and sugar. Heat until sugar is dissolved. Serve hot. Yields 10 (8 ounce) servings.

Mrs. H. Smith (Alyne)

Hot Mulled Cider
Yummy drink on a cold night

1	teaspoon allspice	2	quarts apple cider
1	teaspoon ground cloves	½	cup firmly packed brown sugar
¼	teaspoon salt		
1	stick cinnamon		

Tie allspice, cloves, salt and cinnamon stick into a cheese cloth bag. Place apple cider, brown sugar and spice bag in a saucepan and slowly bring to a boil. Cover and simmer 20 minutes. *May place a clove studded orange wedge in each mug before serving.* Serves 8.

Mrs. Kenneth E. Fry (Jeanne)

Christmas Party Punch

1	can (6 ounces) frozen orange juice	2½ cups pineapple juice
1	can (6 ounces) frozen lemonade	1½ quarts cranberry juice
		Ice cubes

Add water to orange juice and lemonade according to can directions. Pour all ingredients into punch bowl, stir to mix. Add ice cubes. Yields 30 (4 ounce) servings.

Mrs. John B. Isbell (Charlene)

Five Alive Punch

1 can (12 ounces) Five Alive frozen concentrate
1 two quart package Kool-Aid lemonade mix

1½ quarts water
1 can (46 ounces) pineapple juice
1 quart ginger ale, chilled

Thaw Five Alive frozen concentrate. Mix with lemondade mix, water and pineapple juice. Chill. When ready to serve, add chilled ginger ale. Serves 32 in ½ cup servings, or makes 1 gallon of punch. *Ginger ale may be increased to taste.*

Mrs. Lee Radford (Betty)

Fruit Punch

1 can (12 ounces) frozen orange juice concentrate, thawed
3 cans (12 ounces each) water

1 package (16 ounces) frozen strawberries, thawed
1 quart ginger ale

Mix orange juice and water. Purée strawberries in blender. Combine orange juice and strawberries. Refrigerate. Chill ginger ale. Combine all ingredients when ready to serve.

Aggie Mom

Pineapple Jell-O Punch

1½ cups hot water
1 cup sugar
1 box (3 ounces) Jell-O, any flavor

2½ cups pineapple juice
3 ounces frozen lemonade, undiluted

Mix water, sugar, and Jell-O until dissolved. Add remaining ingredients, mix well and refrigerate. *Suggested Jell-O flavors: lemon, lime, apricot, mixed fruit, strawberry or cherry. This punch is excellent when placed in the refrigerator for a day and will thicken slightly.* Yields 20 (4 ounce) servings.

Mrs. Thomas B. Dellinger (Maria)

Punch of the Day

2 small packages (0.21 ounces each) Kool-Aid, any flavor
2 cups sugar

3 quarts water
1 can (46 ounces) pineapple juice

Combine all ingredients. Pour into 1 gallon plastic containers and freeze. Shake occasionally to keep from settling. Remove from freezer several hours before serving. Serve slushy. Yields 24 (6 ounce) servings.

Mrs. W. J. Green (Juanita)

Quite a Punch
Always have a copy of this recipe handy for sharing

4 cups sugar
6 cups water
1 can (6 ounces) frozen lemonade
1 can (6 ounces) frozen orange juice, undiluted

1 can (46 ounces) pineapple juice
6 ripe bananas, mashed
2 quarts ginger ale

Combine sugar and water in saucepan and boil for 3 minutes. Cool. Add lemonade (diluted according to can directions), orange juice, pineapple juice and mashed bananas. Freeze until slushy. Place mixture in a punch bowl and add ginger ale before serving. Yields 1½ gallons. *This punch is good with 1 to 2 cups of rum added at serving time, if desired.*

Mrs. Ben Marek (Pat)

Variation: Add 1 box (3 ounces) Jell-O of any flavor. Decrease sugar to 2 cups.

Mrs. Jack D. Ahlfinger (Julia)

Variation: Orange juice may be deleted for a delicious white punch. Decrease sugar to 3 cups.

Mrs. Kenneth Fry (Jeanne)

Red Holiday Punch

1 small package (0.21 ounces) cherry Kool-Aid
1 small package (0.21 ounces) strawberry Kool-Aid

1 can (6 ounces) frozen orange juice
1 can (6 ounces) frozen lemonade
1 quart ginger ale

Mix Kool-Aid (use water and sugar as package directs). Add orange juice and lemonade (diluted according to can directions), and ginger ale. Freeze for several hours until slushy. *Ginger ale may be added just before serving, instead of before mixture is frozen, if desired.* Yields 1 gallon.

Mrs. J. Michael Cornwall (Sharon)

Lime Mint Frost

1 can (6 ounces) frozen limeade
1 large banana, cut into chunks

2 cups lime sherbet
⅛ teaspoon mint extract

Combine limeade (diluted according to can directions) and banana in blender, blend until smooth. Add sherbet and mint extract. Blend on medium speed until smooth (approximately 10 seconds). Pour into glasses and freeze for 1 hour. Serves 3 to 4.

Mrs. Homer Green (Wilma)

Helen's Peach Slush

1 can (6 ounces) frozen pink lemonade
6 ounces Vodka, use lemonade can to measure

1 package (10 ounces) frozen peaches, partially thawed
12 ice cubes

Combine lemonade, vodka and peaches in blender. Add ice cubes 2 or 3 at a time, until mixture is slushy. Freeze. Remove from freezer about 30 minutes before serving for a slushy consistency. Yields 4 cups. *Use fresh frozen peaches when available.*

Mrs. Charles D. Price, Jr. (Joyce)

Piña Colada

1 can (15 ounces) cream of coconut
1 can (20 ounces) unsweetened pineapple juice

¾ cup water
15 ounces rum

Combine ingredients in large freezer container. As it begins to freeze, stir frequently (very important) to maintain a slushy consistency. Serve in slushy form. Serves 15. *The secrets of this recipe are to stir frequently, do not alter recipe, and do not make in blender.*

Variation: 1 can (16 ounces) crushed pineapple, undrained with no water.

Mrs. Jay D. Smith (Berniece)

Rich's Frozen Margaritas

1 can (6 ounces) frozen limeade, undiluted

6 ounces tequila
3 ounces triple sec

Combine all ingredients in blender and add ice to fill. Blend until smooth. Store in freezer until ready to serve. Dip moistened glass rim in salt before serving. Serves 6.

Mrs. Jay D. Smith (Berniece)

Velvet Hammer

4 cups vanilla ice cream
2 ounces triple sec

2 ounces vodka

Place all ingredients into blender and blend until smooth. Serves 4.

Aggie Mom

HELPFUL HINT:
1 gallon punch will fill 25 punch cups.

White Wine Sangria

2	oranges, juiced	2	quarts white wine
2	limes, juiced	1	quart club soda
1	cup sugar		

Combine juices, sugar and white wine. Best if left to marinate in the refrigerator for a few hours. Add club soda at serving time. Yields 3 quarts. *Looks pretty with slices of orange and lime added when served.*

Aggie Mom

No-Nog Eggnog

2	cups whipping cream	6	egg yolks
6	egg whites	2½	cups milk
¼	teaspoon salt	3	tablespoons vanilla
1	cup sugar		Nutmeg

Several hours before serving, whip cream until stiff and refrigerate until needed. Add salt to egg whites and beat until stiff but not dry. Gradually add sugar, beating continuously. Beat egg yolks until thick and lemon-colored, fold in egg whites and gradually add milk. Just before serving, fold in whipped cream and vanilla. Serve with nutmeg. Yields 16 servings.

Mrs. William O'Connor (Connie)

Instant Spiced Tea

1	jar (1 pound 2 ounces) Tang	2	cups sugar
1	cup Wyler's lemonade mix	2	teaspoons cinnamon
1	cup instant tea	1	teaspoon ground cloves
			Dash salt

Mix all ingredients together. Store indefinitely in airtight container. Use 1 tablespoon per cup of hot water.

Mrs. George Kardell (Roe)

Favorite Coffee Mixes

CAFE CAPPUCINO:

½ cup instant coffee
¾ cup powdered sugar

1 cup dried milk
½ teaspoon orange peel

CAFE VIENNA:

½ cup instant coffee
⅔ cup powdered sugar

⅔ cup dried milk
½ teaspoon cinnamon

SWISS MOCHA:

½ cup instant coffee
½ cup powdered sugar

1 cup dried milk
2 tablespoons cocoa

Mix in blender and store in tightly sealed container. Use 2 teaspoons for each cup of boiling water. *Gift suggestion: Put ½ cup of each of the coffee flavors in plastic baggies, then place all of them in a colorful larger bag and tie with ribbon.*

Mrs. Joy Anderson

Instant Hot Chocolate Mix
Delicious hot chocolate

1 box (8 quarts) Carnation dry milk
1 box (16 ounces) powdered sugar

1 box (16 ounces) Nestle's Quick
1 jar (16 ounces) Cremora

Mix all ingredients together and store in airtight container. Use 2 heaping tablespoons of mix for each cup of hot water.

Mrs. Alvis Reeves (Dolores)

Variation: 1 jar (8 ounces) Cremora. Use ⅓ cup mix for each cup of water.

Mrs. James E. Keeling (Betty)

Soups & Sandwiches

SOUPS

The origin of soups is clouded in the mists of bygone eras. One of the earliest written references to soup or pottage can be found in Genesis 25 where we are told Jacob cooked some pottage and sold it to his brother Esau for his birthright.

Little else is known until medieval times. In 1370 soups are mentioned by Taillevent who was the master chef to Charles VI of France. A little later we have a cabbage soup recipe from the reign of Richard II.

As time went on, kings had tasters to sample food before it was presented to them. Since this was a time-consuming process, often the soups were lukewarm before reaching the monarch. As a result, Louis IV demanded cold soups be served. Vichyssoise is one of the soups developed to serve this need.

After the French Revolution, M. Boulanger opened a cafe in Paris where he served only soups. He named his establishment "Restaurant" which meant "restorative" because of the restorative value of his soups. The name caught on, and by 1794 there were 500 restaurants in Paris serving all kinds of foods, not just soups.

So, today, whether we say soup, pottage, pot-au-feu (pot on the fire) or any of a variety of other names, we are talking about a delightful melding of foods - meat, vegetables or fruits - simmered in a liquid base until the flavors are fully developed. As you try these recipes, we hope you will find them tasty and enjoyable.

Avgolemono Soup
Greek Lemon Soup

2 quarts strong, strained chicken broth (or canned broth, or bouillon made strong)

½ cup raw rice (not instant)
4 eggs
Juice of 2 lemons (real lemons)

Bring broth to a boil and add rice. Cook until rice is tender, about 20 minutes. Remove from heat. Just before serving beat eggs with a rotary beater until they are light and frothy. Slowly beat in lemon juice and dilute mixture with 2 cups of hot soup, beating constantly until well mixed. Add the diluted egg-lemon mixture to remaining part of soup, stirring constantly. Bring almost to boiling point, but do not boil or soup will curdle. Serve immediately. Serves 6 to 8. *Float thin lemon slice on top of each bowl.*

Mrs. John B. Isbell (Charlene)

Olive Soup

3 tablespoons butter
1 medium onion, chopped
6 ribs celery, cut in ½ inch
   pieces
½ cup stuffed green olives
½ cup flour

1½ cups water
2 teaspoons salt
½ teaspoon pepper
½ cup water
2 cups milk

Cook butter, onion and celery together gently for 5 minutes. Cool, turn into blender and add olives, flour, water, salt and pepper. Blend until vegetables are chopped fine. Turn into saucepan and add water and milk. Cook over low heat until smooth and thick. If too thick, add a little milk or water. *This is one of my husband's recipes.*

Mrs. George Kardell (Roe)

Slang-Jang
A cold soup or appetizer

2 cans (14½ ounces each)
   tomatoes (or stewed
   tomatoes) chopped fine
1 can (8 ounces) oysters
1 onion, minced fine

2 small sour pickles, minced
   fine
Hot pepper sauce or Tabasco
   sauce to taste
Salt and pepper to taste

Chop tomatoes in bowl. Drain oysters (reserve oyster juice), chop fine and add to tomatoes. Strain oyster juice and add, along with onion, pickles, pepper sauce or Tabasco, salt and pepper. Chill. Serve in bowls with ice cubes. Eat with soda crackers. *(Family recipe dates back to 1894)*

Mrs. Ralph Plumlee (Stella)

Cheese Soup

¼ cup butter
½ cup finely diced onion
½ cup finely diced carrot
½ cup finely diced celery
¼ cup flour
1½ tablespoons cornstarch
4 cups milk, room
temperature

4 cups chicken broth
⅛ teaspoon baking soda
1 pound Old English cheese,
cut in pieces
1 teaspoon salt
1 teaspoon pepper
1 tablespoon dried parsley
Dash of red pepper

Melt butter in heavy saucepan. Sauté vegetables until tender. Stir in flour and cornstarch. Cook until bubbly. Add milk and broth gradually, blending into a smooth sauce. Add soda and cheese. Stir until thickened. Season with salt and pepper. Add parsley. Do not let boil. Serves 6 to 8. *May be made ahead and reheated in a double boiler. Garnish with paprika, if desired.*

Mrs. Charles E. Allen (Bettie)

Cheddar Cheese Soup

2 cups chopped celery
½ green pepper, chopped
2 cans (10¾ ounces each)
cream of mushroom soup
2 soup cans milk
½ cup tomato puree
¼ teaspoon ground coriander

½ teaspoon white pepper
¼ cup sour cream
2 cups shredded Cheddar
cheese
½ cup dry sherry
2 tablespoons fresh chopped
parsley

Cook celery and green pepper in enough water to cover until tender. Drain. Over low heat blend soup with milk, then puree with cooked celery and green pepper in a blender (or pass through a fine sieve). Cook in a double boiler over hot (not boiling) water. Stirring, add tomato puree, coriander, white pepper, sour cream and cheese until mixture is smooth and hot. Add sherry and parsley. If too thick for your taste, thin with warm milk. Serve very hot. Serves 6 to 8.

Mrs. Bob S. Singer (Janet)

Cheddar Chowder Soup

2 cups boiling water	¼ cup margarine
2 cups chopped potatoes	¼ cup flour
½ cup sliced carrot	2 cups milk
½ cup sliced celery	2 cups shredded sharp
¼ cup chopped onion	Cheddar cheese
1½ teaspoons salt	1 cup chopped ham
¼ teaspoon pepper	

Place potatoes, carrots, celery and onion in water. Simmer covered for 10 minutes. Do not drain. Make white sauce with flour, margarine, salt, pepper and milk. Stir over low heat until smooth. Add cheese and ham. Heat thoroughly. Serves 4. *May be served immediately but is better the second day.*

Mrs. Kenneth Fry (Jeanne)

Monterey Jack Cheese Soup

½ cup finely chopped onion	1½ cups medium white sauce
1 large tomato, peeled and diced	(see below)
	1½ cups milk
1 can (4 ounces) chopped green chilies, drained	¼ teaspoon salt
	Pepper to taste
½ teaspoon garlic powder	1½ cups grated Monterey Jack
1 cup chicken stock or canned chicken broth	cheese

MEDIUM WHITE SAUCE:

3 tablespoons butter	1½ cups milk
3 tablespoons flour	

Over very low heat simmer onion, tomato, chilies and garlic powder for 15 minutes. Remove from heat. Slowly stir in white sauce with wire whisk. Add milk slowly. Add salt, pepper and cheese. Return to low heat, stirring until cheese melts.

MEDIUM WHITE SAUCE: Melt butter, stir in flour and cook three to five minutes. Slowly stir in milk. Stir over medium heat until thickened. Season with salt and pepper. Serves 6. *This recipe is best made a day ahead.*

Mrs. Kenneth Fry (Jeanne)

Gazpacho
Cold Mexican Soup

2 cucumbers, diced	1 cup catsup
2 green peppers, diced	¼ cup vinegar
2 tomatoes, diced	½ cup red wine
1 bunch green onions, diced	Salt, pepper and parsley to
1 quart tomato juice	taste

Mix together cucumbers, peppers, tomatoes and onions. Add remaining ingredients. Mix well and chill for at least 24 hours. Garnish with croutons or onions.

Mrs. Duane C. Uhri (Dee)

Tortilla Soup

2 pounds stew meat, cubed	¼ can (10 ounces) Rotel tomatoes
2 tablespoons cooking oil	
3 garlic buds, diced	1 teaspoon chili powder
1 small onion, chopped	1 teaspoon cumin (seeds or ground)
1 jalapeño pepper, diced	
1 can (10¾ ounces) tomato soup	1 can (16 ounces) tomatoes
	1½ soup cans water
1 can (10½ ounces) beef broth	½ teaspoon pepper
	Tabasco to taste
1 can (10¾ ounces) chicken broth	4 fresh corn tortillas

Brown stew meat in cooking oil, with onion and garlic, in Dutch oven. Add remaining ingredients, except tortillas, and cook at least 1 hour at medium heat. Break tortillas in small pieces and add to soup 10 minutes before serving.

Mrs. Joseph S. Davis (Janelle)

Mexican Chili Soup

1 pound ground beef	1 can (10¾ ounces) tomato
1 clove garlic, crushed	soup
½ green pepper, diced	2 soup cans water
½ onion, chopped	Salt and pepper to taste
1 can (10¾ ounces) chili	1 cup grated Cheddar cheese
beef soup	

Brown beef with garlic, onion and green pepper. Drain off fat. Stir in soups, water, salt and pepper. Heat thoroughly. Sprinkle cheese over top just before serving. Serve with crackers. Serves 6.

Mrs. Robert E. Clark (Sylvia)

Cream of Broccoli Soup

1 quart fresh broccoli heads	1 clove garlic, crushed
(1 large bunch)	2 tablespoons Worcestershire
⅔ cup butter	sauce
½ cup flour	¼ teaspoon Tabasco sauce
3 cups warm milk	2 cups heavy cream
2 cups hot chicken broth	3 egg yolks
2 teaspoons salt	Sherry - optional
¼ teaspoon white pepper	(approximately 1 teaspoon
3 tablespoons lemon juice	per serving)

Wash, trim and dry broccoli. Reserve a few florets for garnish. In saucepan cook broccoli in butter until soft. Blend in flour and simmer until smooth and bubbly, stirring occasionally. Add milk, chicken broth, salt, pepper, lemon juice, garlic, Worcestershire sauce and Tabasco sauce, stirring constantly until smooth and thick. Whirl in blender. *(May be frozen at this point and finished later.)* Stir in cream and bring just to a boil. Remove from burner. Beat egg yolks in small bowl. Whisk a little hot soup into eggs, then pour egg mixture into soup, stirring constantly. Garnish with tiny floret and sherry. Serves 10 to 12.

Mrs. Frank S. Covaro (Genie)

Cream of Asparagus Soup

1 package (10 ounces) frozen
asparagus
1 thin slice of white onion
1½ cups chicken broth

2 tablespoons margarine or
butter
2 tablespoons flour
2 cups cream (add additional
½ cup if desired)

Cook frozen asparagus as directed on package. Drain, saving water. Cut off asparagus tips and save for garnishing. To drained water add stalks of asparagus, onion slice and chicken broth. Boil on low heat 5 minutes. Rub through sieve or put into blender on puree. Melt margarine or butter and blend flour to make paste. Add soup. Cook slowly and stir 5 minutes. Measure soup and add enough cream to make 3 cups total. Add salt and pepper to taste. Add tips and serve immediately. Serves 4.

Dolores Reeves

Grandmother's Vegetable Soup

3½ pounds beef shank with
long shank bone
2 quarts water
Salt to taste
4 onions, chopped
12 sprigs fresh parsley,
broken in pieces
1 can (20 ounces) tomatoes
1 can (14½ ounces)
tomatoes

4 large ribs celery with
leaves, chopped
2 turnips, chopped
(optional)
2 carrots, chopped
¾ small cabbage, chopped in
large pieces
2 packages (10 ounces each)
frozen mixed vegetables

DUMPLINGS (optional):
¾ cup flour
1 egg
¼ teaspoon salt

¼ teaspoon baking powder
3 teaspoons water

In very large pot simmer beef, water, salt, 2 of the onions, half the parsley and the tomatoes for 1½ hours. Add celery, turnips, carrots, 2 more onions and cabbage. Simmer for another hour. Add frozen vegetables and other half of parsley and simmer another hour. If desired, add dumplings and cook another half hour.

DUMPLINGS:
Put all dumpling ingredients in small bowl and mix well. Cut off small chunks (¾ x ¼ inch size) of dumpling mixture and dunk knife into soup to remove dumpling from knife. Serves 12. *Cook at least 4 hours from start to finish for best flavor blend. Make no substitutions on the type of meat.*

Mrs. James A. Brickley (Marge)

Bean Chowder

1	cup dry large white beans	1	cup diced raw carrots
4	cups water	1	cup diced celery and
1	ham bone, if desired		leaves
½	cup minced onion	1	can (16 ounces) tomatoes
2	teaspoons salt	2	tablespoons flour
¼	teaspoon pepper	2	tablespoons butter
1	cup diced raw potatoes	2	cups hot milk

Soak beans overnight in water, or bring water and beans to a boil for 2 minutes and allow to stand, covered, for 1 hour. Do not drain off soaking water. Add ham bone, if using, salt and onion. Bring to boiling point, reduce to simmer. Cover and cook slowly for one hour. Add vegetables and simmer ½ hour. Mix butter and flour to a smooth paste and stir into beans. Simmer until thickened, then add hot milk. If ham bone is used, remove from beans before adding milk. Take meat off bone and add to soup along with milk. *Serve with hot French or homemade bread and a salad.*

Mrs. Lloyd Jones (Marilyn)

Potato Soup

1	large onion, chopped	4	tablespoons butter (more
8	to 10 large potatoes,		or less, as desired)
	peeled and diced	2	cups milk
3	to 4 ribs celery, chopped		Salt and pepper to taste

Cover onions, potatoes and celery with water and simmer 20 minutes, or until potatoes are cooked. Add more water if needed during cooking. Pour in milk, salt and pepper. Add butter. *If thicker broth is desired, add flour to thicken.* Serves 6 to 8.

Mrs. Robert E. Clark (Sylvia)

Potato Bacon Chowder

8 slices bacon	1 cup sour cream
1 cup chopped onion	1¾ cups milk
2 cups cubed potatoes	½ teaspoon salt
2 cups water	Pepper to taste
1 can (10¾ ounces) cream of chicken soup	2 tablespoons chopped parsley

Fry bacon until crisp; drain and reserve bacon. Sauté onion in small amount of bacon fat. Add potatoes and water. Bring to boil, cover and simmer until tender. Stir in soup and sour cream. Gradually add milk, salt, pepper and parsley. Add crisp bacon which has been crumbled. Heat to serving temperature. Don't boil.

Mrs. Bill Hall (Janey)

Lentil Super Soup

1 pound dried lentils	2 beef bouillon cubes
1 medium onion, chopped	2 quarts water
½ cup diced celery	1 tablespoon salt
1 tablespoon chopped parsley	¾ teaspoon Tabasco
1 can (16 ounces) stewed tomatoes	1 pound (about 8) frankfurters, sliced

Pick over lentils, wash and place with remaining ingredients, except frankfurters, in 5 or 6 quart saucepan. Cover and simmer over low heat 2 hours, stirring occasionally. Add sliced frankfurters and cook 10 minutes longer. Yields 3½ quarts.

Mrs. James P. Licandro (Marie)

Louisiana Gumbo Filé

1 (5 pounds) baking hen
Salt and pepper to taste
1½ to 2 dozen oysters or
    2 jars (10 ounces each)
1½ pounds smoked sausage
Water
⅔ cup oil
8 heaping tablespoons flour
1 large onion, finely
    chopped

2 ribs celery, finely chopped
Water
Salt to taste
Red pepper to taste
6 green onions, finely
    chopped
½ cup chopped parsley
2 to 3 tablespoons filé

Wash chicken and cut in serving size pieces. Season with salt and pepper. Drain oysters, reserving liquid. Check for shell pieces. Boil sausage to tenderize, 30 to 40 minutes. *This can be done while preparing balance of recipe.* Heat oil in large pot. Add flour and cook, stirring constantly, until mixture is medium golden brown. Add chicken and continue stirring until browned. Add onion and celery and sauté until tender. Lower heat. Add warm water to cover chicken. Add salt and red pepper. Slice sausage into bite size pieces and add. Cook for 45 minutes, then add green onion and parsley. Simmer over medium heat for 10 minutes. Add oysters and their liquid. Continue cooking for 30 minutes or until chicken is tender. Just before serving sprinkle filé on top. *Do not boil after filé has been added.* Skim excess grease from top and add warm water to keep level up. Serve over hot rice. Serves 6 to 10.

I learned to make this dish by watching my husband's grandmother prepare it. She called it "Gumbo L'Andouille," the name coming from the homemade sausage used as an ingredient. Since I cannot always use the original L'Andouille sausage, I substitute Eckrich smoked sausage. In the original recipe, the water used to boil the sausage was the first water added to the gumbo. I left this out of the instructions, because I find the water from boiling Eckrich contains too much grease. The only way to make use of this water would be to boil the sausage a day ahead, refrigerate the water overnight, and then remove the grease from the top before using it. This, of course, is a lot of extra trouble, especially for someone not familiar with this type of cooking. This is the only change I made in the original method.

Mrs. Joel Lanoux (Carol)

Ham Soup

1 pound cooked ham, cut in ½ to ¾ inch pieces	1 can (16 ounces) tomatoes
1 cup sliced carrots	1 medium onion, chopped
3 cups water	½ teaspoon salt
⅛ teaspoon savory	⅛ teaspoon pepper
1 can (10¾ ounces) condensed cream of celery soup	1 package (10 ounces) frozen okra, ¾ inch pieces (green beans may be used instead)
½ cup uncooked rice	

Combine carrots, onion, water, salt, savory and pepper in Dutch oven. Bring to boil; reduce heat, cover tightly and cook slowly 15 minutes. Stir in celery soup, ham, okra and rice. Cover and continue cooking until rice and okra are done. Cut up tomatoes, stir into soup, and cook slowly for 5 minutes. Makes 5 to 6 servings.

Mrs. Lloyd Jones (Marilyn)

Chuck Wagon Stew
Delicious

2 pounds beef chuck, cut in cubes	1 medium onion
2 tablespoons bacon fat	1 tablespoon salt
4 cups boiling water	½ teaspoon pepper
1 teaspoon Worcestershire sauce	1 teaspoon sugar
1 clove garlic	6 carrots, cut up
	3 medium potatoes, peeled
	6 small onions, peeled

Brown meat in hot fat. Add water, Worcestershire sauce, garlic, onion and seasoning. Simmer 2 hours, stirring occasionally. Add carrots, onions and potatoes. Continue cooking until vegetables are tender. Serves 6.

Mrs. Bobby M. Greenwood (Judy)

3 Hour Stew

3 pounds stewing beef,
cubed (a pot roast of beef)
2 cans (10¾ ounces) cream
of mushroom soup
1 can (6 ounces)
mushrooms, drained

½ envelope dry onion soup
mix
⅔ cup sweet vermouth or red
cooking wine

Combine all ingredients in baking pan. Cover tightly with aluminum foil and bake in 325° oven for 2½ to 3 hours. Serves 6 to 8. *Serve over rice or noodles.*

Mrs. Donald R. Bowen (Carolyn)

Fast Beef Stew

2 pounds stew meat
6 medium size potatoes,
peeled
1 can (16 ounces) onions,
drained

1 can (10¾ ounces) tomato
soup
1 can (10¾ ounces) onion
soup
4 or 5 carrots, peeled and
cut in chunks, optional

Mix all ingredients together in a roasting pan. Cover and bake at 300° for 4 to 5 hours. Serves 4.

Mrs. James Murphy (Rosemary)

SPICE HINTS:
Chicken soup—rosemary, paprika, marjoram
Cranberry juice—cinnamon, cloves
Tomato soup—sage, garlic salt
Vegetable soup—thyme, chili powder

Kentucky Burgoo
From Lexington

¾ pound lean stew meat, cubed
¾ pound pork shoulder, cubed
3 quarts water
1 (3½ pounds) chicken
Water
2½ cups peeled tomatoes
1 cup lima beans
½ cup diced red pepper

4 cups diced green peppers
¾ cup diced onion
1 cup diced potatoes
2 cups corn, fresh cut from cob
1 bay leaf
1 tablespoon Worcestershire sauce
Salt and pepper to taste

Simmer stew meat and pork in water for 2½ hours. In another pot simmer chicken, with water to cover, for 1 hour. Remove chicken bones and combine with meats. Add remaining ingredients. Simmer until vegetables are tender. Serves 8. *Better second day.*

Mrs. T. B. Dellinger (Maria)

Steak Soup
This may be frozen

¼ pound margarine
1 cup flour
½ gallon water
2 cups ground beef
1 cup chopped onion
1 cup chopped carrots
1 cup chopped celery

2 cups frozen mixed vegetables
1 can (15 ounces) tomatoes
2 tablespoons beef base
1 tablespoon Aćcent
1 teaspoon pepper

Melt margarine in large pan and whip in flour to a smooth paste. Stir in water. Sauté ground beef, drain grease and add beef to above. Chop and parboil onions, carrots and celery. Add to above. Add frozen mixed vegetables, tomatoes, beef base, Aćcent and pepper. Bring to a boil, then reduce to simmer until vegetables are done. DO NOT ADD SALT. *The flavor of this soup will depend on the quality of ground beef. I suggest using the best quality that you can find at your supermarket. This recipe is one of George's favorites.*

Mrs. George Kardell (Roe)

SANDWICHES

The sandwich was named for John Montagu, the fourth Earl of Sandwich, when he spent 24 hours at a gaming table in the year 1762 without any other food. He was also interested in naval affairs and exploration. In 1778 the English explorer, Captain James Cook, gave his name to the Sandwich Islands, now known as Hawaii.

A sandwich provides us with a nutritious meal since it is made of bread; meat, cheese or fish; and vegetables such as lettuce, tomato and onion. Teenagers love sandwiches since they are so quick to prepare.

Cucumber and Cheese Sandwiches

1 package (8 ounces) cream cheese
1 large cucumber
1 tablespoon minced onion
½ teaspoon salt, or more to taste

¼ teaspoon pepper
1 large loaf (1½ pounds) white bread, buttered if desired

Soften cream cheese. Peel, seed and mince cucumber. Mix cheese and cucumber with onion, salt and pepper. Spread on bread. Can be cut into halves or quarters. Will keep a number of days in refrigerator. Yields enough filling for 1½ pound loaf of bread.

Mrs. Ted Jones (Marilyn)

Baked Cheese Sandwiches

1 egg
½ cup margarine or butter
¼ pound Cheddar cheese, grated

Salt and pepper to taste
4 slices bread, cut into thirds or quarters

Combine egg and margarine until of spreading consistency. Fold in cheese. Add salt and pepper. Spread on tops and sides of bread slices. Place on cookie sheet and freeze. When frozen, may be put into plastic bag. Will keep frozen for a long time. Bake on cookie sheet at 375° until bubbly on top. Serves 6.

Mrs. Robert E. Clark (Sylvia)

Ribbon Sandwich Loaf

1   loaf unsliced white or
    whole wheat bread,
    decrusted and sliced
    lengthwise (13 slices) to
    melba toast thickness

Spread each layer generously, though not heavily with one of the following fillings, stacking the loaf as it is sliced so it will stand better. Alternate fillings as you go to make the loaf prettier when it is cut. Do not
spread filling on top. Frost sides and top of loaf.

FILLINGS:

Spam with cream cheese

2   cans Spam   2   to 3 pickles
1   package (8 ounces) cream   Mayonnaise
    cheese

Grate Spam, cream cheese and pickles. Mix with mayonnaise until moist
enough to spread.

Egg Salad

1   dozen hard cooked eggs   2   tablespoons finely chopped
12 tablespoons mayonnaise   ripe olives
2   teaspoons Good Seasons   1   tablespoon Woody's
    Onion Salad Dressing Mix   Smoke Sauce
12 drops Worcestershire sauce

Grate eggs and add all other ingredients. Mix well until it is of spreading
consistency.

Chicken Salad

1   chicken   2   bay leaves
1   carrot   8   whole peppercorns
1   onion   ¼   green pepper, sliced
1   teaspoon mild curry   Dash of seasoned salt
    powder

Boil chicken with all listed ingredients. When done, debone and cut up
fine with kitchen scissors. Mix well with the following ingredients:

½ teaspoon mild curry
   powder, optional
Dash of dried onion soup or
   onion powder
2 tablespoons lemon juice

1 cup finely chopped celery,
   optional
Hellmann's mayonnaise to
   moisten

*Other fillings could be tuna or salmon salad, pimiento cheese, ham salad,
potted meat, chopped ham or Underwood deviled ham.*

FROSTING:

1 package (8 ounces) cream
   cheese
½ to 1 cup sour cream
½ cup Hellmann's
   mayonnaise
Dash Tabasco

Dash Worcestershire sauce
Dash onion powder
Dash garlic powder
½ to 1 teaspoon seasoned
   salt

Mix all ingredients together until smooth. To frost, apply frosting to sides
first, holding one hand on top of loaf. Then frost top. Decorate with
pickles and eggs sliced to make flowers. Wrap and chill. Serves 12 to
15, depending on thickness of slices.

Mrs. Jack Starry (Dorothy)

Meat and Pepper Pocket Sandwiches

8 ounces leftover cooked
   beef or pork roast, sliced
¾ cup reserved roast pan
   juices
2 tablespoons flour
¼ teaspoon salt

⅛ teaspoon pepper
1 small green pepper, cut
   into strips
1 small red pepper, cut into
   strips
6 to 8 Syrian bread pockets

Cut sliced meat into ½ inch strips; set aside. In medium saucepan combine reserved pan juices, flour, salt and pepper. Cook and stir until
thickened and bubbly. Add pepper and meat strips. Cover and cook over
low heat for 5 minutes or until peppers are crisp tender. Spoon into bread
pockets. Serves 6 to 8. *You may substitute ¾ cup cream of mushroom
soup for pan juices and omit 2 tablespoons flour. Also, chicken ham
or hamburger could be used instead of roast. Can use Pita pockets instead of Syrian bread pockets.*

Mrs. Jack Starry (Dorothy)

Tuna Burgers

1	can (12½ ounces) chunk light tuna	1	cup mayonnaise
4	tablespoons pickle relish	3	tablespoons diced olives, optional
4	tablespoons grated onion	6	Kaiser rolls
1	cup grated cheese		

Mix all ingredients well and spread on Kaiser rolls. Wrap in foil; warm in 350° oven for 15 to 20 minutes. Serves 6.

Mrs. William B. Heye (Joan)

Sandwich Pizzas
Good and easy for a teenager's party

2	cans (10 each) refrigerated biscuits	Catsup or Pizza sauce

MEAT TOPPING:

½	pound ground beef	¼	teaspoon Italian seasoning
¼	teaspoon Worcestershire sauce		Pepper
¼	teaspoon garlic salt	10	tomato slices
		10	slices American cheese

To prepare meat topping, brown ground beef; drain. Add Worcestershire sauce, garlic salt, Italian seasoning and pepper. Mix well. Heat oven to 425°. On ungreased cookie sheet, flatten each biscuit and spread 10 biscuits with catsup or pizza sauce. Top with meat mixture, then a tomato slice. Let biscuits stand 15 to 20 minutes. Bake 10 to 15 minutes. Top each filled biscuit with a plain one, then a slice of cheese. Bake 5 minutes longer or until cheese melts. Yields 10 small pizza sandwiches.

Variation: Use sausage or pepperoni instead of beef.

Mrs. Margaret Levy

Chicken Fried Hamburgers

1 pound ground round
1 onion, chopped
¼ cup milk

1 cup bread crumbs
Salt and pepper to taste
4 hamburger buns

BATTER:
2 eggs, beaten
2 tablespoons water

1 cup flour or bread crumbs
Oil for frying

CHEESE SAUCE:
¼ pound Velveeta cheese

½ can (10 ounces) Rotel tomatoes

Mix ground round, onion, milk, bread crumbs, salt and pepper to form patties. For batter, mix well egg and water. Dip hamburger in batter and then in flour or bread crumbs. Fry in oil. Serve on toasted hamburger buns with cheese sauce.

CHEESE SAUCE: Mix cheese with tomatoes and heat.

Aggie Mom

Bar-B-Q Sandwiches

3 pounds chuck roast
1 medium onion, diced
2 ribs celery, diced
½ small bottle (14 ounces) catsup
2 teaspoons salt

Pepper to taste
1 tablespoon chili powder
2 tablespoons bottled barbecue sauce
Hamburger buns

Cut roast into chunks, saving bones for soup. Combine all ingredients in heavy pot or skillet and bring to boil. Simmer 5 to 6 hours or until meat is tender. Shred meat on platter with two forks after removing excess fat. Return to pot and simmer another 30 minutes. Serve on fresh hamburger buns. Serves 6 to 8. *This can be easily doubled and frozen for large groups.*

Mrs. Alvis Reeves (Dolores)

Ham and Cheese Sandwiches

SPREAD:

1 cup margarine, softened
¼ cup prepared mustard
2 tablespoons sweet pickle
relish

2 tablespoons minced onion
2 tablespoons poppy or
sesame seed (or both)

18 slices ham
18 slices Swiss cheese

36 slices white sandwich style
bread

Mix margarine, mustard, pickle relish, minced onion and poppy seed, and let stand overnight. Spread on both insides of bread.

Fill sandwiches with layers of ham and Swiss cheese. Wrap in foil and bake for 20 minutes at 300°. Yields about 18 sandwiches. *Spread will keep well in refrigerator for several weeks.*

Mrs. Lloyd Jones (Marilyn)

Golden Sandwiches

8 slices bread
4 slices Swiss cheese
4 slices American cheese

4 slices ham
4 slices turkey
4 slices chicken breast

BATTER:

1¼ cups ice water
1 egg yolk, beaten
1½ cups self-rising flour
Dash salt

1 egg white, beaten until
stiff
Oil for frying

Make 4 sandwiches using bread, cheeses, ham, chicken and turkey. Cut into fourths and secure with toothpicks. Dip into batter. Fry in deep hot oil until golden brown. Drain on paper towels. Serves 8.

BATTER: Add half of water to egg yolk. Stir in flour, salt, and add remaining water. Then fold in beaten egg white. *A pretty fruit cup would be a nice accompaniment.*

Mrs. Jack Starry (Dorothy)

Salads

SALADS

Salsus, salade, ensalada, salat, insalata or salad - in any language the salad has evolved through the centuries to become a welcome and essential part of a well balanced diet. The word "salad" is derived from the Latin word "salsus" which leads historians to believe the first salads were served in early Roman times and were probably made with herbs and greens sprinkled with salt.

For many years, salads were considered to be a nobleman's food. Later, and especially in America, the salad was known as a "lady's dish." But today, in our nutrition and diet conscious world, the salad plays an important role in meal preparation and dining for everyone.

A salad is very versatile. It can be simple or elaborate, hot or cold, tossed, congealed or constructed, appetizer, main course or dessert. Salad preparation affords one the opportunity to use color and creativity while never neglecting nutrition and good taste.

We think you will enjoy the following salad selections. Perhaps you will find an old friend, a tried and true standby, and hopefully a new favorite from our *Hullabaloo in the Kitchen.*

Fluffy Pink Salad

¼ cup lemon juice
1 can (14 ounces) Eagle Brand milk
1 can (11 ounces) Mandarin oranges, drained
1 container (9 ounces) Cool Whip
1 can (8¼ ounces) crushed pineapple, drained
2 cups miniature marshmallows
1 can (21 ounces) cherry pie filling
½ cup chopped pecans
1 cup coconut

Stir lemon juice into milk. Let set for few minutes. Combine remaining ingredients with milk mixture and chill. Serves 8 to 10. *This may also be served as pie in graham cracker crust. Will make two 8 inch pies.*

Mrs. James E. Keeling (Betty)

Frozen Fruit Salad

1 can (20 ounces) pineapple
chunks, undrained
1 package (10 ounces) frozen
strawberries, thawed and
undrained
2 or 3 large bananas, sliced

1 can (6 ounces) frozen
orange juice, thawed
1 can (6 ounces) frozen
lemonade, thawed
12 ounces Seven-Up, can be
sugar free
¾ cup sugar

Combine all ingredients. Stir to mix well. Pour into 9 inch square container and freeze. Thaw 1 to 1½ hours before serving, depending on weather. Cut into squares. Make at least 1 day ahead. Serves 9.

Mrs. Frank S. Covaro (Genie)

Presbyterian Pineapple Salad

4 cups bread crumbs
2 cans (20 ounces each)
chunk pineapple, drained
or 1 can chunk pineapple
and 1 can crushed
pineapple, drained

3 eggs
2 cups sugar
1 cup melted margarine
1 cup milk

Mix bread and pineapple. Beat eggs, sugar, margarine and milk together. Add to bread mixture. Pour into greased 3 quart baking dish. Bake 40 to 50 minutes at 325°. Serves 10 to 12. *This is called a salad; however, I usually serve it as a dessert. Biscuit crumbs are especially good.*

Mrs. S. G. Evetts (Darlene)

Summer Fruit Salad

1 cantaloupe cut into ¾ inch cubes

1 can (20 ounces) pineapple chunks, undrained

1 apple, unpeeled and cubed

2 peaches, cut into wedges

2 bananas, cut into ¼ inch slices

1 cup strawberries, halved

1 can (6 ounces) frozen orange juice concentrate, thawed and undiluted

Layer fruits in large clear bowl in order given. Spoon orange juice over top. Cover and chill 6 to 8 hours or overnight. Serves 8 to 10.

Aggie Mom

Apricot Mousse

1 package (6 ounces) apricot Jell-O

1 can (20 ounces) crushed pineapple, undrained

¾ cup sugar

1 package (8 ounces) cream cheese, softened

2 small jars apricot baby food

1 can (13 ounces) evaporated milk, chilled two or three hours

Mix Jell-O, pineapple and sugar. Cook about 5 minutes. Add cream cheese and cook until melted. Add baby food. Cool. Whip milk and add to cooled mixture. Pour into 9x12 inch container greased with margarine. Refrigerate. Serve in squares on lettuce leaf. Serves 10 to 12.

Mrs. R. H. Stauch (Janet)

CHRISTMAS TREE
AND BOUTIQUE SALE

The Dallas A&M University Mothers' Club serves Texas A&M University in many ways. Working together, Dallas Aggie Moms have established a fund for a President's Endowed Scholarship. In addition, each year tens of thousands of dollars are contributed to a wide variety of scholarships, Aggie student activities and programs.

Annually, the first weekend in December finds Aggie Moms cheerfully selling the freshest Christmas trees and intriguing boutique items at the Texas A&M University Research and Extension Center. Workdays held year-round find busy Moms bringing forth products of creative minds for sale at boutiques, club meetings and the Annual Federation of Texas A&M University Mothers' Club Meeting on the A&M campus in April.

Pictured in the atrium of the beautiful reception hall of the Texas A&M University Research and Extension Center are the popular "Aggedy Ann and Andy" dolls, afghans, Christmas tree ornaments, canned goods, candy and baked items. Each represents the unfailing dedication of Dallas Aggie Moms to support financially the excellence of Texas A&M University.

COLOR PHOTOGRAPHY:
Rick Cook, Designer
Michael Wilson, Photographer
Mrs. Cynthia Jubera, Food Stylist
Mrs. Rosanne Greene, Food Stylist
Lambert's Landscape: Plants

CANDY AND BAKED ITEMS pictured: Kiss Cookies (p.99), Chocolate Crackles (p. 276), Orange Mincemeat Delights (p. 285), Maroon Velvet Cake (p. 74), Coconut Pound Cake (p. 37), Peanut Brittle (p. 336), Chocolate Fudge (p. 90), Austrian Crescents (p. 180) and Dilly Bread (p. 193).

Carolyn's Blueberry Jell-O

2   packages (3 ounces each)
    black cherry Jell-O
2   cups boiling water
1   can (15 ounces)
    blueberries, undrained
1   can (8 ounces) crushed
    pineapple, undrained

1   package (8 ounces) cream
    cheese, softened
¼   cup sugar
½   pint sour cream
½   teaspoon vanilla

Dissolve Jell-O in water. Add blueberries and pineapple. Pour into 10x12 inch dish. Refrigerate until congealed. Beat cream cheese and sugar until fluffy. Add sour cream and vanilla. Mix well. Spread over Jell-O. Refrigerate until ready to serve. Serves 10 to 12.

Mrs. J. Hal Brown (Eva Gay)

Congealed Mandarin Orange Salad

1   package (3 ounces) orange
    Jell-O
½   cup sugar
1   cup hot water

1   can (11 ounces) Mandarin
    oranges, drained
1   can (8¼ ounces) crushed
    pineapple, drained
½   pint sour cream

Dissolve Jell-O and sugar in water. Refrigerate until partially set. Add oranges, pineapple and sour cream. Refrigerate until set. Serves 6 to 8.

Mrs. Lee C. Leissler (Bonnie)

Use egg yolks in cooked salad dressings and Hollandaise sauce.

Cranberry Salad I

1 can (16 ounces) cranberry
    sauce
½ cup hot water
1 envelope gelatin
¼ cup cold water

Ground pulp and rind of 1
    orange
⅓ cup diced celery
⅓ cup chopped nuts
¼ teaspoon salt

Crush cranberry sauce. Add hot water and heat thoroughly. Soak gelatin in cold water for 5 minutes. Add to hot sauce. When starting to congeal fold in remaining ingredients. Pour into mold or individual cups. Refrigerate until set. Serves 6.

Aggie Mom

Cranberry Salad II

2 packages (3 ounces each)
    cherry Jell-O
3 cups boiling water
2 cups fresh cranberries

2 cups sugar
1 cup chopped celery
½ cup chopped pecans

Mix Jell-O and water. Set aside to cool. Grind cranberries in blender. Add sugar, celery and nuts. Let stand until sugar is dissolved. Blend Jell-O and cranberry mixture. Refrigerate. Serves 6 to 8.

Mrs. Jay D. Smith (Berniece)

Holiday Salad

1 box (6 ounces) raspberry
    Jell-O
2 cups boiling water
1 can (20 ounces) crushed
    pineapple, undrained

1 cup whole cranberry sauce
1 cup finely chopped celery
½ cup chopped walnuts

Combine Jell-O and boiling water, stirring until dissolved. Add pineapple and cranberry sauce. Stir well. Add celery. Pour into flat 8x10 inch container. When slightly chilled, sprinkle walnuts over top. Serve in squares on lettuce leaf. Serves 12 to 15.

Mrs. George Kardell (Roe)

Coconut Supreme

1½ cups milk, scalded
½ cup sugar
1½ packages plain Knox
    gelatin (1½ tablespoons)
¼ cup cold water

1 can (3½ ounces) Baker's
    angel flake coconut
½ teaspoon almond extract
1 cup whipping cream,
    whipped

SAUCE:
1 cup sugar
1 cup firmly packed brown
    sugar
1 tablespoon butter

1 cup whipping cream (do
    not whip)
1 pint ripe fresh strawberries

Mix milk and sugar. Soak gelatin in cold water and stir until softened. Add to hot milk and stir until dissolved. Add coconut and almond extract. Chill until partially set. Fold in whipped cream and pour into greased ring mold. Refrigerate until congealed. Serve with strawberries in center of mold. Top with sauce.

SAUCE: Combine sugars, butter and cream in top of double boiler. Cook until thickened. Serve with coconut mold and strawberries. Delicious.

Mrs. Jack Starry (Dorothy)

Jell-O Fruit Salad
My Pet Recipe

1 can (29 ounces) fruit
    cocktail
1 package (3 ounces) Jell-O
    lime, lemon or orange
1 envelope Knox gelatin

¼ cup boiling water
1 package (8 ounces) cream
    cheese, softened
1 cup evaporated milk
¾ cup mayonnaise

Drain fruit cocktail, reserving syrup. Heat syrup. Dissolve Jell-O in syrup. Dissolve gelatin in boiling water. Add to Jell-O. Cool. Beat cream cheese until smooth. Add milk, mayonnaise and Jell-O mixture. Fold in fruit. Pour into oiled container. Refrigerate until set. Serves 10 to 12.

Mrs. Heriberto M. Gonzalez (Laura)

Heavenly Salad

1 box (3 ounces) lemon
  Jell-O
1 box (3 ounces) orange
  Jell-O
1 cup boiling water
1 can (20 ounces) crushed
  pineapple, drained (reserve
  juice)

3 cans (11 ounces each)
  Mandarin oranges
8 ounces miniature
  marshmallows
½ cup chopped pecans

Combine Jell-O and boiling water. Add juices of fruit. Stir well. Stir in pineapple, oranges, marshmallows and nuts. Pour into 6 cup container. Refrigerate. Serves 8 to 10.

Mrs. James P. Licandro (Marie)

Sinful Strawberry Salad

1 package (6 ounces)
  strawberry Jell-O
1 cup boiling water
3 medium bananas, mashed
1 cup chopped pecans

2 packages (10 ounces each)
  frozen strawberries,
  thawed and drained
1 can (20 ounces) crushed
  pineapple, drained
1 pint sour cream

Combine Jell-O and boiling water. Stir until dissolved. Cool. Add bananas, pecans, strawberries and pineapple. Pour half of mixture into 8x12 inch container. Refrigerate until set. Keep remaining mixture at room temperature. Spread sour cream over set mixture. Pour on remaining mixture. Cover and refrigerate until set, about 1½ hours or overnight. Serves 12. *Each serving about 225 calories.*

Mrs. Robert Fredrickson (Mary Ann)

Variation: Use 2 packages (6 ounces each) strawberry Jell-O and 2 cups boiling water. Do not drain fruit.

Mrs. Anthony Marma (Grace)

Variation: Decrease strawberries to 1 package (10 ounces), pineapple to 1 can (15¼ ounces).

Mrs. W. J. Green (Juanita)

Wine Salad

2   packages (3 ounces each)
    raspberry Jell-O
2   cups boiling water
1   cup Port wine
1   can (20 ounces) crushed
    pineapple, undrained

1   can (16 ounces) whole
    cranberry sauce
½   cup chopped nuts
1   cup finely chopped celery

Dissolve Jell-O in water. Cool slightly. Add wine and chill until slightly thickened. Stir in remaining ingredients. Pour into oiled container and chill until firm. Serves 8 to 10. *This recipe won "Best Taste Overall Salad," American Women's Club of Bogota, Colombia. This was a Salad Tasting Luncheon in 1971 and judged by the best restaurant owners of Bogota.*

Aggie Mom

Cauliflower/Broccoli Salad

1   head cauliflower
1   bunch broccoli
¼   cup chopped onions, or
    4 teaspoons onion flakes
1   cup grated Cheddar cheese

1   cup Miracle Whip
1   tablespoon sugar
1   tablespoon vinegar, or
    lemon juice
Paprika to taste

Cut cauliflower and broccoli into florets or bite size pieces, including peeled stems. Add remaining ingredients. Mix well. Refrigerate overnight. Serves 8.

Mrs. Bob Hamblen (Jan)

Sprinkle dill or caraway seed over coleslaw.

Cauliflower Salad

4 cups thinly sliced raw
   cauliflower
1 cup sliced ripe olives

⅔ cup chopped green pepper
½ cup chopped pimiento
½ cup chopped red onion

DRESSING:
3 tablespoons lemon juice
9 tablespoons salad oil
3 tablespoons wine vinegar

½ teaspoon salt
1 teaspoon sugar
Pepper to taste

Toss vegetables. Combine dressing ingredients. Pour over vegetables and marinate at least 2 hours in refrigerator. Stir once or twice. Serves 8.

Mrs. George Kardell (Roe)

Corn and Bean Salad

1 package (10 ounces) frozen
   corn
1 can (16 ounces) kidney
   beans, drained
1 onion, finely chopped

1 green pepper, diced
1 cup salad oil
½ cup vinegar
¼ cup sugar
½ teaspoon salt

Cook corn according to package directions. Drain and cool. Mix beans with onion, green pepper and corn. Blend oil, vinegar, sugar and salt thoroughly. Pour over corn mixture. Chill several hours or overnight. Drain before serving. Serves 8 to 10.

Aggie Mom

Corn Pepper Salad

1 cup canned white shoe peg
   corn
1 cup chopped walnuts
2 green peppers, chopped
¾ cup sour cream

3 tablespoons lemon juice
1 teaspoon sugar
1 teaspoon salt
Olive oil or peanut oil, not to
   exceed ⅓ cup, optional

Combine all ingredients. Chill. Serve on lettuce. Serves 4.

Mrs. Lewis Gross (Jean)

Greek Salad

1 large bunch broccoli
1 head cauliflower
1 cup sliced fresh
   mushrooms
1 red onion, sliced
1 can (8 ounces) water
   chestnuts, drained and
   sliced

1 package (1.25 ounces)
   Good Seasons Italian dry
   dressing mix
3 tablespoons Lawry's Italian
   Seasoning

Cut broccoli and cauliflower into bite size pieces. Mix with mushrooms, onion and water chestnuts. Prepare dressing mix according to directions. Add seasoning. Pour over vegetables and marinate 24 to 36 hours, tossing occasionally. Serves 10 to 12.

Mrs. Raymond Noah (Cynthia)

Kathy's Vegetable Salad

1 can (17 ounces) small
   English peas, drained
2 cans (17 ounces each)
   whole kernel corn, drained
½ cup chopped celery
1 onion, chopped
1 bell pepper, chopped

2 jars (2 ounces each)
   pimientos, chopped
⅔ cup sugar
½ cup salad oil
½ cup vinegar
½ teaspoon pepper
½ teaspoon celery salt

Combine vegetables. Combine sugar, oil, vinegar, pepper and celery salt. Mix well. Pour over vegetables. Marinate in refrigerator overnight. Serves 12 to 16. *Keeps well in covered container in refrigerator.*

Mrs. Judy Dees

Layered Salad

1   small head lettuce
½   cup chopped celery
½   cup chopped bell pepper
½   cup chopped onion
1   package (20 ounces) frozen
    green peas cooked lightly
    and drained

1½ cups mayonnaise
2   tablespoons sugar
2   cups shredded Cheddar
    cheese
8   slices bacon, cooked and
    crumbled or 1 small jar
    Bacon Bits

Shred lettuce in large bowl. Layer remaining ingredients in the order listed.
Serves 8. *Can be made day ahead. Keeps well in covered container in refrigerator.*

Mrs. Floyd Trimble (Nancy)

Mary's Green Salad

1   head lettuce
½   cup chopped green onions
1   cup sliced celery
1   cup diced green pepper

1   cup grated Mozzarella
    cheese
1   cup mayonnaise
Parmesan cheese

Tear lettuce into bite size pieces. Layer lettuce, onions, celery and green
pepper into airtight bowl. Cover with layers of Mozzarella cheese and
mayonnaise. Top with layer of Parmesan cheese. Seal and refrigerate.
Serves 8. *Will keep overnight.*

Mrs. J. Hal Brown (Eva Gay)

*Toss toasted croutons in melted butter seasoned with basil,
marjoram or onion salt.*

Norwegian Coleslaw

3	medium heads cabbage, shredded
2	tablespoons salt
1	stalk celery, chopped
1	red sweet pepper, chopped
1	green pepper, chopped

4	cups sugar
2	cups white vinegar
1	cup water
1	tablespoon celery seed
1	tablespoon mustard seed

Shred cabbage, add salt and mix well. Let stand for 2 hours at room temperature. Squeeze dry, add celery and peppers. Mix sugar, vinegar, water, celery seed and mustard seed. Boil 15 minutes. When syrup is cool, add to cabbage, celery and peppers. Refrigerate 24 hours before serving. *Will keep for weeks! Excellent for unexpected guests.*

Mrs. James Thompson (Charlotte)

Spinach Salad I

1	pound fresh spinach
4	hard cooked eggs, mashed

8	to 10 strips bacon, cooked and crumbled (reserve 2 tablespoons drippings)

DRESSING:

½	cup vinegar
1	cup sugar
1	teaspoon salt
1	teaspoon paprika
½	teaspoon prepared mustard

½	onion, cut into chunks
1½	cups salad oil
2	tablespoons bacon drippings

Wash spinach. Drain and tear into bite size pieces. Refrigerate. Combine and dissolve dressing ingredients except onion, oil and drippings in saucepan. Boil for 1 minute. Cool to lukewarm. Pour into blender. Add onion. Pulverize. Continue blending while adding oil and drippings. Pour over spinach just before serving. Sprinkle eggs and bacon over top. Serves 8. *A favorite with men.*

Mrs. Kenneth Fry (Jeanne)

Spinach Salad II

2 cups finely chopped cabbage

2 cups finely chopped spinach

2 cups finely chopped celery

DRESSING:

½ cup salad oil
2 tablespoons vinegar
2 tablespoons catsup
½ teaspoon salt, no more

½ teaspoon paprika
½ teaspoon pepper
¼ teaspoon celery seed
1 clove garlic, crushed

Mix vegetables. Refrigerate. Mix dressing ingredients and let set 1 hour. Stir and toss with salad shortly before serving. Serves 6.

Mrs. H. Peyton Smith (Alyne)

Spinach Salad III

1 pound fresh spinach
1 can (8 ounces) water chestnuts, drained and sliced

5 strips bacon, cooked and crumbled
½ cup chopped green onions

DRESSING:

½ cup salad oil
Dash of salt
¼ cup sugar

¼ cup wine vinegar
1½ teaspoons Worcestershire sauce

Wash spinach, pat dry. Remove stems and tear into small pieces. Combine spinach, water chestnuts, bacon and onions. Refrigerate. Combine dressing ingredients. Shake occasionally until sugar is dissolved. Pour on before serving and toss well. Serves 6 to 8.

Mrs. Louis Rosen (Mary)

Spinach Salad IV

2 pounds fresh spinach	1 bunch green onions, finely
1 can (8 ounces) water	chopped
chestnuts, drained and	3 hard cooked eggs,
sliced	chopped
1 can (16 ounces) bean	1 pound bacon, cooked crisp
sprouts, drained	and crumbled

DRESSING:

1 cup salad oil	2 teaspoons salt
¾ cup sugar	1 teaspoon lemon juice
½ cup vinegar	1 teaspoon Worcestershire
⅓ cup catsup	sauce

Tear spinach in bite size pieces. Mix with water chestnuts, bean sprouts, onions, eggs and bacon. Refrigerate. Mix dressing ingredients. Toss all together when ready to serve. Serves 12.

Mrs. John Shea (Arlene)

Spinach Salad with Lemon French Dressing

1 to 2 pounds fresh spinach	1 large red onion, sliced thin
½ pound fresh mushrooms,	2 cans (11 ounces each)
sliced	Mandarin oranges, drained

DRESSING:

⅔ cup salad oil	1 clove garlic, crushed
⅓ cup fresh lemon juice	¼ teaspoon dry mustard
¼ teaspoon sugar	1 teaspoon salt
⅓ teaspoon freshly ground	
pepper	

Mix vegetables and fruit. Refrigerate. Combine dressing ingredients and shake until blended. Refrigerate. When ready to serve, pour dressing over vegetables and fruit and toss. Serves 8.

Mrs. J. Hal Brown (Eva Gay)

Zucchini Salad

⅔ cup thinly sliced carrots
5 thinly sliced zucchini
¼ teaspoon caraway seed, optional
1 tablespoon chopped onion
⅛ cup white wine vinegar
¾ cup sugar

1 teaspoon salt
½ teaspoon pepper
⅓ cup salad oil
⅔ cup cider vinegar
½ cup chopped green pepper
½ cup chopped celery

Cook carrots until slightly soft. In large bowl combine all ingredients and let stand 6 hours or overnight.

Mrs. John W. Bailey (Virginia)

Macaroni Salad

1 package (8 ounces) elbow or shell macaroni
½ cup chopped celery
½ cup chopped green pepper
¼ cup chopped green onion
1 tomato, diced

1 tablespoon prepared mustard
1½ teaspoons salt
½ teaspoon paprika
½ cup mayonnaise

Cook macaroni according to package directions. Rinse well and drain. Combine with other ingredients. Refrigerate until serving time. Serves 8 to 10. *If prepared day ahead, add tomato 1 or 2 hours before serving.*

Mrs. Louis Rosen (Mary)

Spinach Salad Dressing

1 cup salad oil
⅓ cup red wine vinegar
2 tablespoons sugar
¼ cup chopped fresh parsley

1 teaspoon salt
¼ cup sour cream, or plain yogurt
2 whole cloves garlic, peeled

Blend well. Refrigerate. Remove garlic after 6 hours.

Mrs. John H. Vandeven (Norma)

Yummy Rice Salad

1 tablespoon vinegar
2 tablespoons corn oil
¾ cup Hellmann's
   mayonnaise
1 teaspoon salt
½ teaspoon curry powder

1⅓ to 1½ cups uncooked rice
2 tablespoons chopped
   onion
1 cup chopped celery
1 package frozen English
   peas, undercooked

Mix vinegar, oil, mayonnaise, salt and curry powder. Cook rice until just done. Add rice to curry mixture. Add onion while rice is hot. When cooled, add celery and peas. Refrigerate. Serves 6 to 8. *Better the second day.*

Mrs. Jay D. Smith (Berniece)

Corned Beef Salad

1 envelope Knox gelatin
¼ cup cold water
½ cup tomato juice
1 teaspoon lemon juice
½ teaspoon salt
1 can (12 ounces) corned
   beef, shredded

3 hard cooked eggs,
   chopped
1 cup chopped celery
2 tablespoons chopped
   onion
1 cup mayonnaise
½ cup chopped stuffed olives

Combine gelatin and water. Heat tomato juice. Add to gelatin. Stir well. Add lemon juice and salt. Refrigerate until partially set. Combine remaining ingredients and add to gelatin mixture. Chill overnight. Cut into squares to serve. Serves 10 to 12.

Mrs. W. C. Marks (Belle)

Chicken Apple Salad

1½ cups cooked, diced
    chicken or turkey
1½ cups diced apples
½ cup chopped celery

¼ cup raisins
1 tablespoon lemon juice
⅓ cup mayonnaise

Combine all ingredients and chill thoroughly. Serve on salad greens.
Serves 4.

Mrs. Ralph Plumlee (Stella)

Molded Chicken Salad

FIRST LAYER:
1 envelope Knox gelatin
½ cup cold water
1 can (16 ounces) whole
    cranberry sauce
1 cup crushed pineapple,
    drained

1 tablespoon fresh lemon
    juice
½ cup chopped nuts,
    optional

SECOND LAYER:
1 envelope Knox gelatin
¾ cup cold water
1 cup mayonnaise
3 tablespoons fresh lemon
    juice
¾ teaspoon salt

2 cups cooked, diced
    chicken
½ cup finely chopped celery
1 to 2 tablespoons chopped
    fresh parsley

FIRST LAYER: Dissolve gelatin in water and heat on low to melt. Add
cranberry sauce, pineapple, lemon juice and nuts. Pour into 9x13 inch
container. Refrigerate until set.

SECOND LAYER: Prepare gelatin as above. Add remaining ingredients.
Pour over first layer. Refrigerate until set and ready to serve. Serves 10
to 12.

Mrs. Jerry L. Ewing (Claudette)
Mrs. W. C. Marks (Belle)

Fresh Vegetable Marinade

4 stalks fresh broccoli	1 cup sugar
1 small head cauliflower	2 teaspoons dry mustard
8 large fresh mushrooms, sliced	1 teaspoon salt
	½ cup vinegar
1 medium green pepper, chopped	1½ cups vegetable oil
	1 small onion, grated
3 ribs celery, chopped	2 tablespoons poppy seeds

Remove florets from broccoli. Cut into bite size pieces. Break cauliflower into florets. Combine vegetables. Toss lightly. Combine remaining ingredients and mix well. Pour over vegetables. Chill at least 3 hours. Serves 10 to 12.

Mrs. Wm. H. Ohmsieder (JoAnn)

Hot Chicken Salad
From Tel Aviv to Aggieland

2 cups chopped cooked chicken	1 can (4½ ounces) sliced mushrooms
1 cup chopped celery	1 can (10¾ ounces) cream of chicken soup
½ cup chopped onion	
¾ cup mayonnaise	½ cup lemon juice
1 jar (2 ounces) chopped pimientos	2 cups Uncle Ben's converted long grain cooked rice
1 can (3 ounces) Chow Mein noodles	1 cup crushed potato chips
	Salt and pepper to taste

Combine all ingredients except chips. Pour into oiled baking dish. Top with chips. Bake at 350° for 30 to 40 minutes. Serves 8. *This salad was served at a bridge luncheon in Tel Aviv to a group of American and Israeli ladies.*

Mrs. Charles D. Price, Jr. (Joyce)

Chicken Salad

2 cups cooked, diced
   chicken
½ to 1 cup chopped celery
½ cup sliced pitted black
   olives

½ cup almonds, blanched,
   slivered and toasted
1 cup mayonnaise

Combine all ingredients and mix only until well blended. Refrigerate until
ready to serve. Serves 6 to 8.

Mrs. L. B. Terry (Jeane)

Shrimp Salad

1 can (10¾ ounces) tomato
   soup
1 package (8 ounces) cream
   cheese, softened
2 envelopes Knox gelatin
½ cup cold water

1 cup mayonnaise
1 cup chopped celery
½ cup chopped onion
1 pound shrimp, cooked and
   cooled

Heat soup; do not boil. Add cream cheese. Stir until dissolved. Dissolve
gelatin in cold water. Add to soup and cheese mixture. Blend in mixer.
Cool. Add mayonnaise. Blend again. Add celery and onion. Coarsely
chop shrimp and combine with other ingredients. Pour into oiled 1½
quart container. Refrigerate until set. Serves 6 to 8.

Mrs. H. Peyton Smith (Alyne)

Waldorf Tuna Salad

1 can (6½ ounces) white
   chunk tuna
3 hard cooked eggs, mashed
1 cup chopped apple

½ cup chopped pecans
½ cup Miracle Whip
¼ cup diced Kosher dill
   pickle

Flake tuna into mixing bowl. Add remaining ingredients. Mix well. Serve
with crackers in tomato cups or as a sandwich spread. Serves 4 to 6.

Aggie Mom

Breads

BREADS

Included in the section on breads are both quick breads and yeast breads. The quick breads - corn bread, waffles, fruit and nut bread, pancakes, biscuits, fritters, and muffins - are easily and quickly prepared, as compared to yeast breads which require rising time before baking.

In the Middle Ages, bread served as a plate for meat and vegetables. After the meat and vegetables were eaten, the bread was eaten. Bannock, a biscuit-like dough that is rolled and cut and then fried on a griddle, is still eaten in the British Isles. Biscuits were served in Southern plantation homes before the Civil War, always dripping with butter and only slightly cooled. A dough cake with currants, made in Wiltshire County in England, probably was the beginning of fruit and nut breads.

The ancient Egyptians were the first to mill flour and apparently discovered that allowing wheat dough to ferment and form gases provided a light, expanded loaf. Before that, cavemen made bread cakes of grain and water and baked them in the sun. Similar flat breads are still eaten, especially in Asia and Africa. Other kinds of flat breads are whole meal chapatties made in India, corn tortillas in Latin America and cassava cakes in Brazil.

In the European countries in medieval times, dark rye bread was eaten by the working people, while white bread was eaten by the rich. In the Far East, the people have preferred rice as a grain, but in the last half of the Twentieth Century, they began to use Western breads. In Germany, Russia and Scandinavia, raised black bread is made from rye. In the United States we eat lighter rye bread, whole wheat bread, gluten bread, and Vienna and French bread. Also, we enjoy rolls, buns and sweet breakfast rolls, which are all made with yeast. Whether you bake quick or yeast breads, your kitchen artistry will be appreciated.

Ruth's Buttermilk Pancakes

1¼ cups all-purpose flour
½ teaspoon baking powder
½ teaspoon soda
¾ teaspoon salt

3 tablespoons Wesson oil
¾ cup plus 2 tablespoons buttermilk

Mix flour, baking powder, soda and salt together, and stir in oil and buttermilk. Cook on a hot griddle. You can keep this mix covered in the refrigerator up to 3 days. Serve with butter and hot syrup.

Mrs. G. Wayne Evans (Dorothy)

Heavenly Waffles

2 cups Bisquick biscuit mix
1 egg

⅓ cup cooking oil
1⅓ cups club soda

Mix all ingredients well and bake in a preheated waffle iron. Serves 4.

Mrs. George Kardell (Roe)

Raised Potato Doughnuts

2 cups milk
1 cup sugar
½ cup Crisco
1½ teaspoons salt
1 cup smoothly mashed potatoes (3 medium boiling potatoes, cooked and drained)

1½ packages (1½ tablespoons) yeast
¼ cup lukewarm water
3 eggs, beaten
½ teaspoon lemon flavoring
½ teaspoon cinnamon
8 cups sifted all-purpose flour
Crisco oil for frying

GLAZE:
¼ cup water
1½ cups powdered sugar

1 teaspoon vanilla

Heat milk until it is hot and film forms on top. Do not boil. Add sugar, shortening, salt and mashed potatoes; cool until lukewarm. Soften yeast in lukewarm water; let stand 5 minutes. Add yeast to milk and potato mixture with eggs, lemon flavoring and cinnamon. Add flour, part at a time, working smoothly to a nice dough with a strong spoon. Scrape into a clean greased bowl. Cover and let rise in a warm place for 50 minutes or until doubled in bulk. Punch down to release air bubbles. Turn out on lightly floured board and roll out to about ¼ inch thickness. Cut out with doughnut cutter and place doughnuts on clean floured dish towel. Cover with another towel. Let rise until doubled in bulk. Deep fry in Crisco Oil heated to 375° until golden brown. Drain on paper towels. Yields 5 to 6 dozen doughnuts.

GLAZE: Blend water into powdered sugar. Mix until smooth, and add vanilla. Dip one side of each doughnut into glaze and drain on rack.

Variation: Doughnuts can also be dipped into a cinnamon and sugar mixture. *Doughnuts cook very quickly.*

Mrs. T. B. Dellinger (Maria)

Austrian Crescents

1   package (1 tablespoon) dry yeast
3   cups all-purpose flour
1   cup butter
3   egg yolks

1   carton (8 ounces) sour cream
½   cup sugar
¾   teaspoon cinnamon
½   cup chopped pecans

GLAZE:
2   cups powdered sugar

3   tablespoons milk

Combine yeast and flour. Add butter and mix well. Stir in egg yolks and sour cream. Make 4 balls of mixture. Wrap in wax paper and refrigerate overnight. Roll balls, one at a time, ¼ inch thick. Spread with mixture of sugar, cinnamon and pecans, and cut into small pie shaped wedges. Roll from wide end and place on baking sheet. Shape into crescents. Bake at 350° for 18 minutes or until light brown. Glaze while still warm.

GLAZE: Mix well powdered sugar and milk, and spread on warm crescents. Yields 3 to 4 dozen, depending on how large the crescent wedges are cut.

Mrs. Kenneth Fry (Jeanne)
Mrs. Charles D. Price, Jr. (Joyce)

Croissants

1   cup milk, scalded
¼   cup shortening
½   cup sugar
1   teaspoon salt

1   package (1 tablespoon) dry yeast
3   eggs
4½ to 5 cups all-purpose flour
Melted butter

Scald milk. Add shortening, sugar and salt. Cool till slightly warm. Add yeast and eggs. Stir in 4 to 4½ cups flour with wooden spoon one cup at a time. Knead in about ½ cup more flour. Put dough in greased bowl, turning to grease top. Let rise 1 hour. Punch down. Divide into thirds and roll each third into a circle. Cut each circle into 16 pie-shaped wedges. Spread with melted butter. Roll each wedge from large end. Put on greased cookie sheet, tip down. Curve ends into crescent shape. Let rise 1 hour. Bake 10 minutes at 400°, until *light* brown. Yields 4½ dozen rolls.

Mrs. Richard Williams (Wanda)

Cinnamon Crisps

1   can (8 ounces) Pillsbury
    Refrigerated Crescent Rolls
1   tablespoon butter or
    margarine, melted
2   tablespoons sugar

¼   cup finely chopped nuts
2   teaspoons cinnamon
½   cup sugar
1   teaspoon cinnamon

GLAZE:

⅓   cup powdered sugar
½   teaspoon butter or
    margarine, softened

1   to 3 teaspoons milk

Separate dough into 2 rectangles. Place end to end to form one long narrow piece of dough. Press perforations to seal. Brush dough with butter. Combine 2 tablespoons sugar, nuts and 2 teaspoons cinnamon. Sprinkle over dough. Starting at short end, roll up and seal other end. Carefully cut into 8 slices. Dip both sides of each slice in ½ cup sugar mixed with 1 teaspoon cinnamon. Press until very thin, about ⅛ inch thick and about 5 inches in diameter. Bake on a very lightly greased cookie sheet 10 to 15 minutes at 375° or until golden brown. Place on cooling rack. Blend powdered sugar, margarine and milk for glaze, and drizzle over warm crisps. Makes 8 cinnamon crisps.

Variation: For sweet rolls instead of crisps, dip in cinnamon sugar, but don't press flat. Can be frozen.

Mrs. Frank S. Covaro (Genie)

Angel Biscuits

1   yeast cake
2   tablespoons tepid water
4   cups all-purpose flour
1   teaspoon soda
3   teaspoons baking powder

4   tablespoons sugar
1   teaspoon salt
1   cup shortening
2   cups buttermilk

Soften yeast in water. Sift flour, soda, baking powder, sugar and salt together; make a well. Add shortening and yeast, and work in. Gradually work in buttermilk. Roll and cut as biscuits. Bake at 400° about 20 minutes or until done. Dough may be kept for several days in a covered bowl in refrigerator, needed amount being pinched off each day.

Mrs. W. C. Marks (Belle)

Danish Puff Pastry

PASTRY:

1   cup all-purpose flour   2   tablespoons water
½ cup butter

FILLING:

½ cup butter or ¼ cup   1   teaspoon vanilla
     butter and ¼ cup cream 1   cup sifted all-purpose flour
     cheese   3   eggs
1   cup hot water

FROSTING:

1   cup powdered sugar   ½ teaspoon vanilla
2   tablespoons warm milk   Pecans or almonds, optional

PASTRY: Put flour in bowl. Cut in butter. Sprinkle with water and mix well with fork. Round into a ball and divide in half. Pat dough with hands into two long strips, about 3x12 inches. Place strips 3 inches apart on ungreased baking sheet.

FILLING: Add butter to hot water in saucepan. Bring mixture to rolling boil. Add vanilla and remove pan from heat. Add flour all at once to keep it from lumping. When mixture is smooth and thick, add eggs one at a time, stirring after each addition until mixture is velvety smooth. Divide mixture in half and spread evenly over the two strips of dough. Bake one hour at 350° until top is crisp and golden brown. Pierce with toothpick to be sure center is done. Frost when slightly cool so frosting does not soak into pastry.

FROSTING: Combine sugar, milk and vanilla; mix well. Drizzle over pastry. Spread with knife for a swirl effect. Pecans or almonds may be sprinkled over top if desired. Yields 18 to 24 pieces. *Important! Make these the day they are to be served, or they may become soggy.*

Mrs. Charles D. Price, Jr. (Joyce)

Butter biscuits or muffins, sprinkle with mixture of sugar and cinnamon, then toast.

Magic Marshmallow Crescent Puffs
Great!

¼ cup sugar	16 large marshmallows
1 teaspoon cinnamon	¼ cup butter or margarine,
2 cans (8 ounces each)	melted
Pillsbury refrigerated	¼ cup chopped nuts, if
quick crescent dinner rolls	desired

GLAZE:
½ cup powdered sugar   2 to 3 teaspoons milk
½ teaspoon vanilla

Combine sugar with cinnamon. Separate crescent dough into 16 triangles. Dip a marshmallow in melted butter; roll in sugar-cinnamon mixture. Wrap a dough triangle around each marshmallow, completely covering marshmallow and squeezing edges of dough tightly to seal. Dip in melted butter and place buttered side down in deep muffin cups. Repeat with remaining marshmallows. Place pan on foil or cookie sheet during baking to guard against spillovers in oven. Bake at 375° for 10 to 15 minutes until golden brown. Immediately remove from pans and drizzle with glaze. Sprinkle with nuts. Serve warm or cold. Yields 16 rolls.

GLAZE: Combine powdered sugar and vanilla with enough milk to make it thin enough to drizzle.

To make ahead, prepare and cover. Refrigerate for 2 or 3 hours and bake as directed. To reheat, wrap in foil and heat for 5 to 10 minutes at 375°. Puffs may be frozen and reheated from frozen state, wrapped in foil, for 10 to 15 minutes at 375°. Do not glaze before freezing. Glaze after puffs have been reheated from frozen state.

Mrs. Alice Wagnon

Easy Pan Coating

½ cup flour   ½ cup Crisco

Mix together and store in sealed container. Can be refrigerated or frozen for weeks.

This eliminates greasing and flouring cake pans, as both ingredients are combined. Always cool cakes 15 to 20 minutes before removing from pan.

Mrs. John B. Isbell (Charlene)

Southern Kitchen Cinnamon Rolls

DOUGH MIXTURE:

½ cup milk
½ cup butter
⅓ cup sugar
½ teaspoon salt

1½ teaspoons dry yeast
2 tablespoons warm water
2¼ cups all-purpose flour
1 egg

CINNAMON SUGAR MIXTURE:

1 cup sugar
½ cup firmly packed light
  brown sugar

1 tablespoon cinnamon
6 tablespoons butter

DOUGH MIXTURE: Scald milk, add butter and stir until the butter is melted. Allow to cool to lukewarm. Add sugar and salt and stir until dissolved. Dissolve yeast in warm water and add to milk mixture. Add 1 cup flour and beat well. Add egg, which has been beaten lightly, and beat about 2 minutes. Add 1 cup of flour and beat well. Then add rest of flour and mix well. Place on floured board and knead very lightly - about 8 times. Put in well greased bowl, cover and let rise until double in bulk. *This is a very soft dough. If needed, more flour can be added; however the texture will not be the same.*

CINNAMON SUGAR MIXTURE: Mix sugar, brown sugar and cinnamon together until well blended. Roll dough out to 8x20 inches. Completely cover with 1 tablespoon melted butter. Spread cinnamon sugar mixture evenly over surface, reserving about ¾ cup for top. Roll up and cut into 24 even pieces. Melt 5 tablespoons butter in 7x10½ inch pan and put rolls in pan placing cut side up. Press down to force butter up around rolls. Then spread remaining sugar mixture evenly over top. Press down. Let rise until double. Bake at 375° until done - about 20 minutes. Serve warm.

Mrs. Clifford Slagle (Henrietta)

Banana Muffins

2 tablespoons margarine,
  melted
1 egg
1 cup mashed ripe bananas

¼ cup milk
2 cups Bisquick
¼ cup sugar

ICING:
1 tablespoon water

½ cup powdered sugar

Combine margarine, egg, bananas and milk. Blend well, then stir in Bisquick and sugar. Bake in greased muffin tins at 400° 20 to 25 minutes for large muffins, or 12 to 15 minutes for small muffins. Yields 12 large muffins, about 24 small muffins.

ICING: Combine water and sugar and pour over warm muffins.

Mrs. Jack M. Fahrner (Marilyn)

Bunnie's Buttermilk Bran Muffins

1 box (15 ounces) Raisin
  Bran
1½ cups sugar
5 cups all-purpose flour
5 teaspoons soda
2 teaspoons salt

1 cup pecans, optional
1 cup raisins, optional
4 eggs, beaten
1 cup oil
4 cups buttermilk

Mix Raisin Bran, sugar, flour, soda, salt, pecans and raisins in large mixing bowl. Add eggs, oil and buttermilk and mix just until blended. Refrigerate overnight. Fill greased muffin tins ⅔ full. Bake at 375° for 15 to 20 minutes or until brown. Yields about 5 dozen muffins. *Do not remix batter before spooning into muffin tins. Mixture will keep 6 weeks in refrigerator.*

Mrs. Bill Heaton (Gladys)

Rice Gems

1	cup buttermilk	1	teaspoon baking powder
½	teaspoon soda	1	egg
1	cup flour	1	cup cooked rice
1	teaspoon salt	1	tablespoon butter, melted

Grease muffin rings and preheat in 450° oven. Mix buttermilk and soda. Mix flour, salt and baking powder in a bowl. Gradually stir in egg, buttermilk and soda. Blend in rice and butter. Pour batter into hot rings and bake for 15 minutes. Yields 12 muffins. *These cook best and look prettiest if baked in fluted iron muffin rings.*

This recipe of my great-grandmother's was a favorite at her hotel in Middle Tennessee. The Estes House served meals family style to guests who came to Primms Springs to drink the mineral water. In the 1800's rooms were 50 cents a day!

Mrs. James Thompson (Charlotte)

Banana Bread I

½	cup shortening	¼	teaspoon salt
1	cup sugar	3	large ripe bananas,
2	eggs		mashed
2	cups all-purpose flour	½	cup chopped nuts
1	teaspoon soda	1	teaspoon vanilla

Cream shortening and sugar. Add eggs, one at a time. Sift flour, soda and salt. Combine dry ingredients with creamed mixture until blended. Stir in bananas, nuts and vanilla. Pour into greased loaf pan 9x5 inches. Bake at 350° for 1 hour. Cool for 5 minutes in pan. Turn out onto wire rack and cool completely. Wrap in foil and let stand for 24 hours before serving. Yields 1 loaf.

Mrs. Lee Radford (Betty)

Banana Bread II

½ cup margarine	1 teaspoon soda
1½ cups sugar	3 large bananas, mashed
2 eggs	1 teaspoon vanilla
4 tablespoons sour milk	1 cup chopped pecans
1½ cups all-purpose flour	

Cream margarine and sugar. Add eggs, sour milk, flour, soda, bananas, vanilla and pecans. Mix well. Pour into 1 greased 9x5 inch loaf pan or 2 small loaf pans. Bake at 275° to 300° for 1 hour. *May be frozen.*

Mrs. Sam Harting (Sandra)

Hawaiian Banana Bread

2 cups sugar	2½ cups cake flour
1 cup shortening	1 teaspoon salt
6 ripe bananas, mashed	2 teaspoons soda
4 eggs, beaten	½ cup nuts

Cream sugar and shortening. Add bananas and eggs. Sift flour, salt and soda, then blend into creamed mixture. Stir in nuts. Do not overmix. Pour into 2 greased and floured 9x5 inch loaf pans. Bake 1 hour at 350°. Yields two loaves. *This is a very moist bread that keeps well.*

Mrs. Bruce Lowry (Elena)

Cranberry-Pumpkin Bread

3½ cups all-purpose flour	½ cup cooking oil
2 teaspoons soda	4 eggs
1 teaspoon salt	⅔ cup milk
1 tablespoon pumpkin pie spice	1½ cups pumpkin
3 cups sugar	1 cup whole raw cranberries
	1 cup nuts

Combine and blend flour, soda, salt and pumpkin pie spice. Stir in sugar, oil, eggs, milk, pumpkin, cranberries and nuts. Beat well. Pour into 2 greased and floured 9x5 inch loaf pans. Cook at 325° for 45 minutes or until done.

Mrs. Lucille Hatcher

Gingerbread

3 tablespoons butter
½ cup sugar
1 egg
1 teaspoon cinnamon
1½ cups flour

1 teaspoon ground ginger
1 teaspoon soda
½ cup milk
½ cup Brer Rabbit molasses
½ cup raisins

Cream together butter, sugar and egg. Add remaining ingredients. Mix well. Pour into 8 inch square baking pan. Bake at 350° for 30 to 40 minutes.

Mrs. Ralph Plumlee (Stella)

Grapenut Bread

1 cup sour milk
½ teaspoon baking soda
½ cup sugar
2 cups all-purpose flour

Pinch of salt
1 teaspoon baking powder
½ cup Grapenuts

Add soda to sour milk, then add sugar. Combine flour, baking powder and salt. Add to sour milk mixture. Stir in Grapenuts. Bake in greased 9x5 inch loaf pan at 350° for ¾ to 1 hour. Yields 1 loaf. *This recipe contains no eggs, so it would be good for low cholesterol diets.*

Mrs. Bruce I. Wilcoxson (Sue)

Leah's Mandel Brodt

1 cup shortening
1 cup sugar
3 eggs
1 teaspoon vanilla
4 cups flour

1 teaspoon salt
2 teaspoons baking powder
½ cup chopped almonds or pecans

Cream shortening, sugar, eggs and vanilla. Sift together flour, salt, baking powder and add to creamed mixture. Add nuts and mix well. Shape into 3 long rolls. Place on greased pans. Bake at 350° for 20 to 25 minutes or until golden brown. Let cool. Cut into slices and toast for about 4 minutes on each side.

Mrs. Charles D. Price, Jr. (Joyce)

Kemishbrote

1 cup sugar	¼ teaspoon salt
1 cup margarine	1 package (6 ounces) sliced
4 eggs	almonds
1 teaspoon vanilla or lemon	1 package (1 ounce)
extract	choco-bake
4 cups flour	1 to 2 teaspoons cinnamon
1 teaspoon baking powder	½ cup sugar

Cream 1 cup sugar and shortening. Add beaten eggs and vanilla or lemon extract to creamed ingredients. Stir in flour, baking powder, salt and almonds and mix well. Form into 3 loaves. Pour choco-bake over top and work in with fork. Place loaves on cookie sheets and bake in preheated oven at 350° for 20 to 25 minutes. Allow to rise but not to bake completely; remove from oven and allow to cool. Slice with sharp knife. Combine ½ cup sugar and cinnamon. Lay slices on cookie sheet and sprinkle with cinnamon and sugar mixture. Place in oven and toast until lightly brown. Yields 3 dozen slices.

Mrs. Edwin Lax (Ruth)

Mountain Bread

4 cups whole wheat flour	1½ teaspoons baking powder
⅓ cup wheat germ	1½ teaspoons salt
¼ cup sesame seed	1 cup water
¾ cup brown sugar	½ cup honey
3 tablespoons dry powdered	⅓ cup oil
milk	¼ cup molasses

Mix together flour, wheat germ, sesame seed, sugar, powdered milk, baking powder and salt. In separate bowl, mix water, honey, oil and molasses. Stir mixtures together until smooth. Pour into greased 8 inch pan. Bake at 300° about 1 hour, or until it pulls away from sides of pan. Cool. Cut into squares. Yields 12 to 16 pieces. *This is a heavy trail bread. Keeps well in backpack. Sweet enough to satisfy. We like it with a piece of cheese and fruit for a trail lunch.*

Mrs. S. G. Evetts (Darlene)

Pineapple Zucchini Bread
A marvelous bread!

3 eggs	1 teaspoon baking powder
2 cups sugar	1 teaspoon baking soda
1 cup oil	1 teaspoon salt
2 teaspoons vanilla	1 cup crushed pineapple
2 cups grated zucchini	½ cup golden raisins
3 cups all-purpose flour	1 cup chopped nuts

Combine eggs, sugar, oil and vanilla, and beat until fluffy. Add zucchini, flour, baking powder, soda and salt, and mix well. Stir in pineapple, raisins and nuts. Pour into 2 greased and floured 9x5 inch loaf pans. Bake at 350° for 1 hour. Yields 2 loaves. *Bread should not be kept unrefrigerated for more than a day because the pineapple ferments.*

Mrs. T. B. Dellinger (Maria)

Pumpkin Bread
Great for gift giving!

2 cups sugar	1 teaspoon salt
1½ cups vegetable oil	2 teaspoons soda
5 eggs	1 teaspoon cinnamon
1 can (16 ounces) pumpkin	½ teaspoon nutmeg
2 packages (3 ounces each) coconut pudding mix	½ cup chopped dates
	1 cup chopped pecans
2 cups all-purpose flour, sifted	

Mix sugar and oil in bowl. Add eggs, one at a time, mixing thoroughly. Add pumpkin and mix well. Add pudding mix, flour, salt, soda, cinnamon, nutmeg, dates and pecans. Mix thoroughly. Divide equally into greased and floured loaf pans. Bake at 350° about 35 minutes or until toothpick inserted comes out dry. Yields three 9x5 inch loaves or five small loaves. *Very moist and keeps well.*

Mrs. Alvis Reeves (Dolores)

Pumpkin Nut Bread

1 cup butter or margarine, softened
3 cups sugar
3 eggs
1 teaspoon vanilla
1 can (16 ounces) solid pack pumpkin
3 cups sifted all-purpose flour

1½ teaspoons salt
1 teaspoon baking soda
1 teaspoon baking powder
1½ teaspoons cinnamon
1 teaspoon cloves
½ teaspoon nutmeg
1 cup chopped walnuts
1 cup dark or golden raisins

Preheat oven to 350°. Cream butter and add sugar gradually. Beat in eggs and vanilla. Add pumpkin, mixing to combine well. Sift together flour, salt, soda, baking powder, cinnamon, cloves and nutmeg. Blend with pumpkin mixture. Add nuts and raisins. Pour batter into 2 greased and floured 9x5 inch loaf pans. Bake 60 to 65 minutes or until bread tests done with a wooden pick. Let stand 10 minutes. Remove from pans and cool on rack. Wrap and store overnight before slicing. Yields 2 loaves.

Variations: Add any one of the following, or use one for half the raisins in the basic recipe: 1 cup fruit and raisin granola, 1 cup all bran buds, ½ cup sesame seeds or ½ cup diced dates. *Fresh cooked pumpkin makes loaves wonderfully moist.*

Mrs. Larry N. Arcury (Dee)

Strawberry Bread

3 cups all-purpose flour, sifted
1 teaspoon soda
2 cups sugar
1 teaspoon salt
1 teaspoon cinnamon

4 eggs
2 cups frozen strawberries, thawed
1 cup oil
1¼ cups chopped nuts

Mix flour, soda, sugar, salt and cinnamon. Mix eggs, strawberries, oil and chopped nuts. Make a well in dry ingredients and pour egg mixture into the well. Hand mix until all dry ingredients are moist. Bake in two 9x5 inch loaf pans for one hour at 350°. Yields 2 loaves.

Mrs. W. J. Green (Juanita)

French Bread

1¼ cups warm water
1 package (1 tablespoon) dry yeast or 1 ounce compressed yeast
1½ teaspoons salt

1 tablespoon softened shortening
1 tablespoon sugar
3½ cups all-purpose flour, sifted
Yellow cornmeal

CORNSTARCH GLAZE:
1 teaspoon cornstarch
1 teaspoon cold water

½ cup boiling water

BREAD: Measure water into large mixing bowl. Add yeast and stir until dissolved. Add salt, shortening and sugar. Stir in flour to make soft dough. Turn out on lightly floured board and knead 8 to 10 minutes or until dough is elastic and doesn't stick to board. Place in greased bowl and grease surface of dough slightly. Cover and let rise in warm place until doubled (about 1 hour). Punch dough down and let rise again until doubled (about 30 minutes). Turn out on floured board and cut dough into 2 equal parts. Roll each into an oblong 8x10 inches. Beginning with wide side, roll each up tightly. Seal by pinching edges together, Roll gently back and forth to lengthen each loaf to about 16 inches, and taper ends. Place loaves on greased baking sheet that is dusted with yellow cornmeal. Brush loaves with cornstarch glaze. Let rise, uncovered, for 1½ hours. Brush again with glaze. With sharp knife, make ¼ inch slashes in dough at 2 inch intervals. Bake at 400° for 10 minutes. Remove from oven, brush again with glaze and return to oven to bake about 30 minutes longer, or until golden brown. Yields 2 loaves.

GLAZE: Combine all ingredients and mix until smooth.

Mrs. Rex Corey (Robyn)

SPICE HINTS:
Coffeecake — anise, enough to taste
Doughnuts — mace, cinnamon sugar
Dumplings — parsley flakes
Rolls — caraway seed, dill seed

Dilly Bread

1 package (1 tablespoon) dry yeast	1½ tablespoons butter
¼ cup warm water	2 tablespoons dill seed
1 cup cottage cheese	1 teaspoon salt
2 tablespoons sugar	½ teaspoon soda
1 tablespoon instant minced onion	1 egg
	2¼ to 2½ cups all-purpose flour

Soften yeast in warm water. Heat cottage cheese until lukewarm. To cheese, add sugar, onion, butter, dill seed, salt, soda and egg; mix well. Add softened yeast and flour. Cover and let rise in a warm place until double in size. Stir down and turn into a well greased 9x5 inch loaf pan. Bake at 350° for 40 to 50 minutes. Yields 1 loaf.

Mrs. Jerry L. Ewing (Claudette)

Monkey Bread

1 cup milk	1 teaspoon salt
1 cup butter or margarine, melted and divided in half	1 package (1 tablespoon) dry yeast
4 tablespoons sugar	3½ cups all-purpose flour

Combine milk, ½ cup butter, sugar and salt in a saucepan. Heat until butter is melted. Cool to 105° to 115°. Stir in yeast until dissolved. Add flour and pour in milk mixture. Stir until blended. Cover dough, and let rise until doubled in bulk, about 1 hour and 20 minutes. Turn out dough on floured surface. Roll ¼ inch thick and cut into 3 inch squares. Dip each square into remaining ½ cup butter. Layer squares in a 10 inch tube or Bundt pan. Let rise until doubled in bulk, about 30 to 40 minutes. Bake at 375° for 30 to 40 minutes.

Mrs. Lucille Hatcher

Aunt Dell's One Hour Rolls

1   package (1 tablespoon) dry
   yeast
1   teaspoon sugar
2   tablespoons warm water
2¼ cups all-purpose flour

½   teaspoon salt
1   tablespoon sugar
¼   teaspoon soda
¾   cup buttermilk
¼   cup oil or melted butter

Mix yeast, 1 teaspoon sugar and water, and let stand. Mix flour, salt, 1 tablespoon sugar and soda in large bowl. Heat buttermilk and oil or butter to lukewarm. Add yeast and buttermilk mixtures to flour and mix. Let rise in bowl for 10 minutes. Put on floured board and knead 10 times. Shape into rolls and let rise for 30 minutes. Bake about 20 minutes at 375°. Yields 18 rolls. *These are super tasty. If you are out of buttermilk, substitute 1 teaspoon of baking powder and ¾ cup sweet milk for the soda and buttermilk.*

Mrs. Bill Heaton (Gladys)

Yeast Rolls

½   cup Crisco
½   cup sugar
½   cup boiling water
1   teaspoon salt
1½ packages (1½ tablespoons)
   dry yeast

½   cup warm water
1   egg, beaten
3   cups all-purpose flour
⅛   to ¼ cup all-purpose flour

Mix Crisco, sugar, boiling water and salt. Cool to lukewarm. Soften yeast in warm water (105° to 115°), and add to Crisco mixture. Add egg and flour; mix together well. Cover and let rise for 1 hour in warm place or until doubled in size. Punch down. Add a little (⅛ to ¼ cup) extra flour to dough to make it less sticky as you make out the rolls. Pinch off balls of dough and place into greased muffin tins. Cover and let rise in warm place until doubled in size, about an hour. Bake in 400° oven for 20 minutes until golden brown. Yields 24 rolls.

This dough can be refrigerated for a few days in a covered bowl. After letting it rise for an hour, punch down and cover tightly; then put in refrigerator. To make rolls, pinch off as many as you desire, let rise, and bake as in above directions.

Mrs. Lee Radford (Betty)

Bran Rolls

1 cup warm water	⅓ cup vegetable oil
1 package (1 tablespoon) dry yeast	2 tablespoons sugar
	1 egg
1 cup bran (Bran Buds, All Bran, 100% Bran)	¼ teaspoon salt
	2½ cups all-purpose flour

Dissolve yeast in warm water for one minute. Add bran, then oil, egg, salt and sugar. Mix; add 1 cup flour and beat two minutes. Add remaining flour. Finish mixing by hand. Dough will be soft and sticky. Cover with damp cloth and let rise until double in size in a warm place. On a well floured surface, divide into 12 pieces and place in oiled muffin pans. In a warm place, let rise until doubled. Bake in 400° oven about 15 minutes. Yields 12 rolls.

Mrs. Harry C. Holmes (Lillian)

Italian Bread Sticks

1 package (1 tablespoon) dry yeast	1 teaspoon salt
1½ cups warm water	¼ cup vegetable oil
⅓ cup instant dry milk	1 egg
2 tablespoons sugar	5 cups all-purpose flour

TOPPING:

1 egg, beaten	¼ cup sesame seed

Dissolve yeast in water. Add milk, sugar, salt, oil and egg. Mix. Add 2 cups of flour and beat 1 minute. Add remaining flour (finish mixing by hand). Dough will be slightly sticky. Cover bowl with damp cloth and let rise in warm place until doubled. Roll out on floured board to about ⅔ inch thickness. Cut into strips ½ inch to ¾ inch wide and to desired length. Place in oiled or Teflon pans, leaving space for spreading. Brush each stick with beaten egg, then sprinkle with sesame seeds. Let rise until doubled in warm place. Bake in preheated 425° oven for 12 to 15 minutes, depending on size and whether you like them soft or hard. Yields about 2½ dozen bread sticks, depending on size. *This recipe also makes good "hard" rolls.*

Mrs. Harry C. Holmes (Lillian)

Philadelphia Sticky Buns

⅓ cup milk
¼ cup sugar
½ teaspoon salt
¼ cup butter or margarine
¼ cup warm water (105° to 115°)

1 package (1 tablespoon) dry yeast
2½ cups all-purpose flour, unsifted
1 egg

TOPPING:

¼ cup butter or margarine, softened
¼ cup light brown sugar

½ cup pecan or walnut halves

FILLING:

¼ cup butter, softened
½ teaspoon cinnamon

½ cup chopped raisins

BUNS: In small pan, heat milk just until bubbles form at edge of pan; remove from heat. Add sugar, salt and butter; stir to melt. Cool to lukewarm (drop on wrist is not warm). Check temperature of warm water with thermometer. Sprinkle yeast over water in large bowl; stir to dissolve. Stir in lukewarm milk mixture. Add egg and 2 cups flour; beat with mixer until smooth. Add remaining flour; mix with hand until dough is smooth and leaves side of bowl. Turn out dough onto lightly floured pastry cloth. Knead until dough is smooth and blisters appear. Place in lightly greased large bowl; turn to bring up greased side. Cover with towel. Let rise in warm place (85°) free from drafts, until double, about 1 to 1½ hours.

TOPPING: In small bowl with wooden spoon cream butter and brown sugar. Spread on bottom and sides of 9 inch square pan. Sprinkle with pecans.

FILLING: Roll dough on lightly floured cloth into a 16x12 inch rectangle. To fill the rolls, spread dough with soft butter; sprinkle with cinnamon and raisins. Roll up from long side, jelly roll fashion; pinch edge to seal. Cut crosswise into 12 pieces; place cut side down in pan. Cover and let rise in warm place (85° free from drafts) 1 to 1½ hours until doubled (rises to top of pan). Meanwhile, preheat oven to 375°. Bake 25 to 30 minutes or until golden brown. Invert on board or plate; let stand 1 minute; remove pan. Serve warm. Yields 12 buns.

Mrs. John Schimmer (Jane)

Texas Corn Fritters

1½ cups sifted all-purpose
   flour
2 teaspoons baking powder
¾ teaspoon salt

2 cups cut fresh corn (6
   ears) or 1 can (12 ounces)
   whole kernel corn, drained
   and liquid reserved
Milk added to reserved liquid
   to make 1 cup
1 egg, beaten

Sift together flour, baking powder and salt. Combine corn, milk mixture and beaten egg; then add to dry ingredients. Mix just until flour is moistened. Drop batter from tablespoon into deep, hot oil (375°). Fry until golden brown, about 3 minutes. Drain on paper towels. Serve with warm maple-flavored syrup. Yields about 18 fritters.

Mrs. Margaret Levy

Dodger Corn Bread

2 cups white cornmeal
½ cup all-purpose flour
1 teaspoon baking powder
½ teaspoon salt

1 tablespoon sugar, optional
4 tablespoons shortening
1½ cups boiling water
Oil for frying

Mix cornmeal, flour, baking powder, salt and sugar. Add shortening. Pour boiling water over all and mix to form a thick paste. Make into patties about 2½ inches round and ¾ inch thick. Fry in deep hot oil until golden brown. Yields about 15 patties. *This is an old recipe from my mother. She used to prepare these every Saturday for the noon meal with a big pot of brown beans.*

Mrs. Charles D. Price, Jr. (Joyce)

Jalapeño Corn Bread

3   eggs, beaten
2½ cups milk
3   cups corn bread mix
½   cup cooking oil
3   teaspoons sugar
1   large onion, grated

1   can (17 ounces) yellow
    cream corn
1½ cups grated sharp cheese
1   teaspoon baking powder
½   can (12 ounces) diced
    jalapeños

Mix all ingredients together well. Pour into greased 9x13 inch pan. Bake at 450° until golden brown. Serves 12 to 20.

Mrs. Jes McIver (Marilyn)

Corn Bread Dressing

1   bunch celery
3   onions
1   cup Crisco shortening
2   cans (10½ ounces each)
    cream of chicken soup
2   cans water
5   hard cooked eggs

3   quarts corn bread (9x13
    inch pan)
1   quart bread, toasted (8
    slices)
Pepper, red pepper, sage and
    poultry seasoning

Chop celery and onions; sauté in Crisco. Add soup and water. Chop eggs, crumble corn bread and bread and add to soup mixture. Add seasonings and mix well. Pour into large casserole dish. Bake at 350° for about 30 minutes or until heated. Yields 1 large *full* casserole.

Mrs. Joy Anderson

Vegetables

VEGETABLES

As our knowledge of nutrition increases, so does our respect for vegetables. After generations of considering meat to be the mainstay of the American diet, we now know that the vegetable is a superior source of nutrition as well as fiber. Vegetables have long been staples of man's diet. Preserved fragments of squash and pumpkin have been discovered in prehistoric cemeteries in South America dating back to 1200 A.D.

Peas were a common food in ancient Egypt long before the birth of Christ, and okra was produced as a food source in the ancient Nile Valley. Broccoli, from the cabbage family, was perfected by the Danish, and it didn't make it to the American table until about a century ago. Brussels sprouts have also been a popular dish in the United States for about a hundred years but have been served in Europe much longer. The cucumber, however, has been around at least 2,000 years, having first been cultivated in Asia and Africa. Corn is one of the more important food crops in the world today, and the American Indian is credited for its development. Beans were found in cultivation by the American Indians also, and over 500 varieties are native to America. Other bean types and lentils are native to the Old World.

The mighty potato (solanum tuberosum) is probably the world's leading vegetable crop today. The potato is native to South America and was cultivated by the ancient Incas. However, it did not become an important food source worldwide until about the Seventeenth Century. Rich in vitamins, minerals and carbohydrates, the potato enjoys a culture which is practically universal today.

You will find many delicious and attractive recipes in this section. Try them all and treat your family to good nutrition!

Asparagus-Pea Casserole

1   can (15 ounces) asparagus spears, drained (or cut)

1   can (16 ounces) small English peas, drained

1   can (10¾ ounces) cream of mushroom soup, undiluted

1   can (8 ounces) sliced water chestnuts

Buttered bread slices, finger sliced

Layer asparagus and peas in 9x13 inch buttered baking dish. Mix together the mushroom soup and water chestnuts. Spread evenly over vegetables. Top with bread slices and bake at 350° until heated thoroughly and topping is toasted. Serves 8.

Aggie Mom

Asparagus In The Round

1 cup Pepperidge Farm herb stuffing mix, blue package
¼ cup butter or margarine, melted
1 can (4½ ounces) sliced mushrooms, drained (reserve liquid)
1 can (10½ ounces) asparagus spears

2 tablespoons sliced green onions
¼ cup butter or margarine
2 tablespoons flour
½ teaspoon salt
½ teaspoon dry mustard
1 cup half-and-half
¼ cup Parmesan cheese

Combine stuffing mix, ¼ cup butter and liquid from mushrooms. Line bottom of 9 inch pie plate with this mixture. Top with asparagus. Sauté onions and mushrooms in the remaining ¼ cup butter. Stir in flour and seasonings, blending well. Gradually stir in half-and-half. Cook over low heat stirring constantly until thickened. Pour over asparagus and sprinkle with cheese. Bake at 375° fifteen minutes, until bubbly. Serves 6 to 8. *You can substitute cooked frozen 10 ounce package of broccoli.*

Mrs. Frank S. Covaro (Genie)

Baked Bean Casserole

2 tablespoons bacon drippings
1 tablespoon prepared mustard
¼ pound boiled ham, in thin strips

2 tablespoons minced onion
1 can (15 ounces) red beans
2 small apples, thinly sliced
¼ cup brown sugar

Heat bacon drippings in a heavy skillet over low heat. Stir in mustard. Add ham strips and onion, sauté until onions are clear. Mix in the red beans and pour in baking dish. Place apple slices on top of bean mixture, sprinkle evenly with brown sugar, and bake 350° for 30 minutes, until apples are tender and beans piping hot. Serve at once.

Mrs. Lewis Eidson (Mary John)

Baked Beans I

6 strips bacon	1 tablespoon vinegar
1 onion, chopped fine	1 tablespoon prepared
½ cup brown sugar	mustard
½ cup dark molasses	2 cans (16 ounces each) Van
½ cup catsup	Camp pork and beans

Fry bacon until crisp. Remove bacon. Sauté onion in bacon fat. Mix together all other ingredients with bacon fat and sautéed onion. Add crumbled bacon. Put in baking dish and bake in slow oven for 2 hours. Serves 8.

This recipe was given in 1957 when I was a featured guest on radio and television programs as Best Cook in the Best Cook of the Week Specials, sponsored by Stokely-Van Camp, Inc. Our Club received from Stokely-Van Camp several cases of canned fruit, later served at Club luncheons.

Mrs. Ralph Plumlee (Stella)

Baked Beans II

3 cups dried beans	½ teaspoon pepper
Water to cover	4 tablespoons molasses
½ cup brown sugar	1 pound bacon fat or salt
½ teaspoon dry mustard	pork, cut in chunks
1 teaspoon salt	1 medium onion, diced

Wash beans and sort for quality. Cover with water and parboil until skin blows back when you blow on a teaspoonful. Rinse thoroughly in cold water. Save hot bean liquor. In a small bowl, mix sugar, mustard, salt, pepper and molasses. Place half of the bacon on the bottom of bean pot or casserole. Add beans, bean liquor, other ingredients and place rest of bacon on top. Bake at 300° covered, for 6 to 7 hours. Watch liquid level carefully, keeping beans covered with liquid.

Mrs. Arthur Collins (Mary)

Baked Eggplant Casserole

1 pound eggplant, peeled	2 eggs, slightly beaten
½ pound dried bread crumbs	1 tablespoon chopped
½ cup evaporated milk	pimiento
¼ cup whole milk	2 teaspoons salt
¼ cup melted butter or	½ teaspoon pepper
margarine	¼ teaspoon sage
¼ cup finely chopped onion	⅛ teaspoon monosodium
¼ cup finely chopped green	glutamate
pepper	1½ cups (4 ounces) grated
¼ cup finely chopped celery	Cheddar cheese

Cut peeled eggplant into 1 inch cubes and soak in salt water in refrigerator overnight. Drain eggplant and place in pan. Cover with water and simmer until tender. Soak bread crumbs in milk. Sauté onion, green pepper and celery in melted butter 15 minutes, or until tender. Combine cooked eggplant, bread crumbs, sautéed vegetables, and add eggs, pimiento and seasonings. Blend thoroughly. Place in greased baking dish and bake at 350° 45 minutes. Top with grated cheese and return to oven until cheese melts.

Mrs. Sam E. Stock (Frances)

Baked Corn

2 eggs	1 can (17 ounces) creamed
½ cup sugar	corn
1 teaspoon cornstarch	Salt and pepper to taste
¼ cup (scant) milk	Butter

Beat eggs and mix all ingredients well. Place in a greased 9 inch square casserole dish, dot with butter and bake at 350° for one hour. Serves 4.

Mrs. William Sleeper (Mica)

Maize Casserole

1   can (17 ounces) yellow
    cream style corn
1   egg
½   cup milk
1   cup biscuit mix
2   tablespoons salad oil

1   teaspoon dried parsley
8   ounces grated sharp
    Cheddar cheese
1   can (4 ounces) chopped
    green chili peppers

Combine corn with slightly beaten egg, milk, biscuit mix, salad oil and parsley, and stir until well blended. Spread half of this mixture in a greased 1½ quart flat baking dish. Spread with cheese and green chilies. Cover with the remaining corn mixture. Bake at 400° for 30 minutes. Serves 6 to 8.

Aggie Mom

Black "Eyes of Texas" Casserole

2   cans (15¼ ounces each)
    jalapeño black-eyed peas,
    drained
1½ pounds lean ground beef
1   large onion, chopped
2   cloves garlic, chopped
1   can (10 ounces) tomatoes
    with green chilies
1   can (10¾ ounces) cream
    of chicken soup, undiluted

1   can (10¾ ounces) cream
    mushroom soup, undiluted
1   can (10 ounces) enchilada
    sauce
¼   teaspoon liquid hot pepper
1¼ dozen corn tortillas
2   cups grated sharp Cheddar
    cheese

Sauté ground beef, onion and garlic until lightly browned, stirring to crumble the meat. Stir in remaining ingredients, except tortillas and cheese. Cut the tortillas into ⅛ths. Alternately layer the mixture of meat and tortillas, beginning and ending with meat mixture in 9x13 inch baking pan. Sprinkle with cheese. Bake at 350° for 35 minutes, or until bubbly. Serves 8. *Freezes well.*

Mrs. James E. Keeling (Betty)

Broccoli Casserole

1 small onion, chopped	5 tablespoons Cheese Whiz
½ cup chopped celery	or Velveeta cheese
1 tablespoon margarine	1 can (10¾ ounces) cream
1 package (10 ounces) frozen	of mushroom soup
chopped broccoli	1 cup Minute rice
½ cup water	

Sauté onion and celery in margarine. Add frozen broccoli and water and cook for 5 minutes. Add Cheese Whiz or Velveeta, mushroom soup and Minute rice. Stir until well mixed. Cover and bake at 350° about 25 minutes. Serves 4 to 6.

Mrs. J. O. Ward (Kaye)

Broccoli Imperial

2 packages (10 ounces each)	2 eggs, beaten
frozen chopped broccoli	¼ teaspoon salt
1 can (10¾ ounces) cream	¼ teaspoon pepper
of mushroom soup	Dash Lawry's seasoned salt
1 cup mayonnaise	1 teaspoon Cavender's All
1 cup grated sharp cheese	Purpose Greek Seasoning
1 large onion, chopped	½ cup grated cheese

Cook broccoli until barely done. Drain. Add mushroom soup, mayonnaise, sharp cheese, onions, eggs and seasonings. Place in greased 9x13 inch baking dish. Top with grated cheese. Bake at 350° until bubbly. Serves 8. *May be prepared ahead of time and refrigerated, then baked at serving time.*

Mrs. James P. Newberry (Mary Jane)

Clara's Cabbage

CABBAGE:
1   firm head of cabbage   Water to cover
Salt to taste

SAUCE:
2   tablespoons margarine   Dash pepper
2   tablespoons flour   1   cup milk
¼   teaspoon salt   Cracker crumbs

CABBAGE: Cut washed cabbage into large pieces and cook in lightly salted water until tender. Drain cabbage and arrange in oiled baking dish. Pour white sauce over cabbage and sprinkle top with crushed cracker crumbs. Bake 10 to 15 minutes at 350°.

SAUCE: While cabbage is cooking, melt margarine over low heat in saucepan. Blend in flour and seasonings. Stir until mixture is smooth and bubbly. Remove from heat. Stir in milk. Bring to boil, stirring constantly, and cook until slightly thickened. *This amount of sauce is sufficient for 1 small head of cabbage. Double recipe for a larger head.*

Mrs. James E. Doherty (Clara)

Carrots Lyonnaise

6   medium carrots   1   tablespoon flour
1   can (10¾ ounces) chicken   ¼   teaspoon salt
    broth   Dash pepper
4   tablespoons butter   ¾   cup water
2   medium onions, sliced   Pinch of sugar

Pare carrots and cut in julienne strips (about 3x¼ inch). Cook covered in chicken broth for 10 minutes. Melt butter in skillet and add onions. Cook covered for 15 minutes, stirring occasionally. Stir in flour, salt, pepper and water. Bring to boil. Add carrots to broth and simmer uncovered for 10 minutes more, or until carrots are tender. Add a pinch of sugar just before serving.

Mrs. John B. Isbell (Charlene)

Mustard Carrots

1	pound carrots	2	tablespoons brown sugar
¼	teaspoon salt	2	tablespoons corn syrup
2	tablespoons butter	2	tablespoons mustard

Peel carrots and cut diagonally into 1 inch slices. Simmer in salted water until tender, about 20 minutes; drain. Combine butter, brown sugar, syrup and mustard in saucepan. Cook until blended, stirring constantly. Pour mixture over carrots, tossing gently until coated. Serves 4.

Mrs. Kenneth D. Cheairs (Dorothy)

Grits Souffle

4	cups water	1	cup grated mild Cheddar
1	cup grits		cheese
3	egg yolks, beaten		Garlic powder to taste
½	cup margarine	3	egg whites, beaten

Cook grits in water. Blend in egg yolks. Stir in margarine and cheese. Add garlic powder to taste. Fold beaten egg whites into mixture and pour into greased 2 quart round casserole dish. Bake covered for 30 minutes at 350°. *Dash of Tabasco may be added.*

Mrs. Fred D. Sewell (Ann)

Mushroom Casserole

1	pound mushrooms (washed and sliced)	1	tablespoon prepared mustard
⅓	cup melted butter	1	teaspoon salt
1	tablespoon chopped parsley	⅛	teaspoon red pepper
1	tablespoon minced onion	⅛	teaspoon nutmeg
		1½	tablespoons flour
		1	cup heavy cream

Place mushrooms in casserole dish. Mix together butter, parsley, onion, mustard, salt, red pepper, nutmeg and flour, and spread over mushrooms. Pour cream over all and bake uncovered at 375° for 55 minutes. Serves 4.

Mrs. Bruce I. Wilcoxson (Sue)

Special Mushrooms

1 pound mushrooms, washed and dried (reserving stems)	½ cup grated sharp cheese
	3 tablespoons bread crumbs
	½ teaspoon salt
¼ cup butter or margarine	½ teaspoon pepper
1 tablespoon Worcestershire sauce	½ teaspoon oregano
	½ teaspoon garlic salt

Chop mushroom stems and add to melted butter, Worcestershire, cheese, crumbs and seasonings. Fill the cleaned mushrooms with above mixture and broil 8 to 10 minutes.

Mrs. James P. Newberry (Mary Jane)

Kitty's Potato Casserole

4 or 5 potatoes	Butter
2 rolls Kraft Jalapeño cheese	Salt and pepper
1 large onion, sliced	

Butter casserole dish. Peel and slice potatoes. Place half of potato slices in dish. Cover with half the sliced onion and one roll of cheese. Dot with a little butter and salt and pepper. Repeat layer. Bake covered at 375° for about 45 minutes.

Mrs. Joe Cointment (Kay)

Lynda's Mashed Potatoes

1 package (8 ounces) instant mashed potatoes	1 package (1.5 ounces) potato toppers
½ cup sour cream	1 cup grated cheese

Prepare mashed potatoes according to directions. Stir in other ingredients. Place in greased baking dish. Sprinkle more grated cheese over top. Bake uncovered for 20 minutes at 350°.

Mrs. J. Hal Brown (Eva Gay)

Peas International

2   packages (10 ounces each) frozen peas
1   cup boiling water
1   cup celery, cut crosswise
1   tablespoon butter
½   cup water

2   tablespoons cornstarch
2   cubes chicken bouillon
1   can (8 ounces) thinly sliced water chestnuts, drained
Toasted slivered almonds

Crisp cook peas and celery in boiling water for 4 minutes. Drain and add butter. Combine water and bouillon cubes. Mix well. Add cornstarch and blend to a smooth paste. Add to peas. Heat quickly just until hot. Add the water chestnuts and top with the toasted slivered almonds. Serves 10 to 12. *DO NOT OVERCOOK. Tester suggests using only 2 teaspoons cornstarch.*

Mrs. W. C. Marks (Belle)

Rice and Green Chili Casserole

4   cups cooked Minute rice (measure ⅔ cup uncooked for each cup)
1   carton (16 ounces) sour cream
2   teaspoons salt

6   ounces chopped green chilies
4   tablespoons butter
3   packages (12 ounces each) Monterey Jack cheese, grated
1   onion, chopped

Combine cooked rice, butter, green chilies, sour cream and 2 packages of cheese and pour into large greased casserole. Top with remaining cheese. Bake at 350° for 30 minutes or until bubbly.

Mrs. J. M. Brundrett (Billye)

Scalloped Rice

½ cup chopped onion	½ cup sour cream
½ cup chopped green pepper	3 cups cooked rice
1 tablespoon water	½ teaspoon salt
1 can (11 ounces) condensed Cheddar cheese soup	¼ teaspoon pepper
	1 cup grated Cheddar cheese

Steam onions and green pepper in water for two to three minutes in covered saucepan. Set aside. Blend soup and sour cream. Add rice, steamed vegetables and seasonings. Pour in greased shallow 1½ quart casserole. Sprinkle with grated cheese. Bake at 350° for 30 minutes, or until hot and bubbly.

Mrs. Frank S. Covaro (Genie)

Orange Rice

½ cup butter	½ cup dry white wine
1 cup rice	1 orange, juice and rind
½ teaspoon salt	Salt and pepper
2 cups chicken broth	Parsley

Place butter, rice, salt, broth and wine in a casserole. Cover. Bake at 350° for 45 minutes. Add juice from the orange and the rind. Cook 10 minutes more. Add salt and pepper to taste, toss with fork and sprinkle parsley on top. *I sometimes add sliced almonds for a delicious taste and omit parsley.* Serves 6 to 8.

Mrs. Jack McAuliff (Betty)

SPICE HINTS:
Beets—tarragon, tarragon vinegar
Cabbage—caraway or mustard seed
Carrots—ginger
Coleslaw—caraway or dill seed
Corn—chili powder
Eggplant—basil or thyme
Fruit salad—allspice or mace
Peas—mint flakes or savory
Potatoes—dill seed, rosemary

Spinach Casserole I

2 packages (10 ounces each)
   frozen chopped spinach
¼ cup finely chopped onion
1 tablespoon butter or
   margarine

6 eggs, beaten
   Salt and pepper to taste
16 ounces sour cream
½ to ¾ pound Cheddar
   cheese, grated

Thaw spinach. Sauté onion in butter. Add eggs, spinach, salt and pepper; scramble until set. Place layer of egg-spinach mixture in bottom of greased casserole. Top with the sour cream and grated cheese. Repeat layers. Place in 350° oven only until cheese melts.

Mrs. Bill Frazier (Ruby)

Spinach Casserole II

2 packages (10 ounces each)
   frozen chopped spinach
1 can (10¾ ounces) cream
   of mushroom soup
2 packages (3 ounces each)
   Philadelphia cream cheese

1 can (3 ounces) French fried
   onion rings
½ cup butter or margarine
   Cracker crumbs

Prepare spinach according to package directions. Drain. Heat soup and cream cheese until cheese melts. Add spinach and onion rings. Pour into greased casserole dish. Melt the butter and add enough cracker crumbs to absorb butter. Sprinkle on top of spinach. Bake at 350° for 25 minutes. Serves 8.

Mrs. S. G. Evetts (Darlene)

Mother's Squash Casserole

2 cups cooked, drained
   yellow squash
3 tablespoons minced onion
Salt and pepper to taste
1 can (10¾ ounces) cream
   of mushroom soup

3 eggs, beaten
½ cup melted margarine
2 cups grated American
   cheese
½ cup crushed Ritz crackers

Mash the cooked squash and add onion, salt, pepper, mushroom soup, beaten eggs, margarine and grated cheese. Place in greased 2 quart baking dish. Top with finely crushed Ritz cracker crumbs. Bake 1 hour at 350°.

Mrs. George D. Neal (Carolyn)

Squash and Corn Casserole

6 to 8 large yellow squash
1 small onion, chopped fine
2 cans (12 ounces each)
   Mexicorn, drained
1 carton (8 ounces) sour
   cream

1 teaspoon sugar
1 egg
1 can (4 ounces) chopped
   green chilies, drained
Sliced Velveeta cheese

Cook and drain the yellow squash. Combine with the chopped onion, corn, sour cream, sugar, and slightly beaten egg. Stir in the chilies, and place in greased cooking dish. Top with slices of Velveeta and bake 30 minutes at 375°, until cheese is slightly browned.

Mrs. William Nelson (Janet)

Baked Summer Squash

4 medium crookneck squash	1 jar (2 ounces) chopped
3 tablespoons butter	pimiento
1 cup sour cream	½ cup grated Swiss cheese
¼ teaspoon allspice	¼ cup dry sherry
	Salt and pepper to taste

Scrub squash and trim ends. Steam whole for 20 minutes or until barely tender. Cut in half and arrange side by side in well oiled baking dish. Melt butter and blend in sour cream, allspice, pimiento with juice, cheese, sherry, salt and pepper. Stir until smooth. Pour over squash. Bake for 15 minutes at 350°. Serve immediately. Serves 8.

Mrs. Bob S. Singer (Janet)

Squash Casserole I

3 pounds yellow crookneck squash, sliced	2 cans (4 ounces each) green chilies, chopped
2 eggs	2 teaspoons salt
1 package (8 ounces) cream cheese	2 teaspoons Accent
	Bread crumbs or crushed crackers

Cook and drain squash. Beat eggs; add cheese, green chilies and seasonings. Mix cheese mixture with squash. Place in greased casserole. Top with bread or cracker crumbs. Bake at 350° for 30 minutes. Serves 8 to 10.

Zucchini can be substituted for all or part of yellow squash.

Mrs. Robert Clark (Sylvia)

Squash Casserole II

2　cups cooked squash,
　　mashed
1　teaspoon sugar
½　cup mayonnaise
½　cup finely chopped onion,
　　sautéed in 1 tablespoon
　　butter
1　egg, slightly beaten

½　cup grated Swiss cheese
Salt and pepper to taste
¼　cup finely chopped green
　　pepper
¼　cup butter, melted
½　cup cracker crumbs
½　cup chopped nuts

Mix together first 8 ingredients and pour into casserole dish; top with buttered crumbs. Bake at 350° for 20 minutes; sprinkle nuts over top and gently press into crumb topping. Bake another 10 minutes. Serves 6 to 8.

Mrs. Opal V. Jones

Tomatoes with Dill Sauce

DILL SAUCE:
½　cup sour cream
¼　cup mayonnaise
2　tablespoons finely chopped
　　onion

1　teaspoon snipped fresh dill
　　weed, or ¼ teaspoon
　　dried dill weed
¼　teaspoon salt

TOMATOES:
4　large, firm, ripe tomatoes
Salt and pepper to taste

Butter

DILL SAUCE: Mix sour cream, mayonnaise, onion, dill weed and ¼ teaspoon salt. Chill.

TOMATOES: Core tomatoes. Cut in half crossways. Season cut surface with salt and pepper. Dot with butter. Broil, cut side up, 3 inches from heat, about 5 minutes or until hot. Top with dill sauce. Sprinkle with more dill weed, if desired. Serve immediately. Serves 8.

Mrs. Bill Sleeper (Mica)

Vegetable Casserole I

1 package (10 ounces each)   ½ cup mayonnaise
   chopped broccoli, regular   ½ cup whipping cream
   cut green beans, baby   ½ cup grated Cheddar cheese
   limas, and green peas   ½ cup Parmesan cheese

Cook vegetables as directed on boxes until just tender. Do not overcook. Mix the mayonnaise with whipping cream, and stir all vegetables into the cream mixture. Combine cheeses and top casserole. Bake in greased casserole 25 minutes at 325°. Serves 16 to 18.

Mrs. Jean Gross

Vegetable Casserole II

1 can (16 ounces) shoe peg   1 can (10¾ ounces) cream
   corn, drained   of mushroom soup
1 can (16 ounces) French-   1 cup sour cream
   style green beans, drained   ¾ cup grated cheese
½ cup chopped onion   Almond slices, optional
¼ cup chopped green pepper Butter
                          Crushed Ritz crackers

Mix together the corn and beans. Stir in onion, pepper, soup, sour cream, cheese and almond slices. Pour into a greased 9x13 inch baking dish and dot with butter. Top with crushed Ritz crackers and bake at 375° for 30 minutes. Serves 8.

Aggie Mom

Cheesed Zucchini

6 medium zucchini,
  quartered lengthwise
Salt
Garlic salt
Oregano
Coarse pepper

3 ripe tomatoes
2 medium onions, sliced
1 package (8 ounces) sharp
  process American cheese
6 slices bacon

Place zucchini to cover bottom of shallow greased 7x12 baking dish. Sprinkle with salt, garlic salt, pinch of oregano and coarse pepper. Slice unpeeled tomatoes, and place over squash, season same as zucchini. Slice enough onions to make a layer; season as before. Over onions, layer cheese slices. Top with layer of bacon. Bake uncovered in 350° oven 45 minutes.

Mrs. Robert Ennis (Ruth)

Zucchini Casserole

7 or 8 medium zucchini, cut
  in ¼ inch slices
1 cup water
8 slices bacon, diced
1 large onion, chopped
1 large garlic clove, minced
4 slices white bread, diced

2 cups shredded Cheddar
  cheese
1 teaspoon salt
1 teaspoon Italian seasoning
Dash pepper
1 can (15 ounces) tomato
  sauce
¼ cup grated Parmesan
  cheese

In large saucepan, cook sliced zucchini in boiling water until tender, about 5 minutes; drain. In medium skillet, cook bacon until crisp, remove from pan. Add onion and garlic to skillet and sauté until onion is tender; drain. Stir onion-bacon mixture into drained zucchini. Add remaining ingredients *except* Parmesan cheese and toss until well coated. Spoon into 9x13 inch baking dish, sprinkle with Parmesan cheese. Bake 350° for 20 minutes. Serves 10 to 12. *200 calories per 10 servings. 165 calories per 12 servings.*

Mrs. Mary Ann Fredrickson

Continental Zucchini

1 pound zucchini	1 teaspoon salt
1 can (12 ounces) whole kernel corn	¼ teaspoon pepper
½ teaspoon garlic powder	½ cup shredded Mozzarella cheese
2 tablespoons salad oil	

Cut zucchini into bite size pieces. In large skillet, stir together the ingredients, reserving the shredded cheese. Cover. Cook over medium heat, stirring occasionally for about 10 minutes. Stir in cheese and heat to melt.

Mrs. Bonnie Leissler

Turkish Onions

1 large white onion	2 teaspoons lemon juice
2 teaspoons salt	Dash of pepper
2 teaspoons salad oil	

Slice onion as thin as possible; separate into rings. Place in colander. Salt heavily with the 2 teaspoons salt. Let set for not less than 3 minutes, nor more than 5 minutes. Place under cold running water and squeeze to bruise rings as you rinse them; drain. Toss with salad oil, lemon juice and dash of pepper. *Serve with any meat. Good with steak.*

Mrs. Ben Marek (Pat)

Pickled Green Beans

1 can (16 ounces) whole green beans	Dash of red pepper
½ cup Wesson oil	Dash salt
½ cup vinegar	2 or 3 cloves garlic, finely minced

Drain beans. Combine oil, vinegar, seasonings, minced garlic and pour over beans. Refrigerate at least 24 hours.

Mrs. James P. Newberry (Mary Jane)

Fresh Vegetable Marinade

4 stalks fresh broccoli	3 ribs celery, chopped
8 to 10 large fresh mushrooms, sliced	1 cup sugar
	2 teaspoons dry mustard
1 medium green pepper, chopped	1 teaspoon salt
	½ cup vinegar
1 medium onion, chopped	1½ cups vegetable oil
1 small cauliflower, broken into florets	2 tablespoons poppy seeds

Remove florets from broccoli and cut into bite size pieces. Reserve stalks for other use. Combine broccoli, mushrooms, pepper, onion, cauliflower and celery. Toss lightly.

DRESSING: Combine the sugar, mustard, salt, vinegar, vegetable oil and poppy seeds. Mix well and pour over vegetables. Chill at least 3 hours. Serves 10 to 12. *I use only half the dressing and reserve the rest in the refrigerator. It stores well for later use.*

Mrs. James E. Keeling (Betty)

FOR A DIFFERENT TASTE:

Add mustard to cheese sauce for vegetables.

Add parsley to lemon butter; spoon over asparagus just before serving.

To season glazed carrots, add mint or ginger.

Over cubed potatoes pour medium white sauce, sprinkle with crumbs and grated cheese. Bake until brown.

Main Dishes

MAIN DISHES

From cave cook to modern cook, meat has been the focal point of every meal. The first meats were probably eaten raw, after having been arduously hunted over rough terrain, and were highly prized. Today one has a vast array of meat choices as easily accessible as the local supermarket with innumerable ways of preparation.

Progression of modern technology, food tastes and nutrition knowledge has made us more creative. Pasta, cheese and eggs have become acceptable, and often desirable meat substitutes or alternatives. However, meat has remained through the centuries as a favored choice of foods.

Fish or fowl, beef, pork or lamb, wild game, casserole or meat alternative will be the center piece of a well planned meal. Wisely chosen, carefully prepared, and appealingly presented, this segment can be both a nutritious and delicious dining experience.

And so, from gourmet feast to "home town" cooking, you will find main dish recipes to fit every need, taste and occasion in this section of our *Hullabaloo in the Kitchen.*

Baked Chicken

2 fryers, cut up or 6 legs
  and 4 breasts
4 tablespoons butter, melted
1 can (10¾ ounces) cream
  of mushroom soup

½ pint whipping cream
1 cup grated Cheddar cheese
¼ cup sliced scallions
½ cup chopped mushrooms

Pour butter into baking dish. Add chicken and bake at 325° for 50 minutes, turning chicken after 30 minutes. Combine remaining ingredients. Pour over chicken. Bake for 25 to 30 minutes. Serve over rice. Serves 6 to 8. *My husband, an Aggie, makes this favorite family recipe.*

Mrs. Bill Kivyta (Barbara)

Barbecued Chicken

3 tablespoons catsup
2 tablespoons Worcestershire sauce
2 tablespoons vinegar
1 tablespoon lemon juice
2 tablespoons butter

3 tablespoons brown sugar
1 teaspoon salt
1 teaspoon paprika
1 teaspoon dry mustard
1 (2½-3 pounds) chicken, cut up

Combine all ingredients except chicken. Heat thoroughly. Place chicken in baking dish. Pour sauce over chicken and bake at 325° for 1 hour. Baste every 20 minutes.

Mrs. James P. Newberry (Mary Jane)

Chicken à la King

¼ cup chopped green pepper
1 can (2 ounces) sliced mushrooms, drained
¼ cup margarine, melted
¼ cup flour
1 teaspoon salt
⅛ teaspoon pepper

1 cup chicken broth
1 cup half-and-half
1 cup diced cooked chicken
¼ cup chopped pimientos
1 package frozen patty shells, baked

Sauté green pepper and mushrooms in margarine in a 10" skillet until green pepper is tender. Combine flour, salt and pepper and add to vegetables. Stir until well blended and cook 1 minute, stirring constantly. Gradually add chicken broth and half-and-half. Cook over medium heat, stirring constantly, until thickened and bubbly. Stir in chicken and pimientos. Cook until thoroughly heated. Divide filling evenly among patty shells. Serves 6. *May be served over rice or toast instead of patty shells.*

Mrs. Rex Corey (Robyn)

Chicken and Stuffing Scallop

1 package (8 ounces) Peppridge Farm herb seasoned stuffing mix	½ cup flour
	¼ teaspoon salt
	Dash pepper
4 cups cooked cubed chicken	4 cups chicken broth
½ cup margarine	6 eggs, slightly beaten

SAUCE:

1 can (10¾ ounces) cream of mushroom soup	¼ cup chopped pimiento
	1 cup sour cream
¼ cup milk	

Prepare stuffing by package directions for *dry* stuffing mix. Spread in 9x13 inch baking dish. Top with chicken. In large saucepan, melt margarine, blend in flour and seasonings. Add cooled broth, cook and stir until thickened. Stir small amount of hot mixture into eggs; return to hot mixture. Pour over chicken. Bake in 325° oven for 40 to 45 minutes, or until knife inserted in center comes out clean. Let stand 5 minutes before cutting into squares. Serve with sauce.

SAUCE: Combine sauce ingredients, heat and stir. Do not boil. Serves 12.

Mrs. Louis S. Rosen (Mary)

Chicken Breasts with Wine Sauce
Easy and Elegant

6 boned chicken breasts	1 jar (2½ ounces) sliced mushrooms
1 jar (2½ ounces) dried beef	
1 can (10¾ ounces) cream of mushroom soup	½ teaspoon parsley flakes
	½ teaspoon rosemary
	½ cup white wine or sherry

Lay dried beef on bottom of buttered shallow casserole dish. Place chicken on dried beef, tucking under edges to make neat servings. Pour soup over chicken and scatter mushrooms evenly over top. Cover and bake at 350° for 1½ hours. Remove cover, sprinkle with parsley flakes and rosemary; add wine. Bake uncovered for 30 minutes longer. Serves 6. *Wild rice is a nice accompaniment.*

Mrs. Kenneth E. Fry (Jeanne)

Chicken and Wild Rice Bake

1 package (6 ounces) Uncle Ben's long grain and wild rice
1 tablespoon margarine
⅓ cup chopped onion
1 clove garlic, chopped
4 cups cubed, cooked chicken
1 can (10¾ ounces) cream of celery soup
1 jar (4 ounces) chopped pimiento
1 can (8 ounces) sliced water chestnuts
2 cans (16 ounces each) sliced green beans, drained
2 cups mayonnaise
½ teaspoon salt
¼ teaspoon Worcestershire sauce
5 drops Tabasco sauce
½ cup Parmesan cheese
Paprika

Prepare rice according to package directions. Set aside. Sauté onion and garlic in margarine. Combine all ingredients, except cheese and paprika. Pour into 9x13 inch baking dish and 8 inch square pan. Top with cheese and paprika. Bake at 350° for 30 to 40 minutes. Serves 16 to 20.

Mrs. Louis Rosen (Mary)

Chicken Cacciatore

2 pounds chicken parts
2 tablespoons shortening
1 can (10¾ ounces) tomato soup, undiluted
¼ cup water
¼ cup dry red wine or 1 tablespoon vinegar
2 large cloves garlic
1 teaspoon oregano
¼ teaspoon salt
½ medium green pepper, cut in strips
¼ cup chopped onion

In skillet, brown chicken in shortening. Pour off fat, add remaining ingredients, cover and cook over low heat for 45 minutes. Uncover and cook until sauce thickens, about 5 minutes. Serves 4 to 6. *Serve with rice.*

Mrs. H. Smith (Alyne)

Chicken Chop Suey

1 can (16 ounces) bean sprouts	½ cup chicken broth
½ cup sliced onion	2 tablespoons cornstarch
2 tablespoons margarine	¼ teaspoon salt
1½ to 2 cups diced, cooked chicken	¼ cup water
1 cup sliced celery	2 tablespoons soy sauce
1 can (5 ounces) water chestnuts, drained and sliced	4 cups cooked rice or fried chow mein noodles

Drain bean sprouts, reserving liquid. Sauté onion in margarine until tender. Add chicken, celery, water chestnuts, broth and bean sprout liquid. Heat to boiling. Combine cornstarch, salt, water and soy sauce. Add to chicken mixture stirring constantly until thickened. Add bean sprouts and heat through. Serve over rice or noodles. Serves 4 to 6.

Variation: 1 chicken bouillon cube dissolved in ½ cup water for ½ cup chicken broth.

Mrs. James P. Licandro (Marie)

Chicken Mexicana

2½ to 3 pounds broiler-fryer, cut up, or 8 chicken breasts	1 can (4½ ounces) enchilada sauce
½ cup butter or margarine	1 cup shredded Cheddar cheese
1 teaspoon salt	½ cup chopped green onion
½ teaspoon paprika	1 can (2¼ ounces) pitted black olives, sliced
Dash pepper	
1 package (6 ounces) tortilla chips	

Wash chicken under cold water; dry with paper towels. Arrange in single layer skin side up, in a 10x14 inch pan. Melt butter and pour over chicken, then sprinkle with salt, paprika and pepper. Bake uncovered 60 minutes at 375°. Coarsely crumble tortilla chips and sprinkle over chicken. Cover with enchilada sauce and sprinkle evenly with cheese, onion and olives. Return to oven for 15 minutes or until cheese is melted. Serves 8.

Mrs. Bobby M. Greenwood (Judy)

FAMILY PICNICS OR "SPREADS"

Mrs. H. L. Peoples of Dallas organized the first Aggie Mothers' Club in 1922. Inspired by her love and concern for students' welfare, scrumptious "spreads" continue to be favorites that warm the hearts of our students. Aggies eagerly look forward to picnics, "tailgate parties" or cookouts held in beautiful settings around the Texas A&M University campus. Before games or on casual weekends, Aggie families and friends are served meals prepared with Aggie Moms' spirit.

The lawn of the President's home offers one of the many cherished sites for the legendary "spread." In its picturesque background is Kyle Field, home of the Fightin' Texas Aggie football team. Dallas Aggie Moms are proud to have been part of the heritage of this important tradition.

COLOR PHOTOGRAPHY:
Rick Cook, Designer
Michael Wilson, Photographer

TODAY'S PICNIC includes: Fried Chicken, Festive Potato Salad (p. 104), Corn and Bean Salad (p. 166), Deviled Eggs, Relish Tray, Texas A&M Mild Peppers, Cucumber Apple Rings, Cantaloupe, Watermelon, Peaches, Italian Bread Sticks (p. 195), and Peppermint Ice Cream (p. 39).

Chicken Parmesan

1½ cups Progresso Italian bread crumbs	1 teaspoon pepper
½ cup Parmesan cheese	2 sticks butter, melted
2 teaspoons salt	8 chicken breast halves, deboned

Combine bread crumbs, cheese and seasonings. Melt butter. Dip chicken in butter and roll in bread crumb mixture, coating heavily. Place in baking dish, skin side up. Bake 30 to 35 minutes at 350°. Serves 8. *Freezes well before or after baking.*

Mrs. J. D. Cointment (Kay)

Chicken Pecan

1 chicken, cut up	½ cup finely chopped pecans
1 cup Bisquick	½ cup evaporated milk
1 teaspoon salt	½ cup melted butter, or
1 teaspoon paprika	margarine
½ teaspoon poultry seasoning	

Skin chicken. Set aside. Combine dry ingredients. Dip chicken in milk and roll in dry mixture. Melt butter. Place chicken in baking dish. Pour butter over top. Bake at 400° for 40 to 50 minutes. Serves 4 to 6.

Mrs. John H. Vandeven (Norma)

Chicken-Rice Casserole

1 whole chicken	1 can (10¾ ounces) cream of mushroom soup
Water	
1 package (6 ounces) Uncle Ben's wild rice	1 can (10¾ ounces) cream of chicken soup
	1 medium onion, chopped

Cook chicken in water. Debone and cut into chunks. Cook rice according to package directions. Combine soups and onion. Combine all ingredients in large baking dish. Bake at 375° for 45 minutes. Serves 4 to 6. *Very good with green salad.*

Mrs. Sidney W. King (Georgia)

Chicken Spaghetti

4 to 6 chicken breasts
Water
1 package (12 ounces) spaghetti
1 cup half-and-half
2 cups chopped Velveeta cheese
Salt to taste
Pepper to taste
1 cup celery, chopped
1 medium onion, chopped

¼ cup chopped green pepper
1 can (4 ounces) chopped mushrooms
1 clove garlic, minced
1 tablespoon oil
1 can (16 ounces) tomato juice
1 can (6 ounces) tomato puree
1 jar (2 ounces) chopped pimientos

Boil chicken in water. Remove, reserving broth. Chop chicken and set aside. Cook spaghetti in broth until tender. Drain. Add half-and-half, cheese and seasonings. Set aside. Sauté celery, onion, green pepper, mushrooms and garlic in oil. Add vegetables and chicken to spaghetti. Add remaining ingredients. Place in 4 quart pan and heat well. Serves 12.

Mrs. Lewis Eidson (Mary)

Chicken Sukiyaki

3 to 3½ pound frying chicken, disjointed
3 tablespoons cooking oil
½ cup soy sauce
¼ cup sake (rice wine) or dry sherry
¼ cup sugar

1 can (8 ounces) bamboo shoots, drained
1 can (4 ounces) mushrooms, with liquid
2 bunches green onions with tops, cut in 1 inch pieces

Rinse chicken and drain on absorbent paper. Remove skin; cut meat from bone and cut meat into small pieces. Heat oil in heavy skillet; add chicken and cook until golden, turning frequently. Add remaining ingredients; cover skillet and cook over high heat until chicken is done, about 10 minutes. Serves 4 to 6. *Serve over hot rice.*

Mrs. S. Ward Hughes (Virginia)

Chicken Tetrazzini

2 (3 pounds each) chickens
Water
½ cup margarine or butter
1 medium onion, chopped
¾ tablespoon flour
2 cans (10¾ ounces each) cream of mushroom soup
½ cup milk
2 jars (2 ounces each) chopped pimientos
2 cans (3 ounces each) sliced mushrooms, undrained
1 can (8 ounces) water chestnuts, sliced or chopped

1 can (7¾ ounces) ripe olives, chopped
1 teaspoon lemon pepper, or more to taste
Garlic powder to taste
½ cup sweet white wine or more to taste
1 pound Velveeta cheese, sliced
1 package (12 ounces) green noodles
1 package (12 ounces) noodles

Cook chicken in water. Reserve broth. Bone and chop chicken. Set aside. Melt margarine in Dutch oven. Add onions and sauté. Add flour, stirring until smooth. Add soup, milk, pimientos, mushrooms, water chestnuts, olives, seasonings, wine, cheese and chicken. Cook noodles in reserved broth until tender. Drain. Add noodles to chicken mixture and toss gently. Serve at once or bake at 350° until bubbly. Serves 20. *Freezes beautifully. Blue Nun is a good white wine to use with this recipe.*

Mrs. Eugene Zachary (Nancy)

Chicken Viva

4 chicken breasts
1 dozen corn tortillas
1 can (10¾ ounces) cream of mushroom soup
1 can (10¾ ounces) cream of chicken soup
1 cup milk

1 medium onion, grated
1 can (7 ounces) green chili salsa
1 can (4 ounces) green chilies
1 pound Cheddar cheese, shredded

Wrap chicken in foil. Bake one hour at 350°. Bone and chop coarsely. Cut tortillas into one inch squares. Combine remaining ingredients with chicken and tortillas. Pour into an oiled 9x13 inch pan. Bake 1¼ hours at 300°. Serves 8 to 10. *Can be made in advance and frozen.*

Mrs. Sam E. Stock (Frances)

Company Chicken

6 chicken breasts, split in half	3 tablespoons lemon juice
Garlic salt	1 cup sour cream
Paprika	¼ cup sherry
¼ to ½ cup butter or margarine	¼ to ½ pound fresh mushrooms, sliced
	⅛ teaspoon red pepper

Sprinkle chicken with garlic salt and paprika while butter and lemon juice melt together in a 9x13 inch pan. Roll chicken in butter and juice and bake at 375° for about an hour, or until tender and lightly browned. While chicken is cooking, mix together sour cream, sherry, mushrooms and red pepper. Spoon sauce over chicken pieces and bake an additional 15 minutes. Serves 8 to 12. *A metal pan seems to bake chicken better. This is a super easy dish to prepare and is very tasty.*

Mrs. Bill Heaton (Gladys)

Curried Chicken

5 tablespoons margarine	1 teaspoon dried sweet bell pepper
2 medium onions, chopped	½ jar (2 ounces) pimiento
1 jalapeño pepper, diced	2 bouillon cubes
½ apple, diced	1½ cups boiling water
½ cup raisins	2 cups milk
6 tablespoons flour	Juice of 1 lemon
2 tablespoons curry powder	3 to 4 pounds chicken, cooked and cubed
1½ tablespoons sugar	Rice
1¼ teaspoons salt	
1 teaspoon ginger	

Melt margarine. Add and sauté onions, pepper, apple and raisins. Stir in flour and seasonings. Add bell pepper and pimiento. Dissolve bouillon cubes in water and add. Add milk and simmer until thickened. Just before serving add lemon juice and chicken. Serve over rice with 3 or 4 condiments. Serves 12.

CONDIMENTS:

Grated egg yolk	Crushed peanuts
Shredded coconut	Diced crisp bacon
Chopped green onions	
Chutney	

Mrs. Jes D. McIver (Marilyn)

Easy Chicken Curry

1   can (10¾ ounces) cream
   of chicken soup
1   can (10¾ ounces) cream
   of mushroom soup
¼   cup milk

2½ to 3 pound chicken,
   cooked, boned and
   chopped
Salt, pepper and curry
   powder to taste

Combine and heat soups and milk. Add chicken and seasonings. Serve over Chinese noodles or rice. Serves 4 to 6. *More milk may be added for thinner consistency. Delicious for company or family.*

Mrs. W. C. Marks (Belle)

Green Enchiladas

1   can (10¾ ounces) cream
   of mushroom soup
¼   cup water
1   can (4 ounces) green
   chilies, seeded
1   clove garlic, chopped
1   medium onion, chopped

1   can (14½ ounces) chicken
   broth
1   cup chopped cooked
   chicken
1   cup diced Monterey Jack
   cheese
6   corn tortillas
Sour cream

Purée soup, water, chilies, garlic and onion in blender. Pour into saucepan. Add broth and bring to boil. Cook, stirring constantly, until thickened. Remove from heat. Combine chicken and cheese. Divide equally on tortillas and roll. Place in buttered baking dish. Cover with sauce. Bake at 350° until cheese is melted, about 12 to 15 minutes. Top with sour cream to taste. Yields 6 enchiladas.

Mrs. G. Gross (Jean)

Use pepper, onion, garlic and cloves sparingly in foods for freezer as they tend to grow stronger when stored in freezer over a period of time.

Herbed Chicken Supreme

8   chicken breast halves,
    deboned
Salt, garlic salt, tarragon and
    pepper to taste (or Spice
    Islands Herb Pepper)

8   pats butter
1   pint sour cream
1   cup salad croutons,
    crushed

Flatten each chicken breast and sprinkle with seasonings. Place a butter
pat on each breast. Roll chicken around it. Place in buttered 9x12 inch
casserole. Spoon sour cream over chicken. Top with croutons. Bake at
275° for 2 hours. Serves 4 to 8. *Perfect for a buffet dinner.*

Mrs. Conrad Leissler (Bonnie)

Honeyed Hens with Figs

¾   cup soy sauce
⅓   cup honey
1   tablespoon grated fresh
    ginger
2   cloves garlic, mashed
1   cup butter, melted
4   Cornish game hens
Salt to taste
Pepper, freshly ground, to
    taste
Oil

2   cups bread crumbs
¼   cup butter, melted
Salt and pepper to taste
1½ teaspoons minced onion
1   cup chopped mixed fruit:
    pears, pineapple, prunes
    and oranges
¼   cup chopped pecans
Fresh figs
Fresh parsley

Combine and heat soy sauce, honey, ginger, garlic and butter. Set aside.
Season hens with salt and pepper. Rub with oil. Combine and mix well
remaining ingredients, except figs and parsley. Stuff hens. Roast at 400°
for 15 minutes. Remove and baste with sauce. Return to oven set at 350°.
Roast 1 hour longer or until tender, basting often with sauce. Garnish
with figs and parsley. Serves 4 to 8.

Mrs. Marie LaCombe

Imperial Chicken

2 cups sour cream
1 teaspoon Worcestershire
  sauce
½ teaspoon hot pepper sauce
1¼ teaspoons paprika
2 teaspoons salt
¼ cup chopped onion or 1
  clove garlic, pressed

5 chicken breasts, skinned
  and boned
2 cups fine bread crumbs
1 can (10¾ ounces) cream
  of chicken soup and/or
  2 cups chicken broth
1 can (4 ounces) mushrooms

Mix sour cream and seasonings. Pour over chicken, turning until well coated. Roll chicken in cream mixture. Tuck under the edges of chicken to form croquettes. Cover baking dish tightly with foil and refrigerate overnight. Wipe chicken with paper towel. Roll to coat completely in crumbs. Place in baking dish. Cook at 325° for 1 hour. Combine soup and/or broth. Baste chicken 2 or 3 times while cooking. Combine remaining soup and/or broth with mushrooms. Serve with chicken. Serves 8 to 10.

Mrs. L. C. Eubank (Agnes)

Italian Style Oven Fried Chicken

2½ to 3 pound chicken, cut in
  serving pieces
½ cup olive oil, or Wesson
  oil
1 cup bread crumbs

½ cup grated Parmesan
  cheese
¼ cup oregano
2 garlic cloves, pressed
1½ teaspoons salt
¼ teaspoon pepper

Wash and dry chicken. Roll in oil. Combine remaining ingredients. Coat chicken in crumb mixture and arrange in shallow pan without crowding. Pour remaining oil into pan for extra moisture, if desired. Cover with foil. Bake at 350° for 45 minutes. Uncover and bake 30 minutes. Serves 4.

Mrs. Bruce Lowry (Elena)

Mother's Chicken and Rice

4 cups cooked rice
4 cans (5 ounces each) chicken
2 cans (10¾ ounces each) cream of mushroom, or cream of chicken soup
1 can (17 ounces) English peas, drained
1 jar (2 ounces) chopped pimientos, drained
1 onion, chopped
1 to 2 pounds longhorn Cheddar cheese, sliced or grated

Combine all ingredients except cheese. Place layer of rice mixture in 9x13 inch casserole. Cover with layer of cheese. Continue to layer rice mixture and cheese, ending with cheese. Bake at 400° for 15 to 20 minutes. Serves 12. *Freezes well.*

Mrs. J. Hal Brown (Eva Gay)

Tangy Chicken Tokay

2 cups Tokay grapes
3 small frying chickens, cut into halves
½ cup brown sugar, packed
½ cup cider vinegar
¼ cup chili sauce
¼ cup margarine
1 teaspoon Worcestershire sauce
1 teaspoon soy sauce
½ cup sliced sweet red peppers
1 cup onion rings

Halve and seed grapes. Place chicken halves in large shallow baking dish. Combine sugar, vinegar, chili sauce, margarine, Worcestershire and soy sauce in saucepan; bring to boil and boil rapidly for 5 minutes. Add grapes, peppers and onion rings. Boil 5 minutes longer. Spoon over chicken. Bake at 375° for one hour, basting chicken with grape sauce frequently. Spoon sauce over chicken to serve. Serves 6.

Mrs. Jes D. McIver (Marilyn)

Walnut Chicken

1 cup bamboo shoots, drained	2½ pounds chicken breasts, skinned, boned and cubed
1½ cups diced celery	1 teaspoon salt
1½ cups diced onion	1 tablespoon soy sauce
8 ounces water chestnuts, sliced	½ cup chicken bouillon
5 tablespoons oil	3 tablespoons cooking sherry
2 cups English walnuts, halved	1 tablespoon cornstarch
	Rice

Sauté bamboo shoots, celery, onion and water chestnuts in oil. Remove from pan. Add walnuts and brown. Remove from pan and drain, reserving oil in pan. Sprinkle chicken with salt and soy sauce. Sauté in oil until tender. Add bouillon and heat thoroughly. Combine vegetables and chicken in large pan. Add sherry and cornstarch. Heat thoroughly. Add walnuts. Serve over rice. Serves 8 to 10. *To remove bitter flavor from walnuts, place in pan, cover with cold water. Bring to boil and boil for 3 minutes. Drain immediately.*

Mrs. Alice Wagnon

Smothered Quail

6 quail, dressed	Salt and pepper to taste
6 tablespoons butter	1 can (3 ounces) mushrooms, chopped
3 tablespoons flour	1 box (6 ounces) Uncle Ben's Long Grain Wild Rice
2 cups chicken broth	
½ cup sherry	

Brown quail in butter. Remove to baking dish. Add flour to butter. Stir well. Slowly add broth, sherry and seasonings. Blend thoroughly. Add mushrooms. Pour over quail. Cover and bake at 350° for 1 hour. Serve over rice prepared according to package directions. Serves 6.

Mrs. Conrad Leissler (Bonnie)

Crabmeat Au Gratin

1 package (6 ounces) Wakefield snow crabmeat	¼ cup grated American cheese
2 tablespoons margarine or butter	¼ cup grated Parmesan cheese
1 tablespoon cornstarch	Salt to taste
1 cup cream or milk	Paprika to taste
1 egg yolk	1 cup buttered crumbs

Combine all ingredients except crumbs. Place in small buttered baking container. Top with crumbs. Bake at 350° for 30 minutes. Serves 4.

Mrs. G. Gross (Jean)

Seafood Gumbo

½ tablespoon shortening, melted	Thyme to taste
1 tablespoon flour	1 teaspoon salt
½ cup diced celery	¼ teaspoon pepper
1 onion, chopped	Red pepper to taste
1 clove garlic, minced	Parsley to taste
1 green pepper, diced	½ pound ham, chopped
1½ ounces tomato paste	1 pound shrimp, peeled
1 cup water	½ pound blue crab, shelled
1 quart chicken broth	½ teaspoon filé
1 small bay leaf	Rice

Combine shortening, flour, celery, onion, garlic and pepper. Sauté until clear. Add remaining ingredients, except filé. Simmer 30 minutes. Just before serving, add filé. Serve over steamed rice. *This recipe has been in our family for 35 years.*

Mrs. Purvis J. Thrash (Betty Jo)

Oysters Casino

3 slices bacon, chopped	6 drops Worcestershire sauce
1 small onion, chopped	4 drops Tabasco sauce
1 small celery rib, chopped	¼ teaspoon seafood
1 teaspoon lemon juice	seasoning
1 teaspoon salt	1 pint "standard" oysters,
⅛ teaspoon pepper	shucked and drained

Fry bacon until partially cooked. Add onion and celery and cook until tender. Add lemon juice and seasonings. Arrange oysters in a single layer in foil lined shallow baking pan. Spread mixture over oysters. Bake at 400° until the edges of oysters curl, about 9 to 11 minutes. Yields about 3 dozen appetizers; or serve on toast with the liquid as an entree. Serves 4.

Dr. Sam Gillespie
Assistant Dean, College of Business

This is a nice appetizer. The recipe is written for shucked oysters but can be used with half-shell oysters, if the shells are set in a bed of rock salt. Oysters may also be placed in porcelain scallop shells after cooking in baking dish.

Variation: Scallops may be used instead of oysters. Remember not to overcook scallops as they cook very quickly.

Shrimp Luncheon Dish
Can be made only on an electric range

3 tablespoons margarine	1 clove garlic, minced
¼ green pepper, chopped	1 bay leaf
1 jar (2 ounces) pimientos	1 cup raw rice
½ cup canned mushrooms	2 cups water
1 teaspoon salt	1½ cups shrimp, raw
1 onion, chopped	

Melt margarine in skillet and add other ingredients. Cover skillet while steaming freely. Turn electric switch off and cook 45 minutes on stored heat. Do not remove lid during this time.

Mrs. Jes D. McIver (Marilyn)

Shrimp Mousse

1 can (10¾ ounces) tomato soup
1 package (8 ounces) cream cheese
1½ envelopes (1½ tablespoons) unflavored gelatin
¼ cup cold water
1 cup mayonnaise
2 cans (4½ ounces each) shrimp
1 tablespoon Worcestershire sauce
3 ribs celery
6 scallions or 1 medium onion
Salt and pepper to taste

Warm soup and cheese in saucepan over low heat until cheese melts. Soften gelatin in cold water; add to soup and stir over heat until gelatin dissolves. Put cheese mixture and remaining ingredients in blender and blend until smooth. Pour into 1 quart mold and refrigerate overnight. Unmold and garnish as desired. *Mousse may be made several days before serving. Garnish with grated egg yolk, parsley sprigs and pimiento strips. Serve as a spread on crackers or bread.*

Mrs. J. Peter Jost (Jo Ann)

Shrimp Ratatouille

1 pound raw shrimp, peeled and deveined
¼ cup olive oil
2 small zucchini, unpared and thinly sliced
1 small eggplant, peeled, cut into 1 inch cubes
1 medium onion, thinly sliced
1 medium green pepper, seeded and cut into 1 inch pieces
1 cup sliced fresh mushrooms
1 can (16 ounces) tomato wedges
1 teaspoon crushed basil
1½ teaspoons garlic salt
1 teaspoon dried parsley
¼ teaspoon pepper

Cut shrimp in half lengthwise. In large pan, sauté zucchini, eggplant, onion, green peppers and mushrooms in oil for 10 minutes or until crisp tender. Add shrimp and cook, stirring frequently for approximately 2 minutes. Add tomatoes, basil, garlic salt, parsley and pepper. Cover and simmer about 5 minutes. Serves 6. *Serve with rice or noodles.*

Mrs. James P. Licandro (Marie)

Shrimp Rice Quiche
A new twist

2 eggs	½ cup sliced green onion
3 cups cooked rice	¼ cup chopped pimiento
1 cup grated Swiss cheese	1 can (4 ounces) sliced
1½ cups half-and-half	mushrooms, drained
4 eggs	1 teaspoon salt
8 ounces shrimp, cooked	¼ teaspoon pepper
1 cup grated Swiss cheese	Dash Tabasco sauce

Beat 2 eggs and combine with rice and 1 cup of cheese. Press firmly over bottom and sides of greased 9x13 inch baking dish. Heat half-and-half, do not boil. Beat 4 eggs and gradually add half-and-half to eggs. Stir in remaining ingredients and pour into rice shell. Bake at 350°for 30 to 35 minutes, or until a knife inserted near the center comes out clean. Cool 5 minutes. Cut into squares. Serves 10 to 12.

Mrs. Frank S. Covaro (Genie)

Salmon and Egg Pie

1 unbaked (9 inch) pie shell	2 teaspoons chopped parsley
3 hard cooked eggs, sliced	¼ teaspoon basil
1 can (16 ounces) salmon	¼ cup butter, melted
2 eggs, beaten	

SAUCE:

⅓ cucumber	2 teaspoons parsley
1 slice onion	½ cup sour cream or plain
¼ cup mayonnaise	yogurt
2 teaspoons vinegar	Salt and pepper to taste

Chill eggs. Line bottom of pie shell with egg slices. Combine salmon, eggs and seasonings. Spread over eggs. Pour butter over top. Bake at 425° for 20 to 25 minutes.

SAUCE: Grate cucumber and onion. Press out juices. Combine juices with remaining ingredients. Pour over pie, or serve as a side dish.

Mrs. John H. Vandeven (Norma)

Filet of Sole Bonne-Femme

1 cup white wine	1 pinch white pepper
3 shallots, chopped	2 pounds filet of sole
1 can (4 ounces) mushrooms	½ cup heavy cream
1 teaspoon finely chopped parsley	Juice of ½ lemon
2 pinches salt	2 egg yolks

Preheat oven to 375°. Combine wine, shallots, mushrooms, parsley and seasonings in pan. Add sole. Cook for 10 minutes. Remove sole. Add cream to pan. Cook until sauce thickens. Stir in lemon juice and egg yolks. Place sole on oven proof platter. Pour sauce over and broil for ½ minute. Serve immediately. Serves 4.

Mrs. Marie LaCombe

Stewed Fish
Less than 225 calories per serving.

2 pounds frozen fish fillets, partially thawed	¼ cup dry white wine
2 tablespoons olive oil	1 teaspoon dried basil
1 clove garlic, minced	1 can (28 ounces) tomatoes, coarsely chopped
1 small onion, diced	2 tablespoons minced parsley, optional
1 teaspoon salt	
½ teaspoon lemon flavored pepper	

If desired, chicken stock may be substituted for white wine. Cut block of partially frozen fish into one inch cubes. Heat olive oil in large skillet and sauté garlic and onion while covered until tender. Season fish with salt and pepper and add to skillet. Add wine, basil and tomatoes. Simmer about 15 to 20 minutes until fish is just cooked through. Sprinkle with parsley. Serves 6. *Serve over hot fluffy rice.*

Mrs. John D. Waring (Freda)

Sea and Garden Casserole

SAUCE:

6 tablespoons butter or margarine

4 tablespoons Wondra flour

1¼ cups milk

¾ cup asparagus liquid, drained from cans of asparagus

1 can (10¾ ounces) Campbell's cream of mushroom soup

5 tablespoons lime juice

1 teaspoon marjoram

TUNA MIXTURE:

1 can (12½ ounces) Chicken of the Sea tuna

1 can (6½ ounces) Chicken of the Sea tuna

1 can (5 ounces) sliced water chestnuts

1 jar (2 ounces) sliced pimiento

1 can (14½ ounces) cut asparagus

1 can (10½ ounces) cut asparagus

4 hard cooked eggs, cubed

Rice, noodles or mashed potatoes

SAUCE: Melt margarine in 4 to 6 quart double boiler on medium heat. Gradually add flour, mixing thoroughly. Add milk and asparagus liquid. Cook until thickened. Add soup and mix well. Gradually blend in lime juice and marjoram. Sauce may be prepared ahead and frozen. Carefully add tuna, water chestnuts, pimiento, asparagus and eggs. Serve over rice, noodles or potatoes. Serves 6 to 8. *Sauce may be prepared ahead and frozen.*

Variation: For quick cooking substitute cream of asparagus soup and ½ cup milk for butter, flour, milk and asparagus liquid. Leftovers may be reheated and served on toast, English muffins or omelettes.

Mrs. John Otto (Sue)

Tuna Casserole

6 ounces medium noodles
2 cans (6½ ounces each)
tuna, drained
½ cup mayonnaise
1 cup sliced celery
½ cup chopped onion
¼ cup chopped green pepper

¼ cup chopped pimiento
½ teaspoon salt
2 cans (10¾ ounces each)
cream of celery soup
½ cup milk
1 cup grated Velveeta cheese

Cook noodles according to package directions and drain. Combine noodles with tuna, mayonnaise, vegetables and salt. Pour into 2 quart container. Combine and heat soup, milk and cheese in a double boiler. Pour over tuna mixture. Bake for 20 minutes at 425°. Serves 10 to 12.

Mrs. James P. Newberry (Mary Jane)

Escalope de Veau Normande (Veal Scallops)

2 pounds veal, loin or
bottom round, ¼ inch
thick
1 tablespoon oil
3 tablespoons butter, melted
½ cup flour
Salt and pepper to taste

2 large apples, peeled, cored
and cut into eighths
1 ounce Calvados (apple
brandy)
1 pint plus 2 tablespoons
heavy cream

Cut veal into 4 pieces. Place between wax paper and pound until ⅛ inch thick. Roll in oil and 1 tablespoon butter. Sauté lightly each side for approximately 2 minutes. Dip in flour and seasonings to coat. Place in baking dish and set aside. Sauté apples in remaining butter. Pour brandy and cream over apples. Simmer until thickened. Pour over veal. Glaze under broiler for ½ minute. Serves 4.

Mrs. Marie LaCombe

B-B-Q Beef Brisket

1 beef brisket well trimmed
(5-6 pounds)

RUB:

⅓ cup salt
⅓ cup chili powder
2½ tablespoons monosodium
glutamate

1½ tablespoons pepper
1 tablespoon garlic powder

MOP SAUCE:

2 tablespoons soy sauce
¼ cup wine vinegar

1 clove garlic, crushed
½ cup vegetable oil

Heat oven to 250°. Combine salt, chili powder, monosodium glutamate, pepper and garlic powder and mix well. Place brisket in shallow roasting pan and coat well on all sides with dry rub. Bake 5 hours, brushing well with mop sauce each hour. Remove from pan, slice and serve with your favorite barbecue sauce. Serves 10 to 12. *This rub may be used on turkey, ribs or chicken also. Store rub in refrigerator.*

Mrs. William O. Wood, Jr. (Joan)

Beef Tips
Great over noodles or rice

2 pounds lean beef, cubed
1 envelope dry onion soup
  mix
1 can (10¾ ounces) cream
  of mushroom soup

1 can (6 ounces)
  mushrooms, drained
½ to ⅔ cup dry red wine,
  optional

Preheat oven to 300°. Place meat in baking dish, add onion soup mix, mushroom soup, mushrooms and wine. Cover and bake for 3 to 3½ hours. Serves 6. *This may be made in a crock pot allowing 5 to 6 hours to cook.*

Mrs. Robert H. Stauch (Janet)

Beef Barbecue

4 to 6 pounds beef brisket	1 bay leaf
Water	6 cloves
1 onion, thickly sliced	1 clove garlic

SAUCE:

3 cups catsup	1 tablespoon dry mustard
¼ cup Worcestershire sauce	¼ cup brown sugar

Score meat on fat side. Place in large pot. Cover with water and add onion, bay leaf, cloves and garlic. Cover and simmer 3½ to 4 hours. Cool meat in liquid. Remove fat and refrigerate meat overnight. Slice thinly cross-grain and reshape. Place in flat baking dish.

SAUCE: Combine all ingredients. Heat and stir well to blend. Pour over brisket and heat for 30 minutes at 350°.

Mrs. J. D. Cointment (Kay)

Beef Roll Ups

2 pounds round steak	2 bouillon cubes
8 small carrots or 4 medium carrots, cut in half	1 cup hot water
	½ cup chili sauce
2 large dill pickles quartered, optional	2 teaspoons Worcestershire sauce
⅓ cup flour	Noodles
Salt and pepper to taste	Butter
2 tablespoons oil	

Cut steak into 8 pieces. Pound until thin. Roll each meat piece around a carrot cut the same length as meat. Pickle may be added. Secure with toothpicks. Combine flour and seasonings and coat meat. Brown in oil. Drain. Combine remaining ingredients and pour over meat. Cover and cook over low heat for 1½ hours. Serve with buttered noodles. Serves 4 to 8.

Mrs. Kenneth Fry (Jeanne)

Serve chopped roast with gravy over toasted bread.

Corned Beef Casserole

1 package (10 ounces) shell or elbow macaroni
1 can (12 ounces) corned beef
1 medium onion, chopped
½ pound Velveeta cheese, grated
1 can (10¾ ounces) cream of mushroom soup

Garlic salt
Pepper
1 can (5.33 ounces) evaporated milk
5 slices bread, cut in cubes
½ cup butter or margarine, melted

Cook macaroni according to package directions and drain. Mix corned beef, onion, cheese, mushroom soup and evaporated milk together. Season to taste with garlic salt and pepper. Add macaroni and mix well. Place in greased casserole. Mix bread cubes with melted butter and put on top of casserole. Bake at 375° to 400° for 20 minutes or until bubbly. Serves 8.

Mrs. Bill Wilkinson (Laura)

Marinated Brisket
The aroma while cooking is terrific

3 to 5 pound well trimmed brisket
4 ounces liquid smoke
4 ounces Worcestershire sauce
2 ounces soy sauce

⅓ bottle Pickapeppa Sauce
2 tablespoons Dijon mustard
3 tablespoons lemon juice
2 shakes Tabasco sauce
Salt and pepper, if desired

Place brisket in oven proof dish with cover. Mix together all other ingredients and pour over brisket. Cover and place in refrigerator for at least 2 days, turning brisket over each day. The flavor will be even better if it is marinated for 4 days. Place covered dish in oven and bake at 200° to 225°. Bake for 6 to 7 hours. Uncover for the last 30 minutes. *Delicious served on hamburger buns, pita bread, or as a main course with green salad.*

Mrs. Frances Laningham

Beef Rouladen

2 pounds round steak, ½ inch thick
Salt and pepper to taste
3 to 4 slices uncooked bacon
12 to 16 teaspoons chopped onion
½ pound lean ground beef
¼ to ½ pound sausage
¼ cup margarine
2½ cups water
4 to 5 tablespoons flour
Noodles

Remove fat from steak. Cut into 6 to 8 serving pieces. Pound until thin. Season with salt and pepper. On each piece of steak place ½ slice bacon and 2 teaspoons onion. Combine ground beef and sausage. Roll like a hot dog and place on steak pieces. Roll up and secure with toothpicks or twine. Brown *slowly* in margarine. Add 1½ cups water and simmer until tender, about 1½ to 2 hours. It may be necessary to add more water as it cooks. Remove rolls. Make a paste of flour and remaining 1 cup water. Add to pan and stir until smooth. Replace rolls and continue cooking 15 to 30 minutes. Serve over noodles. Serves 4 to 6.

Mrs. K. R. Withrow (Sharon)

Rouladen

4 slices lean beef, 4 to 5 inches wide, 7 to 8 inches long, ¼ inch thick
Mustard
Salt and pepper to taste
4 strips bacon
Bacon fat
1 large onion, sliced
2 medium sour pickles, sliced
1 to 2 teaspoons cornstarch
Water

Pound meat. Spread each slice with mustard, seasonings, bacon, 2 to 3 slices of onion, three pickle slices and roll. Fasten with toothpicks or metal lacing needles. Brown on all sides in bacon fat. Add water not to cover and simmer 1 hour. Add more water as needed. Remove meat from water. Remove toothpicks. Mix cornstarch with ¼ cup water. Strain. Add to water in which meat was simmered. Pour over meat. Serves 4. *Delicious served with boiled potatoes and salad or egg noodles and red cabbage.*

Mrs. Hubert Blessing (Irene)

Salisbury Steak Deluxe

1 can (10¾ ounces) cream of mushroom soup	1 egg, slightly beaten
1 tablespoon prepared mustard	¼ cup dry bread crumbs
2 teaspoons Worcestershire sauce	¼ cup finely chopped onion
	Salt to taste
1 teaspoon prepared horseradish, optional	Dash pepper
	½ cup water
1½ pounds ground beef	2 tablespoons chopped parsley

Combine soup, mustard, Worcestershire sauce and horseradish. Blend well. Combine beef, egg, bread crumbs, onion, salt, pepper and ¼ cup of soup mixture. Shape into 6 patties and brown in skillet. Drain drippings from pan and discard. Combine remaining soup mixture, water and parsley and pour over patties. Cook over low heat 20 minutes, stirring occasionally. Serves 6.

Mrs. William L. Humphries (Gail)

Smothered Steak

1 pound round steak	¼ cup Crisco
Salt	1 cup hot water
Pepper	¼ to ½ cup diced onions, as desired
Flour	

Trim fat from meat. Pound on both sides to tenderize and flatten slightly. Cut into serving pieces. Salt and pepper both sides, and dredge in flour. Brown on both sides in hot Crisco. Drain off about ½ of the Crisco. Add onions and hot water to cover the meat. Cover tightly and simmer until gravy is thick and meat is tender. Serves 4 to 5.

This is my mother's recipe. She served it to our family as we were growing up. At the time, we thought that this was the only way that steak was cooked. It's really tasty. Liver can be prepared in almost the same way and is very good.

Mrs. Lee Radford (Betty)

Vickie's Beef Stroganoff

2½ to 3 pounds beef
   tenderloin, or sirloin
Salt and pepper to taste
½ cup butter
4 to 6 green onions, white
   part only, chopped
5 tablespoons flour
1 beef bouillon cube

1 cup hot water
1 can (10½ ounces) beef
   consommé
1 teaspoon Dijon mustard
1 can (6 ounces)
   mushrooms, undrained
⅓ cup Sauterne wine
⅓ cup sour cream

Remove fat from beef. Cut across grain into two inch strips. Season. Heat butter in Dutch oven and evenly brown meat. Remove meat. Sauté onions. Remove onions. Combine flour with drippings and stir until smooth. Add meat and onions. Dissolve bouillon in water. Add to meat mixture with consommé. Stir until smooth. Add mustard and cook slowly for one hour. Add remaining ingredients. Serve over rice or noodles. Serves 6 to 8.

Mrs. Bill Hall (Janey)

Apple Ring Beef Patties
An inexpensive but festive dish!

2 pounds ground beef
2 cups cooked rice
2 eggs, slightly beaten
2 teaspoons garlic salt
½ small onion, chopped
1 small green pepper,
   chopped

1 jar (15 ounces) spiced
   apple rings
½ cup Karo syrup
2 tablespoons lemon juice
1 tablespoon cornstarch
1 tablespoon water

Mix meat, rice, eggs, salt, onion and green pepper together and shape into ten thick patties. Place in a shallow baking pan. Drain apple rings, saving juice, and press one apple ring into each patty. Bake uncoverd at 350° for 35 minutes. While patties bake, mix reserved juice, Karo syrup, lemon juice and cornstarch which has been mixed with water. Cook and stir until thickened. Spoon over patties and bake 5 minutes longer. Serves 10.

Mrs. Bill Heaton (Gladys)

Ground Round Cakes
Quick, easy, low cal

1   pound ground round steak   Salt and pepper to taste
¼ to ½ cup milk

Gradually add milk to ground meat, mixing with fork until meat holds together. Form into 6 to 8 cakes. Brown well in hot frying pan. After browning add salt and pepper to taste. Remove cakes from pan. Add 1 cup hot water to pan to make natural gravy. Season gravy and serve. Serves 3 to 4. *Use approximately 1 pound for 3 servings.*

Mrs. John E. Keiser (Sandra)

Favorite Frijoles

½ pound ground beef
1 large onion, chopped
1 pound pinto beans
2 quarts water

3 beef bouillon cubes
1 large bay leaf
1 package (1.25 ounces) Lawry's taco seasoning

Sauté beef and onion. Add beans, water and bouillon cubes. Bring to boil. Boil uncovered 2 minutes. Turn off heat. Cover. Let stand 1 hour. Add remaining ingredients. Simmer 3 to 4 hours. Add more water if necessary. *Delicious with warm buttered flour tortillas.*

Mrs. Purvis J. Thrash (Betty Jo)

Jalapeño Corn Bread Casserole

1½ pounds ground beef
1 cup cornmeal
¾ teaspoon salt
½ cup bacon drippings
1 can (17 ounces) cream style corn

2 eggs
4 to 6 jalapeño peppers, chopped
1 medium onion, chopped
1 cup grated Cheddar cheese

Cook ground beef in hot skillet and drain well; set aside. Mix cornmeal, salt, bacon drippings, corn and eggs together. Put half of corn bread mixture in greased baking dish. Layer meat, onion, peppers and cheese. Cover with remaining corn bread mixture. Bake at 350° for 45 to 50 minutes. Serves 6.

Mrs. Bruce Lowry (Elena)

Crepe Manicotti

SHELLS (Crepes)

4   eggs
1   cup low fat milk or water
1   cup flour

½ teaspoon salt, optional
Pam

Beat eggs with milk or water. Gradually add flour and beat until smooth. Add salt if desired. Batter will be thin. Preheat 6 to 8 inch crepe pan to 275°. Spray pan with Pam. Spoon batter into pan until lightly covered. When firm, turn and cook other side.

FILLINGS:

Meat and Cheese Variety:

1   pound ground round
1¾ pounds Ricotta cheese, grated or cottage cheese
2   tablespoons grated Romano cheese

1   tablespoon chopped fresh parsley
1   egg
1   teaspoon Italian seasoning
Pepper to taste

Brown meat. Drain and cool. Add remaining ingredients. Mix well.

Spinach and Cheese Variety:

1   can (8 ounces) spinach, well drained
2   pounds Ricotta cheese, grated or cottage cheese
¼ to ½ pound Mozzarella cheese, grated

2   tablespoons grated Romano cheese
1   tablespoon chopped fresh parsley
1   egg
1   teaspoon Italian seasoning
Pepper to taste

Combine all ingredients. Mix well.

Spray 8½x11 inch baking dish with Pam. Pour in layer of Meaty Spaghetti Sauce (Recipe follows). As each crepe is made, place approximately 3 tablespoons of desired filling across center diameter line of crepe. Fold each side across center line. Place crepe, seam side down, on sauce in pan. Use only 5 crepes to a pan, as crepes will expand as baked. Spoon more sauce on top. Cover with foil. Bake at 350° for 30 minutes. Sprinkle with Romano cheese and additional sauce as desired.

Meaty Spaghetti Sauce with Italian Sausages

Use 1 quart or more for Crepe Manicotti:

16.5	ounces tomato sauce	2	teaspoons Lawry's
4	cups tomato juice		seasoned pepper
24	ounces tomato paste	4	tablespoons whole oregano
32	ounces stewed tomatoes		leaves
3½	pounds lean ground round, uncooked	4	tablespoons basil
		2	tablespoons tarragon
2	medium onions, chopped	1	tablespoon rosemary
4	tablespoons olive oil	1	cup chopped fresh parsley
4	tablespoons instant beef bouillon	16	mild Italian sausages each 8 inches long
4	tablespoons garlic powder	2	cups red wine
		2	cups Parmesan cheese

Pour tomato ingredients into very large pot. Add ground round and seasonings. Do *not* add salt. Bring to near boil. Lower heat and simmer 3 hours, stirring every 20 minutes. Pierce each sausage 10 times. Boil for 30 minutes in unsalted water. Drain and rinse. When sauce has cooked 3 hours, add sausage and wine. Cook 1 hour or more until sauce is thick. Add Parmesan to mixture as it cools, stirring thoroughly. Yields 10 quarts. *May be frozen.*

Mrs. Diann Contestabile

Stuffed Meat Loaf

2	pounds ground beef	1	medium onion, diced
½	cup catsup	1	cup diced celery
1	can (17 ounces) whole kernel corn, drained		Salt and pepper to taste

Press or roll beef on waxed paper to ½ to ¾ inches thick. Combine catsup and vegetables. Spread evenly over meat. Season. Roll meat into loaf, jelly roll style. Place loaf on heavy aluminum foil and seal. Bake at 350° for 1 hour. Serves 6. *Super for camping. Bake on slow to medium coals, turning frequently, for 1 hour.*

Mrs. H. Peyton Smith (Alyne)

Season meatballs with mustard or garlic powder.

Italian Sauce and Spaghetti
A favorite for many years

2 tablespoons salad or olive oil
1 onion, chopped
1 clove garlic, minced
1 can (16 ounces) whole tomatoes, chopped
1 can (12 ounces) tomato paste
1 can (8 ounces) tomato sauce
12 ounces water
Salt and pepper to taste
1 teaspoon dry Italian seasoning
1 teaspoon ground oregano
1 bay leaf
1 teaspoon sugar
2 pounds ground hamburger meat
½ cup wine, white or red
1½ pounds thin spaghetti
Parmesan cheese

Sauté onion and garlic in oil until clear, but not brown. Add tomatoes, tomato paste, tomato sauce, water and all dry seasonings. Simmer for one to three hours, stirring occasionally. Sauté hamburger meat, drain off fat and add meat to sauce. Add wine and simmer ½ hour longer. Cook spaghetti following package directions. Serve sauce over spaghetti and sprinkle with Parmesan cheese. Serves 8. *Freezes well.*

Mrs. John Meneghetti (Marty)

Swedish Meatballs

2 tablespoons shortening
¾ cup finely chopped onions
½ cup dry bread crumbs
½ cup milk
1 pound ground beef
½ pound ground pork
1 egg, slightly beaten
1 tablespoon sugar
½ teaspoon salt
¼ teaspoon ginger
¼ teaspoon nutmeg
¼ teaspoon allspice
2 tablespoons flour
1 cup milk
1 cup water

Melt shortening in skillet and cook onions until light golden brown. Soak bread crumbs in ½ cup milk, add drained onions, ground beef, ground pork, egg, sugar, salt and spices. Mix well, form into small balls and brown in skillet. Remove from skillet and discard all but 2 tablespoons of fat. Add flour to remaining fat in skillet and brown well. Add milk and water to browned flour and cook over low heat, stirring constantly until thickened. Place meatballs in gravy and cover. Cook 15 minutes on low heat. Serves 6 to 8.

Mrs. George Kardell (Roe)

Manicotti Alla Romana

12 manicotti shells

FILLING:
¼ cup butter
¼ cup chopped onion
1 clove garlic, crushed
1 pound ground beef

1 package (10 ounces) frozen chopped spinach, thawed and well drained
½ cup cottage cheese
2 eggs, slightly beaten
1 teaspoon salt

SAUCE:
¼ cup butter
1½ teaspoons seasoned chicken stock base
¼ cup flour
1½ cups milk
¼ cup chopped parsley

1 jar (15½ ounces) spaghetti sauce with mushrooms
2 teaspoons crushed basil leaves
Parmesan cheese

Cook manicotti according to package directions; set aside.

FILLING: In skillet melt butter; add onion and garlic and cook until onion is transparent. Add meat and brown. Remove from heat. Stir in spinach, cottage cheese, eggs and salt. Fill each manicotti shell with about ¼ cup filling; place in 3 quart buttered baking dish.

SAUCE: In saucepan melt butter; blend in flour and chicken stock base. Remove from heat. Stir in milk. Heat to boiling, stirring constantly. Boil and stir 1 minute. Stir in parsley. Pour over manicotti.

Combine spaghetti sauce and basil leaves. Pour over sauce. Sprinkle with Parmesan cheese. Bake in preheated 350° oven for 30 minutes. Serves 6. *Can be assembled ahead of time, covered and refrigerated. Increase baking time slightly.*

Mrs. M. D. Davidson (Mickey)

Slice meat loaf and spread with catsup. Broil slowly 5 minutes; top with grated cheese and broil 3 minutes.

Julee's Meat Loaf

2 pounds ground beef
Dash ground cumin
Dash garlic salt
Dash pepper
½ teaspoon chili powder or
  more to taste
1 egg
1 can (8 ounces) tomato
  sauce

1 can (5.33 ounces)
  evaporated milk
10 crackers, crumbled
1 medium onion, chopped
4 ounces Velveeta cheese,
  cubed
1 envelope onion mushroom
  soup mix

Combine all ingredients; mix until well blended and place in baking dish. Bake in 350° oven for 55 minutes. Remove from oven, add topping and return to oven for 5 minutes.

TOPPING:
¼ cup catsup
¼ teaspoon nutmeg

Dash dry mustard
3 tablespoons brown sugar

Mix together and spread evenly over top of meat loaf. Serves 6 to 8.

Mrs. Glinn H. White (Bettyeann)

Monday Meat Loaf

1½ pounds lean ground beef
1 cup bread crumbs
1 medium onion, diced
1 egg, slightly beaten

1 teaspoon salt
1 teaspoon dried parsley
½ teaspoon pepper
4 ounces tomato sauce

Lightly mix the above ingredients. Shape into 2 loaves and place in 1½ quart baking dish. Cover with sauce.

SAUCE:
4 ounces tomato sauce
1 tablespoon cider vinegar
1 tablespoon prepared
  mustard

4½ tablespoons brown sugar
½ cup water

Mix ingredients well and pour over prepared meat loaves. Bake in 350° oven for 1½ hours. Do not cover, but baste occasionally. Serves 6.

Mrs. Charles D. Price, Jr. (Joyce)

Venezuelan Meat Loaf

1 egg, beaten
⅓ cup milk
1 teaspoon salt
1 tablespoon soy sauce
⅛ teaspoon hot pepper
   sauce, optional

1½ cups soft bread crumbs
2 pounds lean ground beef
1 package (10 ounces) frozen
   chopped spinach, thawed
   and drained

SAUCE:
1 can (4 ounces) mushroom
   pieces (save liquid)
1 teaspoon flour
1 cup sour cream
2 tablespoons chopped
   chives

⅛ teaspoon hot pepper
   sauce, optional
2 tablespoons chopped
   parsley

MEAT LOAF: Combine egg, milk, salt, soy sauce and pepper sauce. Mix well. Add bread crumbs. Stir until moistened. Add beef and spinach. Mix well. Lightly pack in loaf pan. Bake at 350° for 1 hour.

SAUCE: Drain liquid from mushrooms into small saucepan. Blend in flour. Cook over medium heat stirring constantly until mixture thickens and comes to a boil. Add remaining ingredients. Heat well, but do not boil. Serve with meat loaf. Serves 6.

Mrs. T. B. Dellinger (Maria)

Mother's Casserole

1½ pounds ground beef
½ large green pepper,
   coarsely chopped
½ large onion, coarsely
   chopped
8 medium fresh mushrooms,
   sliced

Lawry's seasoned salt to taste
1 box (14½ ounces) Kraft
   macaroni and cheese
1 can (10¾ ounces) cream
   of mushroom soup,
   undiluted

Combine beef, vegetables and salt. Cook over medium heat until beef is browned. Drain. Prepare macaroni mix according to directions, using 3 quart pot. Add soup and meat mixture. Mix thoroughly. *Tastes even better reheated. For a hot and spicy flavor add Open Pit barbecue sauce.*

Mrs. Nancy Davidsson

Hamburger Stroganoff

½ cup minced onion	1 pound fresh mushrooms,
¼ cup butter	sliced
1 pound ground beef	2 cans (10¾ ounces) cream
2 tablespoons flour	of chicken soup, undiluted
1½ teaspoons salt	1 cup sour cream
¼ teaspoon pepper	2 tablespoons minced
	parsley

Sauté onion in butter over medium heat, add meat and brown. Add flour, salt, pepper and mushrooms. Cook 5 minutes. Add soup, simmer uncovered 10 minutes. Stir in sour cream and heat through. Sprinkle with parsley. Serves 4 to 6. *An 8 ounce can of mushrooms may be substituted for fresh mushrooms. Serve with noodles.*

Mrs. Arlene Shea

Chinese Casserole

6 to 8 pork chops, boned	1 can (4 ounces) mushrooms
1 package (5 ounces) Uncle	1 can (10¾ ounces) cream
Ben's brown and wild rice	of mushroom soup
1 can (16 ounces) Chinese	1 soup can water
fancy vegetables	

Preheat oven to 400°. Brown chops. Set aside. Sprinkle rice in oiled 9x13 inch casserole. Sprinkle seasoning packet from rice on top. Layer vegetables and mushrooms over seasoning. Combine soup and water and pour over top. Place chops on top of mixture. Cover and bake 45 minutes. Uncover. Bake 30 minutes longer. Serves 6 to 8.

Mrs. Alice Wagnon

Creamed Ham, Oysters and Mushrooms

1 pint fresh or frozen oysters with liquor, about 24	1 cup butter or margarine
	¾ cup flour
	2½ cups cooked, diced ham
Half-and-half, about 5 cups	Salt and pepper
1 pound fresh mushrooms	

Cook oysters gently in their own liquor until edges curl. Drain oysters; set aside. Measure oyster liquor and add enough half-and-half to make 6 cups and set aside. Wash and slice mushrooms. Cook in ¼ cup butter until tender and set aside. Melt remaining ¾ cup butter in large saucepan over medium heat. Remove from heat. Blend in flour, salt and pepper to taste; mix well. Slowly add liquid while stirring. Return to medium heat. Cook, stirring constantly, until thick and smooth. Add oysters, mushrooms and ham. Heat well. Serves 8 to 10. *Serve over rice.*

Mrs. Tom J. Lymenstull (Wanda)

El Paso Ham

3 cups chopped, cooked ham	1 can (4 ounces) green chili peppers, seeded and chopped
2 cups shredded Monterey Jack cheese, about 8 ounces	½ cup finely chopped onion
	Hot pepper sauce to taste
1 can (8 ounces) tomato sauce	

Combine ingredients in crockery cooker. Cover and cook for two hours on low heat setting. Serve on hot corn bread or rolled in soft corn tortillas. Serves 6. *Also good as dip with corn chips.*

Mrs. Michael D. Miesch, Jr. (Ann)

Ham'n Cheese Delight

½ cup finely chopped onion	⅔ cup finely crushed
1 tablespoon butter	crackers, about 15
2 cups chopped cooked ham	1½ cups milk
3 eggs, slightly beaten	Dash pepper
4 ounces sharp American cheese, shredded	

Cook onion in butter until tender. Combine with ham, eggs, cheese, crackers, milk and pepper. Mix well. Pour into 10x6 inch baking dish. Bake at 350° for 45 to 50 minutes or until a knife inserted just off center comes out clean. Serves 6.

Mrs. William O. Petty (Marye Jo)

Italian Lasagna

1½ pounds Italian sausage, remove casing and crumble	1 package (8 ounces) wide lasagna noodles
1 large clove garlic, minced	3 cups fresh Ricotta or creamy cottage cheese
1 teaspoon basil	½ cup grated Parmesan or
1 teaspoon salt	Romano cheese
1 can (16 ounces) tomatoes	2 tablespoons parsley flakes
2 cans (6 ounces each) tomato paste	2 eggs, beaten
1 tablespoon oregano	1 teaspoon salt
	½ teaspoon pepper
	1 pound Mozzarella cheese, sliced very thin

Brown meat slowly. Drain. Add garlic, basil, salt, tomatoes, tomato paste and oregano. Simmer 30 minutes, stirring occasionally. Cook noodles according to package directions. Do not overcook. Drain and rinse with cold water. Combine remaining ingredients, except Mozzarella. Place layer of noodles in 9x13 inch baking dish. Spread half of cheese mixture over noodles. Add half of Mozzarella and half of meat sauce. Repeat layers. Bake at 350° for 30 minutes. Let stand for 10 minutes before cutting. Serves 8. *Best prepared and refrigerated one day before serving. The most important ingredient in this lasagna is the quality of the Italian sausage. An Italian market or good meat market generally makes its own.*

Mrs. James W. Kenney (Ann)

Rolled Pork Roast - Apple Jelly Sauce

4   to 5 pounds rolled,   ½   teaspoon garlic powder
     boneless pork roast   ½   teaspoon chili powder
½   teaspoon salt

SAUCE:
1   cup catsup   2   teaspoons vinegar
1   cup apple jelly   1   teaspoon chili powder

Mix salt, garlic powder and chili powder together and rub into roast. Place on rack in roasting pan and bake at 325° for 2½ hours. Remove from oven and allow to stand 10 minutes before slicing.

For sauce, mix all ingredients and heat to boiling point. Serve over sliced pork roast. Serves 8.

Mrs. Jerry R. Wagnon (Alice)

Toad-In-The-Hole
A Goodie

1   cup flour   Pepper to taste
2   eggs   1   pound link pork sausages
1   cup milk   Butter
½   teaspoon salt

Combine flour, eggs, milk and seasonings in blender. Blend at high speed for 2 to 3 seconds. Scrape down, blend again for 40 seconds. Refrigerate at least 1 hour. Preheat oven to 400°. Bake sausages for 15 minutes or until done. Butter a 9x12 inch baking dish. Place sausages 1 inch apart in dish. Pour blender mixture around sausages. Bake 30 minutes. Serves 4. *This is like a Yorkshire pudding. Makes an easy brunch dish.*

Mrs. John B. Isbell (Charlene)

Marinated Pork Roast

½ cup soy sauce
2 cloves garlic, minced
1 teaspoon ginger
½ cup dry sherry
1 tablespoon dry mustard

1 teaspoon thyme, crushed
4 to 5 pound pork loin
    roast, boned, rolled and
    tied

Combine soy sauce, garlic, ginger, sherry, mustard and thyme. Place roast in plastic bag and set in deep bowl. Pour in marinade and close bag tightly. Let set overnight in refrigerator, pressing bag occasionally to spread marinade. Remove roast and place on rack in shallow baking pan. Roast uncovered at 325° for 3 to 3½ hours. Baste with marinade several times during last hour. Serves 8 to 10.

Mrs. Jes D. McIver (Marilyn)

Old Sod Casserole

¾ pound bulk sausage
3 tablespoons flour
1¼ cups milk
1 can (17 ounces) whole
    kernel corn

½ teaspoon salt
⅛ teaspoon pepper
1 teaspoon chopped parsley
1 large tomato, sliced

Brown sausage in skillet. Pour off all but 2 tablespoons fat, add flour and stir until blended. Add milk and liquid from corn, stirring constantly, and cook until thick. Add corn, salt and pepper. Turn into shallow casserole. Lay tomato slices on top. Heat in 375° oven about 5 minutes. Sprinkle with parsley. Serves 2.

Mrs. Maurice L. Levy (Margaret)

Cream ham with mushrooms and chopped hard cooked eggs. Serve on toast slices.

Desserts

DESSERTS

Dessert, to many, is the Piece De Résistance of a formal or informal dinner. Cakes, pies, ice cream and frappés are eaten for pleasure, satisfaction and nutrition. Desserts add a touch of elegance and excitement to entertaining. Let your imagination run "wild" whether making an Old World dessert, an American apple pie or a delightful Texas fruit plate.

Our Old Country heritage of desserts, fancy sweetbreads, cobblers, jelly rolls, coffee cakes, ice creams, cookies, doughnuts, kuchens, tortes, chaussons, flans and tarts came over with the first settlers which influenced our culinary knowledge. The Italians brought home from the Middle East tales of the "enchanting" ices of Persia. They were so captivated by the sorbets that they were inspired to station relays of runners from Rome to the Alps to bring back ice to make the frozen desserts. The French were introduced to ices in 1530, Parisian public in 1660 and England in 1770. Also, an Italian, Francesco Procopio Dei Coltelli, in Paris, France opened a cafe (our first cafe) in 1686 selling coffee and desserts.

Our traditional American desserts are: Angel food cake, brownies, cheesecake, chocolate chip cookies, apple pie, pecan pie, pumpkin pie, pound cake and strawberry shortcake. Americans and chocolate have had a long-standing love affair since Spaniards under Cortez (1519) invaded Mexico. Emperor Montezuma used cocoa beans as money and drank spiced unsweetened chocolate from golden goblets. Chocolate, spices, honey, hard maple syrup and molasses helped American cooks develop their own special magical desserts. Desserts, in the United States, represent a lifetime of memories of special occasions.

Texas developed its own brand of personality and sophisticated, dramatic cuisine under six flags, namely, Spain, France, Mexico, as a Republic, in the Confederacy and lastly the United States. Texas, a Caddo Indian word meaning friendship, is noted for its hospitality, generousity and graciousness. Texans adore food and friends; consequently, Texas hostessess always have desserts "out" and big "Howdy" for friends and strangers alike who appear unexpectedly at her door. Texas Aggies and hostessess in the great State of Texas seem to have their own fraternity steeped in friendliness, traditions, appreciation and love of good desserts!

Wherever Aggies or Former Students congregate, nostalgic reminiscenting of the good ole' days occurs and there comes to mind the aroma of delicious Aggie apricot fried pies. So, whether it's Hullabaloo in the kitchen or Hullabaloo in Aggieland, Aggies and desserts are everyone's favorite! Happy cookin' y'all.

Aggie's Apricot Pie

1 package (10 ounces) dried apricots	Pinch cinnamon
Water	3 tablespoons butter
¾ cup sugar	3 tablespoons sugar
½ lemon (juice only)	1 unbaked (9 inch) pie shell
	Pastry strips

Soak apricots in just enough water to cover for about 3 hours. Slowly boil apricots for about 1 hour, adding sugar at end of boiling. Apricots must be very tender. Do not drain. Stir apricots and sugar with fork. Add lemon juice and cinnamon. Pour apricot mixture in unbaked pie shell. Smooth out and cover with strips of pastry laced on top. Dot top crust with butter and sprinkle with about 3 tablespoons sugar. Bake at 350° for 1 hour. *Brush bottom crust with melted butter for a crisper crust.* Yields 7 pieces.

Variation: Roll out pastry and cut circles 4 to 5 inches in diameter. Spoon about 2 tablespoons of apricot mixture in center of circle, completing 1 at a time. After apricots are placed in center of pastry, fold circle in half, sealing with tines of fork. Fry in butter until brown on both sides. Yields 2 dozen.

Mrs. Dan Scott (Pat)

Jeff's Favorite Apple Pie

2 cups sliced apples	2 tablespoons flour
1 cup sugar	2 tablespoons cinnamon

TOPPING:

½ cup firmly packed brown sugar	⅓ cup margarine
¾ cup flour	1 unbaked (9 inch) pie shell

Peel, core and slice apples. Sprinkle with sugar and place in pie shell. Sprinkle flour and cinnamon over apples.

TOPPING: Mix brown sugar and flour, cut in margarine and sprinkle over apples. Bake at 375° for 45 minutes. Place strips of foil over edges of crust during baking to keep from burning.

Mrs. Sam Harting (Sandra)

George's Sour Cream Apple Pie

CRUST:

1 cup flour, unsifted	⅓ cup margarine
½ teaspoon salt	3 to 4 tablespoons ice water

FILLING:

2 tablespoons flour	1 egg, slightly beaten
½ cup sugar	1½ teaspoons vanilla
¼ teaspoon salt	2 cups pared and sliced
1 cup sour cream	apples

TOPPING:

⅓ cup flour	1½ teaspoons cinnamon
⅓ cup sugar	¼ cup margarine

CRUST: Cut margarine into flour and salt until it resembles coarse meal. Stir in ice water. Mix well and roll on lightly floured board to fit a 9 inch pie plate. Trim edge, leaving ½ inch to fold under and flute.

FILLING: Combine flour, sugar and salt. Add sour cream, egg and vanilla. Beat until smooth. Mix in apples and pour mixture in pie shell. Bake at 425° for 15 minutes. Reduce heat to 350° and bake for another 30 minutes.

TOPPING: Blend all ingredients and sprinkle on top of pie. Bake at 400° for 10 minutes.

Mrs. George Kardell (Roe)

Chocolate Rich Pie

1 can (14 ounces) sweetened condensed milk	½ teaspoon vanilla
4 heaping tablespoons cocoa	1 baked (9 inch) pie shell
2 tablespoons butter or margarine	¼ cup grated semisweet chocolate, optional
2 egg yolks, slightly blended	1 to 2 cups nondairy topping

Stir milk, cocoa, butter, egg yolks and vanilla together in saucepan. Cook slowly, stirring constantly, until mixture is consistency of pudding. Pour into pie shell and cool in refrigerator. Garnish with a nondairy topping and grated chocolate. Serves 6.

Mrs. Charles D. Price, Jr. (Joyce)

Blueberry Cream Pie

1 package (8 ounces) cream cheese, softened
2 tablespoons lemon juice
2 teaspoons vanilla
1¾ cups powdered sugar
1 pint whipping cream, whipped

1 can (21 ounces) blueberry pie filling
2 teaspoons lemon juice
2 bananas, sliced
2 baked (9 inch) pie shells

Combine cream cheese, 2 tablespoons lemon juice, vanilla and powdered sugar and beat well. Fold in stiffly beaten whipping cream. Line pie shells with sliced bananas. Divide cream cheese mixture and spread over bananas. Refrigerate for 1 hour. Add 2 teaspoons lemon juice to blueberry pie filling and spoon on tops of pies.

Mrs. William L. Humphries (Gail)

Chocolate Pie

1 cup sugar
4 tablespoons flour
Pinch salt
5 tablespoons cocoa
2 eggs, separated

2 cups milk
2 tablespoons butter or margarine
1 teaspoon vanilla
1 baked (9 inch) pie shell

MERINGUE:
2 egg whites

2 tablespoons sugar

Mix together in heavy saucepan sugar, flour, salt, cocoa and beaten egg yolks. Add milk. Cook over medium heat until thick, stirring constantly. Remove from heat. Add butter and vanilla. Pour into baked pie shell.

MERINGUE: Beat egg whites with sugar. Place on top of filling. Seal meringue onto edge of crust. Brown in 350° oven. Serves 8.

Mrs. Ernest L. Austin, Jr. (Marvel)

Chocolate Brownie Pie

3 egg whites
Dash salt
¾ cup sugar
¾ cup crumbled chocolate
    cookies

½ cup chopped nuts
1 teaspoon vanilla
1 cup whipping cream,
    whipped and sweetened

Beat egg whites and salt until soft peaks form. Add sugar slowly, beating until stiff. Fold cookies, nuts and vanilla into mixture. Spread into buttered pie pan. Bake 35 minutes at 325°. Cool and spread with whipped cream. Chill. Serves 8.

Aggie Mom

Sheree's Chocolate Velvet Pie

CRUST:

3 egg whites
¼ teaspoon salt
6 tablespoons sugar

3 cups chopped walnuts or
    pecans

FILLING:

6 tablespoons white corn
    syrup
4 teaspoons water
5 teaspoons vanilla

1½ cups semisweet chocolate
    chips
1 cup sweetened condensed
    milk, chilled
2 cups whipping cream

CRUST: Preheat oven to 400°. Beat egg whites and salt to soft peaks. Gradually beat in sugar until stiff. Add nuts. Spread over bottom and sides of 10 inch greased pie plate. Make rim about ¾ inch high. It will be a generous crust. Bake pie shell 12 minutes. Cool.

FILLING: Bring corn syrup and water just to boil and remove from heat. Stir in vanilla and chocolate chips until melted. Cool. Reserve 2 tablespoons of chocolate sauce for top of pie. Combine chocolate sauce with condensed milk and stir well. Add whipping cream and with mixer on low speed, beat well. Beat at medium speed until it stands in soft peaks. Pour chocolate filling into cooled pie shell. Firm pie in freezer. Decorate frozen pie. Wrap and freeze until served. *Chocolate piping on top is optional. Crisscross to make lattice design. Garnish with nuts, whipping cream, Cool Whip or serve plain.* Serves 12.

Mrs. Jack Starry (Dorothy)

Fudge Pie

1 cup sugar
½ cup flour
8 tablespoons butter or margarine, melted
1 square unsweetened chocolate, melted

2 eggs, beaten
1 teaspoon vanilla
½ cup chopped pecans
1 greased (9 inch) pie pan
Peppermint ice cream, optional

Mix together sugar and flour. Add butter and chocolate and mix. Add eggs, vanilla and pecans and blend well. Pour into greased pie pan. Bake at 300° about 30 minutes. Serve with scoop of peppermint ice cream. *These make good brownies by increasing flour to 1¼ cups.*

Mrs. Bill Heaton (Gladys)

Kentucky Bluegrass Fudge Pie

⅔ cup sifted flour
½ cup cocoa
¼ teaspoon salt
1½ cups coarsely chopped walnuts

½ cup butter
1 cup sugar
2 eggs
3 teaspoons vanilla

ICING:
2 tablespoons butter
3 to 4 tablespoons cocoa
2 cups powdered sugar

1 teaspoon vanilla
Milk

Grease an 8 or 9 inch cake pan. Combine flour, cocoa and salt on wax paper. Toast walnuts for 10 minutes at 350°. Beat butter, sugar, eggs and vanilla until light and fluffy. Stir in toasted walnuts. Turn into prepared pan. Bake at 350° for 30 minutes. Do not overbake. Cool on wire rack. Remove from pan. Ice if desired.

ICING: Mix together all ingredients using enough milk to make of spreading consistency. Frost and cool pie. Serves 6 to 8.

Mrs. John Schimmer (Jane)

Egg Custard Pie I

3 eggs	1 teaspoon vanilla
1 cup sugar	¼ teaspoon nutmeg
2 cups milk	1 unbaked (9 inch) pie shell

Beat together eggs, sugar and milk over medium heat until well blended and sugar is dissolved. Add vanilla. Pour into unbaked pie shell. Sprinkle with nutmeg. Bake at 450° for 10 to 15 minutes. Lower temperature to 350°. Cook until set. *This can be put in custard cups (6) and placed in an oblong dish of water and baked as pudding.*

Mrs. Ernest L. Austin, Jr. (Marvel)

Egg Custard Pie II

¾ cup sugar	1 teaspoon vanilla
5 tablespoons flour	1 tablespoon butter
Dash salt	1½ cups milk
4 eggs, separated	1 unbaked (9 inch) pie shell

Mix together sugar, flour, salt, egg yolks, vanilla, butter and milk. Fold beaten egg whites into above mixture gently. Pour in pie shell. Bake at 375° for 15 minutes; reduce to 325° and bake for 30 minutes. Serves 6 to 8.

Mrs. Glinn H. White (Bettyeann)

Nita's Million Dollar Pie

1 can (14 ounces) Eagle Brand sweetened condensed milk	¼ cup lemon juice
	1 pint large, fresh strawberries
1 carton (8 ounces) Cool Whip	2 to 3 bananas, sliced
	1 cup pecans or walnuts
1 can (8 ounces) crushed pineapple, drained	2 graham cracker pie crusts (9 inch)

Mix together all ingredients and place in pie crusts. Chill.

Mrs. J. Hal Brown (Eva Gay)

Peach Praline Pie

CRUST:
½ cup butter
¼ cup firmly packed brown
   sugar

1 cup sifted flour
½ cup chopped pecans

FILLING:
1 quart vanilla ice cream,
   softened slightly
1 to 1½ pounds fresh
   peaches or 1 package (16
   ounces) frozen peaches

¾ cup sugar
½ pint whipping cream,
   whipped

CRUST: Mix together butter, sugar and flour. Add nuts. Press into 9x13 inch pan. Bake at 400° for 7 to 9 minutes or until brown. Remove from oven and stir immediately. Reserve ¼ of mixture for topping. Press remainder into 9 inch pie pan. Cool.

FILLING: Peel and slice fresh peaches. Sprinkle sugar over peaches and let set. Use blender or mixer on low speed and mash peaches (don't puree them). Fold peaches and whipped cream into softened ice cream. Don't let ice cream soften too much. Spoon into pie crust. Sprinkle with reserved crumbs. Cover with foil and freeze several hours or overnight. Let thaw about 15 or 20 minutes before serving. *Don't let pie melt.* When ready to serve, garnish with whipped cream, fresh peaches and pralined pecan halves.

PRALINED PECAN HALVES:
1 cup sugar
½ teaspoon soda
½ cup half-and-half

1 tablespoon butter
1½ cups pecan halves

Combine sugar and soda in deep saucepan. Add half-and-half, and stir well. Cook over medium heat to 234° (soft ball stage), stirring constantly. Remove from heat. Stir in butter and pecan halves. Beat until pecans are well coated and mixture thickens. Pour pecans onto buttered aluminum foil. Quickly separate each pecan with a spoon. Cool.

Mrs. Sam C. Laden, Jr. (Mary Lou)

Pour cream over bananas and sprinkle with nutmeg.

Crunchy Nut Mince Pie

1　unbaked (9 inch) pie shell

1　jar (28 ounces) Borden's None Such mincemeat

TOPPING:

½　cup butter or margarine, softened

1　cup sifted flour

⅓　cup shredded coconut

½　cup firmly packed brown sugar

½　cup chopped pecans

Spoon mincemeat into an unbaked pie shell.

TOPPING: Cut butter into flour with pastry blender until mixture is crumbly. Add coconut, brown sugar and pecans; toss together. Sprinkle evenly on top of mincemeat. Bake at 400° until crust is golden brown, 20 to 25 minutes.

Variation: Instead of 1 jar mincemeat, use 2 boxes (9 ounces each) None Such condensed mincemeat. Crumble mincemeat into 1½ cups water and place over medium heat, stirring constantly. Bring mixture to a boil, and boil 1 minute. Cool before putting into pie shell.

Mrs. Sam C. Laden, Jr. (Mary Lou)

Pumpkin Chiffon Pie

1　tablespoon gelatin

¼　cup cold water

2　eggs, separated

1½　cups canned pumpkin

½　cup firmly packed brown sugar

½　cup milk

½　teaspoon salt

½　teaspoon cinnamon

½　teaspoon nutmeg

¼　cup granulated sugar

1　baked (9 inch) deep pie shell

½　cup whipping cream, whipped

Soften gelatin in water. Combine egg yolks, pumpkin, brown sugar, milk, salt, cinnamon and nutmeg in top of double boiler. Cook, stirring constantly, for 10 minutes or until slightly thickened. Remove from heat. Stir in softened gelatin. Cool. Beat egg whites until foamy. Add ¼ cup sugar gradually, until meringue stands in soft peaks. Fold in pumpkin mixture and pour into baked pie shell. Chill until firm. Garnish with whipped cream. Serves 6 to 8.

Mrs. James P. Licandro (Marie)

Osgood Pie

6 eggs, separated
3 cups sugar
1½ cups pecans, chopped
1 cup raisins
3 tablespoons vinegar
2 tablespoons cinnamon

2 tablespoons butter, melted
½ teaspoon vanilla
2 unbaked (9 inch) pie shells
1 cup whipping cream,
   whipped or ice cream

Mix beaten egg yolks, sugar, nuts, raisins, vinegar, cinnamon, butter and vanilla and cream thoroughly. Fold in stiffly beaten egg whites. Pour into 2 pie shells and bake at 325° for 50 minutes. Garnish with whipped cream or ice cream. Serves 16.

Mrs. Ralph Plumlee (Stella)

Variation: For 1 pie use 2 eggs, separated, 1 cup sugar, 1 teaspoon cinnamon, ½ teaspoon nutmeg, ½ cup pecan halves, ½ cup raisins, 1 tablespoon butter, melted, and 1 tablespoon vinegar. Pour into pie shell and bake for 10 minutes at 400° reduce heat to 350° and bake for about 25 minutes longer.

Mrs. W. J. Green (Juanita)

Pumpkin Pie

1 can (16 ounces) pumpkin
1 box (6 ounces) instant
   vanilla pudding
1 cup Cool Whip
1 cup cold milk

1 teaspoon pumpkin pie
   spice
1 baked (9 inch) pie shell
1 cup whipping cream,
   whipped

Mix together all ingredients and beat for 2 minutes. Pour into pie shell and refrigerate. Top with whipped cream and serve. Serves 8.

Mrs. Tom J. Lymenstull (Wanda)

Pecan Pie

1 cup sugar	1 teaspoon vanilla
1 cup dark Karo syrup	1 cup pecan halves or pieces
3 eggs	1 unbaked (9 inch) pie shell
Pinch salt	

Mix sugar, syrup, eggs, salt and vanilla with mixer. Cover bottom of pie crust with pecans. Pour filling over pecans. Bake at 425° for 15 minutes. Reduce to 325° and bake for 35 to 45 minutes or until middle is set. *Freezes well.* Serves 8.

Mrs. James E. Keeling (Betty)

Variation: Reduce sugar to ½ cup; use 1 cup white Karo; add 2 tablespoons butter, 1 tablespoon flour, ½ teaspoon salt, 1 teaspoon almond extract. Bake 400° for 10 minutes. Reduce heat to 325° and bake 20 minutes.

Mrs. S. Alvin Reeves (Dolores)

Variation: Use white Karo, 3 tablespoons flour, 2 tablespoons butter, 1½ tablespoons cider vinegar, ⅛ teaspoon salt, 1 teaspoon vanilla, chop pecans. Bake at 400° for 10 minutes. Reduce heat to 300° and bake for 30 minutes or until done.

Mrs. Bill Heaton (Gladys)

Southern Lemon Chess Pie

1 unbaked (9 inch) pie shell	¼ cup milk
4 eggs	Dash salt
2 cups sugar	Grated lemon rind
1 tablespoon cornmeal	6 tablespoons butter, melted
1 tablespoon flour	¼ cup lemon juice

Beat eggs well. Combine and add sugar, cornmeal and flour and mix well. Add milk, salt, lemon rind and melted butter. Gradually add lemon juice. Pour into an unbaked pie shell. Bake at 350° until center is set, about 40 to 45 minutes.

Mrs. Sam C. Laden, Jr. (Mary Lou)

Green Tomato Pie

½ cup water
1 quart sliced firm green
  tomatoes
½ cup seedless raisins
1 cup sugar
2 tablespoons flour
¾ teaspoon cinnamon
½ teaspoon ginger
¼ teaspoon nutmeg

2 tablespoons butter
Grated rind of 1 lemon
1½ tablespoons lemon juice
1 wineglass of brandy or
  whiskey (4 tablespoons or
  a little more, to taste)
1 recipe for double crust (9
  inch) pastry

Pour water over tomatoes and simmer 5 minutes or until tomatoes are tender. Add raisins and cook longer. Drain off any remaining liquor, saving juice; dump tomatoes and raisins into pie shell. Sprinkle with sugar, flour, cinnamon, ginger and nutmeg and dot with butter. Add grated rind and lemon juice. Now pour over the whole a "spilling wineglass" (as they say in Kentucky) of brandy or whiskey. If pie will hold it, add a few tablespoons of tomato liquor or enough to moisten tomatoes well. Top with slashed solid crust or use strips across top as you prefer. Bake at 450° for 15 minutes. Reduce to 375° and leave ½ hour longer, or until crust is brown. *A Kentucky specialty. Select firm green tomatoes. Be sure there is no red at all on the tomato.*

Mrs. Thomas Dellinger (Maria)

Strawberry Pie

2 pints fresh strawberries,
  reserve several for garnish
½ pint whipping cream,
  whipped

1 package (3 ounces) cream
  cheese
½ cup sugar
Juice of small lemon
1 baked (9 inch) pie shell

Whip cream very stiff and set aside. Mix cream cheese, sugar and lemon juice until smooth. Fold in whipped cream. Cut up berries into mixture and spoon into shell. Garnish with halved berries and refrigerate.

Mrs. Eugene E. Frantz (Mary)

Extra egg whites may be used in white cakes, tortes, meringues, sherbets or frostings.

Strawberry Meringue Pie

½ teaspoon vinegar
¼ teaspoon vanilla
Dash salt
2 egg whites, beaten

⅔ cup sugar
½ cup nuts, chopped
1 (9 or 10 inch) pie pan
  (glass)

FILLING:
½ pint whipping cream,
  whipped

1 can (1 pound) drained
  strawberries, raspberries
  or fruit cocktail
  Whole frozen strawberries,
  slightly sweetened, may be
  substituted. Let set and
  drain.

SHELL: Add vinegar, vanilla and salt to egg whites. Beat into soft peaks. Gradually add sugar and beat until stiff. Fold in nuts. Put in well buttered pie pan. Bake at 300° for 45 minutes. Cool.

FILLING: Whip cream until stiff. Fold in berries. Pour into pie shell and refrigerate. Serves 8.

Mrs. Bob Hamblen (Jan)

Aunt Lillie's Pie Crust

1 cup flour
¼ teaspoon salt
1 tablespoon sugar

⅓ cup Wesson oil
3 tablespoons milk

Mix together flour, salt and sugar. Add Wesson oil, and milk and mix well. Press into pie plate. Bake at 350° for 10 to 15 minutes, or may be used as unbaked shell.

Aggie Mom

Apricot Bars

48 double graham crackers	1 cup coconut
¾ cup margarine	1 cup graham cracker crumbs
1 cup sugar	
½ cup milk	½ cup chopped pecans
1 egg, slightly beaten	½ teaspoon vanilla
¾ cup chopped apricots	

GLAZE:

2 tablespoons margarine	2 cups powdered sugar
3 tablespoons lemon juice	

Line a 15x10 inch jelly roll pan with 24 double graham crackers. In saucepan, combine margarine, sugar, milk and egg. Cook until slightly thick, stirring constantly, about 5 minutes. Add remaining ingredients. Spread over graham crackers in pan and cover with another layer of 24 double graham crackers. Press down gently. Do not bake.

GLAZE: Mix all ingredients and spread on bars. Yields 48.

Mrs. S. G. Evetts (Darlene)

Aunt Karen's Desperation Bars

½ cup butter, melted	1 cup semisweet chocolate chips
1 cup graham cracker crumbs	
	1 cup chopped nuts
1 cup flaked coconut	1 can (14 ounces) sweetened condensed milk

Mix together melted butter, crumbs and coconut. Press lightly into 9x13 inch pan. Cover with chocolate pieces and sprinkle with nuts. Drizzle sweetened condensed milk over mix. Bake at 350° for 30 minutes. Yields 4 dozen cookie bars.

Mrs. Alexander W. McCracken (Terry)

Boyfriend Cookies

1 cup butter or margarine	1 teaspoon soda
1⅓ cups sugar	3½ cups rolled quick cooking
1⅓ cups firmly packed light	oatmeal
brown sugar	1½ cups chopped salted
2 eggs	peanuts
1 teaspoon vanilla	1 package (6 ounces)
1½ cups flour, unsifted	chocolate chips

In a bowl, cream butter and slowly beat in both sugars. Add unbeaten eggs and vanilla. Beat until fluffy. Sift flour with soda; add oatmeal and stir into sugar mixture. Fold in peanuts and chocolate chips, mixing well. Drop rounded teaspoonfuls on greased cookie sheet. Bake at 375° for 12 minutes. Makes 6 dozen cookies.

Mrs. R. E. Spurling (Margaret)

Brownies

2 squares semisweet	1½ cups flour
chocolate	Dash of cinnamon
¾ cup margarine	4 eggs
2 cups sugar	1 teaspoon vanilla

FROSTING:

½ cup margarine	1 teaspoon vanilla
6 tablespoons milk	½ cup chopped nuts,
4 tablespoons cocoa	optional
1 box (16 ounces) powdered	
sugar	

Melt chocolate and margarine. Mix together sugar, flour, cinnamon, eggs and vanilla. Combine chocolate mixture and flour mixture. Bake in greased and floured 9x13 inch pan for 25 minutes at 350°. Frost brownies while hot.

FROSTING: Combine margarine, milk and cocoa. Heat until margarine is melted and blend together. Beat in powdered sugar and add vanilla. Stir in nuts if desired. Frost brownies and cool. Cut into squares. Yields 24.

Mrs. Charles E. Allen (Bettie)

Honey's Brownies

½ cup butter, melted
4 tablespoons vegetable oil
4 eggs, beaten
⅛ teaspoon salt
1½ teaspoons vanilla
1 cup sugar

1 cup firmly packed brown sugar
1 cup flour
12 tablespoons cocoa
1 cup chopped pecans
1 cup coconut, optional

Mix butter and oil and cool. Beat eggs, salt and vanilla. Add sugars gradually, beating well. Add butter mixture. Sift together flour and cocoa and add all at once to mixture. Stir by hand until barely mixed. Add nuts and coconut. Spread in 9x13 inch greased pan. Bake at 350° for 20 to 25 minutes. Cool and cut.

Mrs. Bill Heaton (Gladys)

Cheesecake Cookies

⅔ cup butter
⅔ cup firmly packed light brown sugar

2 cups flour
1 cup finely chopped pecans

FILLING:
2 packages (8 ounces each) cream cheese
½ cup sugar
2 eggs

¼ cup milk
1 teaspoon vanilla
2 teaspoons lemon juice

Cream together butter and brown sugar. Add flour and pecans; mix together to make a crumb mixture. Reserve 2 cups of mixture for topping. Press remainder of crumb mixture into the bottom of two 8 inch square pans. Bake at 350° for 12 to 15 minutes.

FILLING: Blend cream cheese and sugar; beat until smooth. Add remaining ingredients. Spread cream cheese mixture over baked crust. Sprinkle with remainder of crumb mixture. Bake for 25 minutes at 350°. Cool and cut into squares.

Mrs. William O. Petty (Marye Jo)

Chocolate Crackles
Interesting & Easy

1 package (18.5 ounces) chocolate cake mix
1 egg

1 carton (4 ounces) Cool Whip
½ cup powdered sugar

Mix together cake mix, egg and Cool Whip with wooden spoon. Do not add extra liquid. Shape into 1 inch balls; roll in powdered sugar. Place on greased cookie sheet. Bake at 350° about 10 to 12 minutes. Cookies will flatten as they bake. Yields 4 dozen.

Mrs. S. G. Evetts (Darlene)

Chocolate Chip Meringue Cookies

2 egg whites
½ cup sugar

1 cup chocolate chips

Preheat oven to 450°. Beat egg whites until foamy. Gradually add sugar and beat until stiff peaks form. Fold in chocolate chips. Drop by teaspoons on ungreased cookie sheet. Shut off oven. Leave in oven ½ hour. Yields 2 dozen.

Mrs. James Doyle (Barbara)

Delicious Nut Cookies

1 egg white, unbeaten
¾ cup firmly packed brown sugar

2 cups pecans, chopped

Mix ingredients. Drop in small mounds on well greased cookie sheet. Bake 30 minutes at 250°. Makes 36 cookies.

Mrs. Jack McAuliff (Betty)

Erna's Krum Kake
(Crisp Cone Cookie)

½ cup butter	3 eggs
½ cup light cream	½ teaspoon vanilla, or 3
1 cup flour	crushed cardamon seeds,
1 cup sugar	or 1½ teaspoons ground
½ cup potato starch, or ½	cardamon
cup cornstarch	

Mix above ingredients, but do not beat. Put a teaspoon of butter on Krum Kake iron. Brown slightly on both sides. Roll quickly on wooden cone or cylinder to cool. Store in airtight container. These cones may be filled with sweetened whipped cream or ice cream.

In October, 1982, King Olaf of Norway paid a visit to the Norse Community, Bosque County, Texas. At a tea in his honor at the Bosque County Museum, Clifton, the King selected a Krum Kake from the assortment of sweets, no doubt recognizing it as an authentic Norwegian cookie. This recipe was given to me by my sister-in-law, Mrs. Joe Forson.

Mrs. Charles D. Price, Jr. (Joyce)

Four O'Clock Cookies

1½ cups sifted flour	½ teaspoon vanilla
1 teaspoon soda	½ cup firmly packed brown
¼ teaspoon salt	sugar
½ cup shortening	½ cup sugar
½ cup peanut butter	1 egg, beaten

Sift flour, soda and salt. Blend shortening, peanut butter and sugar. Cream until light and fluffy. Stir in egg and vanilla. Add flour to creamed mixture; mix well. Chill. Form dough into marble size balls. Place on greased cookie sheet, 1 inch apart. Indent with fork. Bake at 375° 12 to 15 minutes. Yields 40 cookies.

Mrs. L. B. Hatcher (Lucille)

Graham Cracker Praline Cookies

24 graham crackers
(2½"x2½")

ICING:
1 cup butter or margarine
1 cup firmly packed brown
   sugar

1 cup pecans
1 teaspoon vanilla

FROSTING:
¼ cup margarine, softened
3 tablespoons half-and-half
½ teaspoon vanilla

¼ cup chopped nuts
1 cup powdered sugar

Place 24 graham crackers side by side on a foil-lined cookie sheet.

ICING: Combine all ingredients and boil 2 minutes. Immediately pour over graham crackers. Bake in preheated 350° oven for 10 minutes. When cool, break into 48 small rectangular cookies.

FROSTING: Mix all ingredients. Spread on cool cookies. *These keep in a tin in dormitory as long as it takes to eat them. Ship well, too.*

Mrs. H. Mathews Garland (Dorothy)

Grandmother's Teacakes
Very old recipe

½ cup shortening
½ teaspoon salt
½ teaspoon nutmeg
½ teaspoon lemon juice
1 cup sugar

2 eggs
2 cups flour
1 teaspoon baking powder
½ teaspoon soda
2 tablespoons milk

Combine shortening, salt, nutmeg, lemon juice, sugar and eggs. Beat until fluffy. Sift together flour, baking powder and soda. Mix with creamed ingredients. Blend in milk and drop from teaspoon on greased cookie sheet. Cover bottom of glass with damp cloth. Use to flatten cookies. Sprinkle with sugar. Bake 375° 10 to 12 minutes. Makes 3½ dozen.

Mrs. William Nelson (Janet)

Honey Bars

2 cups flour	¾ cup oil
1 cup sugar	¼ cup honey
1 teaspoon cinnamon	1 egg, well beaten
½ teaspoon salt	1 teaspoon vanilla
1 teaspoon soda	1 cup nuts

ICING:

1 cup powdered sugar	2 tablespoons water
2 tablespoons Hellmann's mayonnaise	½ teaspoon vanilla

Mix flour, sugar, cinnamon, salt and soda together. Add oil, honey, egg, vanilla and nuts. Dough will be stiff. Press into a 10x15 inch jelly roll pan. Cook 18 minutes exactly at 350°. Remove from oven and immediately pour icing over bars. Set about 8 minutes. Cut into squares.

ICING: Mix together all ingredients and pour over bars.

Mrs. Tom Graham (Norma)

Holly Wreath Cookies
No Baking

½ cup butter	1 teaspoon green food coloring
16 large marshmallows	2½ cups corn flakes
1 teaspoon vanilla	Red hots

Melt butter with marshmallows. Add vanilla and green food coloring. Pour in corn flakes and stir with a fork. Spoon on wax paper in shape of a wreath and decorate with red hots.

Mrs. James R. Jones (Bobbie)

Lemon Meringue Squares

1 cup margarine	½ teaspoon rum extract
1 cup sugar	1 cup flour, sifted
2 eggs, separated	1 cup chopped walnuts
1 teaspoon lemon peel	2 teaspoons lemon juice
¼ teaspoon salt	

Cream margarine with ½ cup sugar, egg yolks, lemon peel, salt and rum extract. Blend in flour. Add ½ cup walnuts. Spread in greased 8 inch square pan. Bake at 350° for 20 minutes. Beat egg whites until stiff. Gradually beat in remaining sugar. Fold in lemon juice and remaining nuts. Spread over the hot baked layer. Bake 25 minutes longer. Cool. Cut in squares.

Mrs. E. E. Frantz (Mary)

Coconut Scotch Squares

½ cup margarine	1 teaspoon vanilla
2 cups firmly packed brown sugar	½ cup coarsely chopped walnuts
2 eggs, unbeaten	½ cup Baker's Angel Flake coconut
1½ cups flour	½ cup powdered sugar
2 teaspoons baking powder	
¼ teaspoon salt	

Combine margarine and brown sugar over low heat until melted. Cool slightly. Add eggs; whisk lightly with fork. Mix well. Sift together flour, baking powder and salt. Add to sugar mixture and stir. Mix in vanilla, walnuts and coconut. Spread in greased and floured 9x12 inch pan. Bake at 325° for 35 to 40 minutes. Top will have a shiny appearance. Do not overbake. Cut into squares while warm. *Bars may be sprinkled with or rolled in powdered sugar if desired.*

Mrs. Jack M. Fahrner (Marilyn)

Little Bits

½ cup butter, softened
1½ cups graham cracker
    crumbs
3   eggs, separated

¾ cup sugar
2   packages (8 ounces each)
    cream cheese, softened

SOUR CREAM FILLING:
1   carton (8 ounces) sour
    cream

¾ cup sugar
½ teaspoon vanilla

Butter 1½ inch muffin tins and coat generously with graham cracker crumbs. Set aside. Cream egg yolks, sugar and cream cheese until fluffy. Beat egg whites until stiff; fold into creamed mixture. Spoon cream cheese mixture into muffin tins, filling ¾ full. Bake at 350° for 20 minutes. Cool 10 to 15 minutes. Centers will fall, forming an indentation. Carefully remove from muffin tins; spoon 1 teaspoon sour cream filling into each indentation. Store in refrigerator. Yields 4 dozen.

FILLING: Combine ingredients in 9 inch pie plate; stir well. Bake at 400° for 5 minutes. Stir well and bake an additional 3 minutes. Yield 1 cup.

Mrs. William Stallings (Bettye)

Marek Munchies

2   cups sugar
2   cups firmly packed brown
    sugar
1   cup margarine, melted
1   cup oil
4   cups flour
1   teaspoon salt
2   teaspoons baking powder
2   teaspoons soda
4   eggs

12 ounces M&M's
12 ounces chocolate chips
12 ounces butterscotch chips
1   cup coconut
1   cup peanuts (or peanut
    M&M's)
1   cup pecans
2   cups corn flakes
2   cups oatmeal

Mix sugars, margarine and oil. Add remaining ingredients. Drop by teaspoons on greased cookie sheet. Bake at 350° for 8 to 10 minutes. Yields 48. *DELICIOUS.*

Mrs. Ben F. Marek (Pat)

Mother B's Frosty Strawberry Squares

1 cup flour	2 tablespoons lemon juice
¼ cup firmly packed brown sugar	1 package (10 ounces) frozen strawberries, unthawed
½ cup chopped pecans	1 carton (10 ounces) Cool Whip
½ cup butter, melted	
2 egg whites, unbeaten	

Mix flour, sugar, pecans and butter together and spread in 12x15 inch pan. Bake at 350° until brown, breaking up and stirring to make crumb mixture. Set aside. Mix together egg whites, lemon juice and strawberries. Cover bowl and mixer with towel while mixing so it will not splatter. Fold Cool Whip into strawberry mixture. Place ½ crumb mixture in bottom of 9x13 inch pan. Spread strawberry mixture on top of crumb mixture. Top with remaining crumbs and freeze overnight. Serves 9 to 12.

Mrs. J. Hal Brown (Eva Gay)

Grandma's Oatmeal Cookies

3 eggs, beaten	2½ cups sifted flour
1 cup raisins	1 teaspoon salt
1 teaspoon vanilla	2 teaspoons soda
1 cup shortening	1 teaspoon cinnamon
1 cup firmly packed brown sugar	2 cups oatmeal
1 cup sugar	¼ cup chopped walnuts

Combine eggs, raisins and vanilla; let mixture stand 1 hour. Cream shortening and sugars. Sift flour, salt, soda and cinnamon into sugar mixture. Mix well. Blend into egg mixture oatmeal and nuts. Dough will be stiff. Drop by teaspoons on ungreased cookie sheet or roll into small balls and flatten. Do not overbake! Bake at 350° for 10 to 12 minutes or until lightly browned. Yields 7 to 8 dozen.

Mrs. Gale Tschantz (Margot)

Oatmeal Carmelitas

1 cup flour
1 cup quick cooking oats
¾ cup firmly packed brown sugar
½ teaspoon soda
¼ teaspoon salt
¾ cup margarine, melted

1 cup semisweet chocolate pieces
½ cup chopped pecans
¾ cup caramel ice cream topping
3 tablespoons flour

Mix flour, oats, brown sugar, soda, salt and margarine in large bowl until crumbly. Press half of crumbs into bottom of 7x11 inch pan. Bake at 350° for ten minutes. Remove from oven. Sprinkle with chocolate pieces and pecans. Mix caramel topping with 3 tablespoons flour and spread carefully over the other layers. Sprinkle with remaining crumb mixture. Bake 15 to 20 minutes longer or until golden brown. Chill 1 to 2 hours. Cut into bars. Yields 24.

Mrs. Ross M. Williams (Jane)

Oatmeal Molasses Cookies

1½ cups flour
1 cup sugar
1 teaspoon baking soda
½ teaspoon salt
1 teaspoon ginger

¼ teaspoon cloves
½ cup shortening
1 egg
¼ cup Grandma's molasses
¾ cup quick cooking oats

Stir together flour, sugar, baking soda, salt, ginger and cloves. Add shortening, egg and molasses. Stir until smooth. Stir in oats and mix well. Drop on ungreased baking sheet. Bake at 375° for 10 minutes. Yields 3 dozen. *Do not overcook.*

Mrs. Joy Anderson

Tea Time Tassies

PASTRY:

1 package (3 ounces) cream
   cheese, softened

½ cup butter or margarine
1 cup flour

FILLING:

1 egg
¾ cup firmly packed brown
   sugar
1 tablespoon butter,
   softened

1 teaspoon vanilla
Dash salt
⅔ cup chopped pecans

PASTRY: Blend cream cheese and butter. Stir in flour. Chill for 1 hour. Roll into 2 dozen one inch balls. Press dough into bottom and sides of miniature muffin tins.

FILLING: Beat together egg, sugar, butter, vanilla and salt until smooth. Divide half of pecans among pastry lined cups, add egg mixture and top with remaining pecans. Bake at 325° for 25 minutes. Cool. Remove from tins. Yields 24.

Mrs. Sam E. Stock (Frances)

Variation: Decrease vanilla to ½ teaspoon. Increase nuts to 1 cup chopped pecans. Bake 350° for 15 to 17 minutes. Reduce heat to 250° and bake for 10 minutes.

Mrs. Duane C. Uhri (Delores)

Cherries Jubilee

1 can (16 ounces) pitted,
   dark, sweet cherries
¼ cup sugar

2 tablespoons cornstarch
¼ cup brandy or Kirsch
Vanilla ice cream

Drain cherries, saving syrup. Blend sugar and cornstarch in saucepan and gradually add syrup. Cook mixture until thickened. Remove from heat. Add cherries. Pour mixture into chafing dish. Heat brandy in ladle, ignite, pour over cherry mixture. Stir to blend into sauce and serve immediately over ice cream. Serves 4 to 6.

Mrs. John B. Isbell (Charlene)

Orange Mincemeat Delights

11 pecan halves, toasted	1 egg
1 box (9 ounces) mincemeat	1 cup sifted flour
1½ cups water	1 teaspoon baking powder
2 tablespoons rum	¼ teaspoon salt
2 tablespoons brandy	2½ cups uncooked rolled oats,
½ cup shortening	quick or old-fashioned
1 cup firmly packed brown	½ cup coconut
sugar	1 cup chopped nuts

ORANGE SUGAR GLAZE:

¼ cup orange juice	1¾ cups sifted powdered sugar

Toast pecan halves in 350° oven about 8 to 10 minutes. Cool. In small saucepan crumble mincemeat; add water. Cook and stir over medium heat until lumps are thoroughly broken. Add rum and brandy and cook 1 minute. Cool. Beat together shortening and sugar until creamy. Add egg and mincemeat. Mix well. Sift together flour, baking powder and salt. Add to creamed mixture; mix well. Stir in oats, coconut and nuts. Drop by teaspoon onto greased cookie sheet. Bake in preheated oven at 350° for 12 to 15 minutes. Cool slightly. Brush with glaze and press pecan half on each. Yields 44 cookies.

GLAZE: Mix together orange juice and powdered sugar; beat well.

Mrs. Sam C. Laden, Jr. (Mary Lou)

Six Threes Ice Cream

3 oranges, juice only	3 cups milk
3 bananas, mashed	3 cups whipping cream or
3 lemons, juice only	half-and-half
3 cups sugar	Dash salt

Mix well and freeze in 1 gallon ice cream freezer.

Mrs. James Thompson (Charlotte)

Pineapple Cheesecake Bars

CRUST:
1 cup flour
½ cup margarine or butter, softened
½ cup sugar
1 teaspoon grated orange peel
1 teaspoon grated lemon peel

FILLING:
1 package (8 ounces) cream cheese, softened
¼ cup sugar
2 tablespoons milk
1 teaspoon vanilla
1 egg, slightly beaten
1 can (8 ounces) crushed pineapple, well drained
1 tablespoon margarine or butter, melted
1 cup coconut

CRUST: Preheat oven to 350°. Combine all ingredients until crumbly. Press mixture into 9 inch square pan. Bake at 350° for 20 to 25 minutes or until light golden brown. Cool.

FILLING: Combine cream cheese and sugar. Mix well. Blend in milk, vanilla, egg and pineapple. Pour mixture over baked crust. Combine margarine, coconut and sprinkle evenly over filling. Bake at 350° for 18 to 22 minutes or until top is light golden brown and filling is set. Cool completely, before cutting into bars. Store tightly covered in refrigerator. Yields 24 bars.

Mrs. Alice Wagnon

Potato Chip Cookies

1 cup margarine
1 cup firmly packed brown sugar
1 cup sugar
2 eggs, well beaten
2 cups flour
1 teaspoon soda
2 cups crushed potato chips
1 package (6 ounces) butterscotch bits

Cream margarine and sugars. Add eggs, flour and soda and mix well. Add potato chips and butterscotch bits. Shape into balls the size of walnuts. Bake at 350° on ungreased cookie sheet for 10 to 12 minutes. Makes 6 dozen.

Mrs. Richard Hatch (Arlene)

Peanut Butter Cups

1 Pillsbury Refrigerated Peanut Butter Cookie roll

36 bite size Reese's Peanut Butter Cups
Pam Spray

Spray miniature muffin pans with Pam. Make 36 balls out of the cookie dough, following the directions on the cookie package. Drop one cookie ball in each muffin cup and bake at 350° for 10 minutes. While cookies bake, remove wrappers from Reese's Peanut Butter Cups. When cookies are removed from the oven, they will fall. Immediately place a peanut butter cup in the middle of each cookie. Press them in a little. Let cookies cool before removing from pan. Yields 36.

Mrs. Heriberto M. Gonzalez (Laura)

Peanut Butter Round-Ups

1 cup soft shortening
1 cup granulated sugar
1 cup brown sugar
2 eggs
1 cup peanut butter

2 cups flour
½ teaspoon salt
2 teaspoons soda
1 cup rolled oats, uncooked

Cream shortening and sugars until light and fluffy. Add eggs and beat well. Blend in peanut butter. Sift together flour, salt and soda; stir into peanut butter mixture. Stir in oats. Roll dough to form small balls, place on ungreased cookie sheets. With tines of fork press to make crisscross on each. Bake in 375° oven 8 to 10 minutes. Yields 5 to 6 dozen.

Mrs. Lloyd G. Jones (Marilyn)

Strawberry Sherbet

4 cups mashed strawberries
2 cups sugar

2 cups buttermilk

Mix together all ingredients. Put in shallow container in freezer portion of refrigerator. When frozen, break up and beat. Refreeze. *A wonderfully refreshing dessert and very simple to make. Never mention the buttermilk and no one will guess it's in it!*

Mrs. Bill Heaton (Gladys)

Pecan Bars

CRUST:

½ cup margarine
½ cup firmly packed brown
  sugar

1½ cups flour

TOPPING:

3 eggs, beaten
1½ cups firmly packed brown
  sugar
¼ cup flour
¼ teaspoon salt

1 teaspoon baking powder
1½ cups coconut
1 cup pecans
1 teaspoon vanilla

CRUST: Cream margarine and sugar. Stir in flour. Spread into 9x13 inch pan. Bake 15 minutes at 350°.

TOPPING: Beat eggs until foamy. Add brown sugar. Beat until thick. Add remaining ingredients and mix well. Spread on crust. Bake 25 to 30 minutes at 350°. Cool. Cut with wet sharp knife.

Mrs. Richard Williams (Wanda)

Refrigerator Cookies

1 cup shortening
1 cup sugar
1 cup firmly packed brown
  sugar
2 eggs
1 teaspoon vanilla

1½ cups flour
1 teaspoon salt
1 teaspoon soda
3 cups oatmeal
½ cup nuts

Cream shortening and sugars. Add egg and vanilla. Beat well. Add sifted flour, salt, soda and oatmeal. Add nuts and mix well. Shape in rolls, wrap in wax paper and chill thoroughly. Slice ¼ inch thick. Bake on ungreased cookie sheet at 350° for 15 minutes. Yields 2 dozen cookies.

Mrs. Lewis Eidson (Mary John)

TEXAS A&M UNIVERSITY
MEMORIAL STUDENT CENTER

Pride and dignity fill the hearts of Aggie faithful when entering the Texas A&M University Memorial Student Center. Dedicated to those who have made possible the freedom and opportunity exemplified by Texas A&M University, this beautiful activity-filled setting is a favorite of Aggie families and friends as they relish the full flavor of campus life.

Elegant Corps unit guidons accentuate the beauty of the student lounge area for a tasteful setting of baked creations certain to command aromatically the attention of every Aggie. A gift of the Texas Federation of A&M Mothers' Clubs to Texas A&M University, the graceful and handsome silver service and matching silver pieces, presented by the former students accentuate delectable dessert selections on display here. Maroon and white standards overlook discriminating settings and dedicated family gatherings, each a vibrant element of life at Texas A&M University.

COLOR PHOTOGRAPHY:
Rick Cook, Food Stylist and Floral Designer
Michael Wilson, Photographer
Floriculture Department, Texas A&M University: Flowers
Mrs. Charlene Isbell, Original Cake Designs: Petits Fours

PARTY FARE pictured: Tea Time Tassies (p. 284), Delicious Nut Cookies (p. 276), Spiced Pecans (p. 328), Petits Fours, Strawberries, Jarlsberg Cheese, Green and Red Grapes, and mints.

Simone's Nutjammer Cookies

1 cup butter	2 cups finely chopped walnuts
1 package (8 ounces) cream cheese	1 jar (12 ounces) apricot or peach jam
2 cups sifted Gold Medal flour	2 teaspoons sugar
½ teaspoon baking powder	⅓ cup powdered sugar

Cream butter and cheese. Sift flour and baking powder and add to creamed mixture. Chill dough 2 to 3 hours. Preheat oven to 375°. Mix nuts, jam and sugar and set aside. Divide dough into 4 equal parts; work with ¼ dough at a time. Refrigerate remaining dough. Roll dough very thin (1/16 inch) on lightly floured cloth covered board; cloth is optional. Cut 2 inch square of dough and place on baking sheet. Place 1 teaspoon nut mixture in center of square and top with another square of dough. *PRESS EDGES TOGETHER* with floured tines of fork. Bake 15 to 20 minutes, or until browned lightly. When completely cooled, sprinkle tops with powdered sugar. Makes about 5 dozen.

Mrs. Jack Starry (Dorothy)

Skillet Cookies

½ cup butter	1 teaspoon vanilla
1 package (8 ounces) dates, diced	1 cup chopped nuts
1 cup sugar	4 to 6 cups Rice Krispies
2 eggs, beaten	1 can (3½ ounces) coconut

Place butter, dates and sugar in skillet. Cook over moderate heat, stirring constantly, until butter, dates and sugar are blended. Add eggs very slowly so they will not curdle. Cook for 15 minutes. Remove from heat and add vanilla and nuts. Add Rice Krispies, 1 cup at a time. Form into balls the size of walnuts and roll lightly in coconut. Yields 6 dozen. *These are very similar to cookies that Original Cake Designs and Neiman's make.*

Mrs. John B. Isbell (Charlene)

Variation: Reduce butter to ¼ cup plus 1 tablespoon, use ½ cup brown sugar and ½ cup granulated sugar. Decrease Rice Krispies to 2½ cups, omit vanilla. Yields 2 dozen.

Mrs Glinn H. White (Bettyeann)

Marion's Sugar Cookies

1½ cups powdered sugar	½ teaspoon almond extract
1 cup butter or margarine	2½ cups sifted flour
1 egg	1 teaspoon cream of tartar
1 teaspoon vanilla	1 teaspoon soda

Cream together sugar and butter. Add egg, vanilla and almond extract. Sift together and stir in flour, cream of tartar and soda; refrigerate 2 to 3 hours. Preheat oven to 375°. Divide dough, roll out and cut into desired shapes. Place on lightly greased baking sheets and bake 7 to 8 minutes or until lightly browned. *The best Christmas cookie recipe I have found.* Yields 7 dozen.

Mrs. Duane C. Uhri (Delores)

Variation: Omit ½ teaspoon almond extract.

Mrs. Robert Fredrickson (Mary Ann)

Soft Sugar Cookies

2 cups sugar	1 cup shortening
4 cups flour	3 eggs
Pinch salt	1 teaspoon vanilla
1 teaspoon soda	½ cup milk
3 teaspoons baking powder	

In bowl, mix dry ingredients. Mix in shortening as for pie dough. In separate bowl, beat together eggs, vanilla and milk. Blend with dry ingredients. Drop on greased cookie sheet. Bake at 400° about 9 to 12 minutes. *Keep in covered container to stay soft.*

Mrs. Arlene Shea

Applesauce Spice Cake

½ cup butter or margarine
2 cups sugar
2 eggs
2 cups applesauce
2 cups flour
2 teaspoons soda

2 teaspoons cinnamon
½ teaspoon cloves
½ teaspoon allspice
½ teaspoon nutmeg
1 cup finely chopped
  walnuts or pecans

PENUCHE ICING:
¾ cup butter or margarine
1½ cups firmly packed light
  brown sugar
6 tablespoons half-and-half

2½ to 3 cups powdered sugar,
  sifted
½ cup chopped nuts

CAKE: Cream together butter and sugar; add eggs beating until light and fluffy. Stir in applesauce. Sift together flour, soda and spices. Gradually add to applesauce mixture and stir until batter is smooth. Stir in nuts. Pour batter into greased and floured 9x13 inch pan. Bake at 350° for 45 minutes or until done. Cool; frost with penuche icing.

ICING: Melt butter and stir in brown sugar. Bring to boil, stirring constantly and cook for 2 minutes. Stir in half-and-half; bring to boil again. Remove from heat. Cool and gradually stir in powdered sugar. Beat until spreading consistency. Ice cake and garnish with chopped nuts.

Mrs. James E. Keeling (Betty)

Fantastic Bundt Cake

2 cups sugar
2 cups flour
1 cup margarine
5 eggs

1 tablespoon flavoring (1
  teaspoon each vanilla,
  almond and lemon, if
  desired)

Ingredients must be at room temperature. Preheat oven to 325°. Grease Bundt pan generously, even teflon pan. Combine sugar, flour, margarine and eggs and beat until smooth, about 10 minutes. Pour into Bundt pan and bake for about 1 hour. *You will note there is no baking powder, milk or baking soda, just simple 2-2-1-5-1 formula. The eggs leaven the cake. It may be glazed, if desired, but we prefer it plain.*

Mrs. Thomas G. Withey (Marilyn)

Kim's Carrot Cake

2　cups sugar
1½ cups Wesson oil
2　cups flour
2　teaspoons baking powder
2　teaspoons baking soda

1　teaspoon cinnamon
1　teaspoon salt
4　eggs, beaten
3　cups grated carrots
1　cup chopped pecans

ICING:
½　cup butter, softened
2　packages (3 ounces each)
　　cream cheese, softened

3　cups powdered sugar
2　teaspoons vanilla

Mix sugar and oil. Add flour, baking powder, soda, cinnamon, salt, then eggs. Mix well and add carrots and pecans. Pour into 3 buttered and floured 9 inch cake pans. Bake at 350° about 25 minutes. Remove from pans and cool.

ICING: Blend butter and cream cheese together. While beating, add powdered sugar and vanilla. Beat until smooth. Serves 12 to 16.

Mrs. Bill Hall (Janey)

Christmas Welcome Cake

1　package (8 ounces)
　　chopped dates
1　teaspoon soda
1　cup hot water
1　cup butter or margarine
1　cup sugar
2　eggs, beaten
1¾ cups flour

Pinch salt
2　tablespoons cocoa
1　teaspoon vanilla
1　package (12 ounces)
　　chocolate chips
½　cup pecans
1　cup whipping cream,
　　whipped

Mix dates, soda and water. Heat to boiling point and remove from heat. Cream margarine and sugar. Add eggs. Stir together flour, salt and cocoa. Combine the 3 mixtures until well blended. Stir in vanilla. Pour batter into greased and floured 9x13 inch pan. Sprinkle ½ package chocolate chips over batter and bake at 350° for 5 minutes. Sprinkle other half package chocolate chips and pecans over cake. Return to oven and bake 25 to 30 minutes. Cut in squares and serve plain or with whipping cream.

Mrs. Laura Wilkinson

Chocolate Cake

2 cups buttermilk
2 teaspoons soda
½ cup Crisco (original recipe called for lard)
2 cups sugar

2 eggs, beaten
1 teaspoon vanilla
5 tablespoons cocoa
2 cups flour
Pinch salt

FROSTING:
½ cup butter or margarine, softened
1 egg yolk, beaten
4 tablespoons coffee or hot water

4 tablespoons cocoa
1 teaspoon vanilla
1 box (16 ounces) powdered sugar

Combine buttermilk and soda and set aside. In large bowl, cream Crisco and sugar. Add eggs and vanilla. Sift together cocoa, flour and salt. Add alternately with buttermilk to creamed mixture. Pour batter into 3 greased and floured 8 or 9 inch cake pans. Bake at 350° for 30 to 40 minutes. *Use ½ recipe for 8½x3⅝ inch loaf cake.*

FROSTING: Beat together all ingredients except powdered sugar. Add powdered sugar, continuing to beat until of spreading consistency. Frost cooled cake layers.

Mrs. Ralph Plumlee (Stella)

Luscious Hot Fudge Sauce

1 package (12 ounces) milk chocolate chips (Hershey or Nestlé)
1 can (14 ounces) Eagle Brand milk

1 can light Karo syrup (use empty Eagle Brand can)
1 cup butter, *not margarine*

Melt all ingredients in double boiler. Stir and simmer 30 minutes. Beat 5 minutes and serve. *This tops Baskin Robbins. Try it and see!*

Mrs. Don Bowen (Carolyn)

Kahlua Chocolate Almond Cake

7½ ounces finely ground
  unblanched almonds
5 eggs, separated plus 2
    yolks

¾ cup sugar
Pinch salt
¾ cup Kahlua

FROSTING:
1 package (6 ounces)
    semisweet chocolate chips
2 teaspoons instant coffee

¼ cup Kahlua
Red and green candied
  cherries

Beat egg whites until foamy. Gradually beat in ¼ cup sugar until stiff. Beat egg yolks with ½ cup sugar to a pale lemon color. Add almonds, salt and ½ cup Kahlua. Mix well and fold gently into egg whites. Pour into greased 9 inch springform pan, bottom lined with greased wax paper. Bake at 300° for 45 minutes. Loosen sides of cake from pan with sharp knife. Cook 5 minutes. Remove sides, invert on rack to remove paper. Turn over and cool. Drizzle cake with ¼ cup Kahlua before frosting.

FROSTING: Melt chocolate chips in double boiler. Cool slightly. Gradually stir in instant coffee dissolved in Kahlua. Mix well. Chill until spreadable. Frost and decorate with candied cherries alternating colors. *This cake was made twice and stacked for 2 layer birthday cake. Delicious. Serve with 1 ounce Kahlua in cup of hot black coffee topped with whipped cream.*

Aggie Mom

To Insure Level Cakes

To be sure of getting level cakes, you can cut out strips of terrycloth twice the height of the side of your cake pan and about an inch longer than the circumference. Fold it in half to exactly the height of the cake pan, then wet it, wring it out and place around outside edge of cake pan. Pin loose ends overlapping.

If wet, this will not burn in your oven. The reason most cakes "hump" in the middle is that the outer edges cook first (area exposed to pan heat); therefore, the batter must go to the middle to continue to rise. By wrapping your pans you will have level heat, allowing the cake to bake level.

Mrs. John B. Isbell (Charlene)

White Chocolate Cake

¼ pound white chocolate	2½ cups flour
½ cup boiling water	1 teaspoon soda
1 cup butter	1 cup buttermilk
2 cups sugar	1 cup chopped pecans
4 eggs, separated	1 can (3½ ounces) coconut
1 teaspoon vanilla	

ICING:

1 can (13 ounces) Pet milk	1 teaspoon vanilla
1 cup sugar	1 can (3½ ounces) coconut
4 tablespoons butter	1 cup chopped pecans
3 egg yolks	

WHITE CHOCOLATE CREAM CHEESE FROSTING:

4 ounces white chocolate	1 teaspoon vanilla
2 teaspoons milk	1 cup chopped pecans
¼ cup butter	1 pound powdered sugar
1 package (8 ounces) cream cheese	

Melt white chocolate slivers in boiling water. Set aside to cool. Cream butter and sugar until fluffy. Mix in egg yolks, 1 at a time, beating well after each addition. Add chocolate and vanilla. Sift together flour and soda. Add to chocolate mixture alternately with buttermilk. Do not over cream. Fold in egg whites, beaten but not stiff. Gently stir in pecans and coconut. Makes three 8 or 9 inch layers. Bake at 350° approximately 25 minutes. Frost either with icing *or* white chocolate cream cheese frosting.

ICING: Combine milk, sugar and butter and bring to boil, stirring constantly. Blend beaten egg yolks into cooked mixture. Add vanilla. Cook until thick over low heat, about 15 minutes. Remove from heat and add coconut and pecans. Beat until fluffy and of spreading consistency.

FROSTING: Melt chocolate in double boiler with milk and butter. Add cream cheese, vanilla, pecans and powdered sugar and beat well. Spread.

Mrs. Jack Starry (Dorothy)

If allowed to become moist, baking powder loses its leavening powers. Check by placing 1 teaspoon baking powder in a glass of water. Should bubble actively.

Wacky Chocolate Cake

2¼ cups flour, sifted
4½ tablespoons cocoa
1½ teaspoons soda
1½ cups sugar
¾ teaspoon salt

7½ tablespoons oil
1½ tablespoons vinegar
1½ teaspoons vanilla
1½ cups cold water

CREAMY CHOCOLATE FROSTING:
3 tablespoons butter or
　margarine
½ cup cocoa
⅓ cup milk

1½ teaspoons vanilla
3½ cups powdered sugar,
　sifted
⅛ teaspoon salt

Grease a 9x13 inch pan. Sift dry ingredients into it. Make three holes (small, medium, large) with back of spoon. Put vanilla in small hole, vinegar in medium hole and oil in large hole. Pour water over all and stir or beat slightly with spoon until well blended and you can't see the flour! Bake at 350° for 30 minutes. Frost when cool with creamy chocolate frosting.

FROSTING: Melt butter and stir in cocoa. Add milk and vanilla. Mix sugar with salt and add gradually to chocolate mixture, blending well.

Mrs. Fred D. Sewell (Ann)

Cathy's Diabetic Cake

2 cups flour
2 teaspoons soda
½ cup butter or margarine
1 egg
1 tablespoon Sweet'n Low
1 teaspoon vanilla

1 cup chopped dates or
　prunes
1½ cups unsweetened apple
　sauce
1 cup chopped pecans
1 teaspoon cinnamon
¼ teaspoon cloves

Sift flour and soda; set aside. Cream butter, egg, sweetener and vanilla. Add dates, apple sauce and pecans. Mix well. Add flour mixture, cinnamon and cloves and beat with electric mixer. Pour in greased 9x5x3 loaf or 10 inch Bundt pan. Bake at 350° for 1 hour.

Mrs. William O. Petty (Marye Jo)

Foolproof Delicious Fruitcake

1 box (18.5 ounces) spice
  cake mix
¼ cup flour
4 cups mixed candied fruit
1 package (8 ounces) pitted
  dates, chopped

1½ cups raisins
2 cups coarsely chopped
  walnuts
1¾ cups brandied mincemeat
3 eggs
Sherry, brandy or cider,
  optional

Grease 2 large loaf or 2 ring pans and line with brown paper. Grease again. In a very large bowl mix together ¾ cup cake mix, candied fruit, dates, raisins and walnuts. Blend remaining cake mix with mincemeat, egg and flour. Add this to fruit and nut mixture. Blend well. Spoon mixture into pans. Place a pan of water in the oven while the cakes bake to keep them moist. Bake at 350° until done, approximately 2 hours. Cool. Peel off brown paper. Brush with sherry, brandy or cider. Wrap in plastic paper, then in foil. Keep in airtight containers or in the freezer.

Mrs. Heriberto M. Gonzalez (Laura)

Lemon Fruitcake

1¾ cups margarine
2 cups sugar
6 eggs, beaten
4 cups flour
2 teaspoons baking powder
1 teaspoon salt

1 bottle (2 ounces) lemon
  extract
1 cup candied cherries
1 cup candied pineapple
1 pound pecans

Blend margarine and sugar until fluffy and add eggs. Sift flour, baking powder and salt. Add small amount at a time to creamed mixture. Beat 2 minutes. Add lemon extract, candied fruit and pecans. Beat just until fruit and pecans are blended. Pour into greased and floured 10 inch tube pan. Bake at 350° for 1 hour. Remove from oven and cool 10 minutes. Run knive around edge and turn out on plate.

Mrs. Gerald E. Dixon (Jane)

Fresh Pear Cake

2 cups sugar	1 teaspoon salt
3 eggs, well beaten	1 teaspoon vanilla
1½ cups salad oil	2 teaspoons cinnamon
3 cups flour	3 cups thinly sliced pears
1 teaspoon soda	

POWDERED SUGAR GLAZE:

1¼ cups powdered sugar, 2 to 4 tablespoons milk
    sifted

Combine sugar, eggs and oil. Beat well. Combine flour, soda and salt. Add to sugar mixture, 1 cup at a time, mixing well after each addition. Stir in vanilla, cinnamon and pears. Spoon batter into greased 10 inch Bundt or tube pan. Bake at 350° for 1 hour. Remove from pan and allow to cool; top with powdered sugar glaze, if desired.

GLAZE: Combine sugar and milk, blending until smooth. Makes ½ cup.

Mrs. J. Hal Brown (Eva Gay)

Pineapple Wonder Cake

1 box (18.25 ounces) yellow cake mix	1 package (3¾ ounces) vanilla instant pudding
1 can (20 ounces) crushed pineapple	3 bananas, sliced
1½ cups sugar	1 carton (8 ounces) Cool Whip
1 package (8 ounces) cream cheese	¾ cup coconut
	¼ cup chopped pecans
	1½ cups milk

Bake cake as directed on package in 8½x13½ glass dish. Combine pineapple and sugar in saucepan and bring to boil. Spread on cake while hot. When cake has cooled, mix cream cheese, pudding mix and milk until smooth and spreadable. *Do not cook.* Spread over pineapple layer. Arrange sliced bananas on top. Frost with Cool Whip and garnish with pecans. Refrigerate. Better if made 2 to 3 days in advance. Serves 16.

Mrs. Wm. Fuhrmeister (Sophia)

Coconut Pound Cake

½ cup margarine
⅔ cup Crisco
3 cups sugar
5 eggs
1½ teaspoons coconut extract
3 cups flour

½ teaspoon salt
1 teaspoon baking powder
1 cup milk
1 cup Baker's Angel Flake coconut

Cream margarine, Crisco and sugar. Add eggs one at a time; beat well. Add coconut extract. Add flour, salt and baking powder alternately with milk, mixing well after each addition. Add coconut and mix well. Pour into greased and floured 10 inch Bundt pan or use two 9x5 inch loaf pans. Bake at 325° for 1 hour or until done. Cool on rack for 10 to 15 minutes. *Makes nice loaf cakes to give at Christmas.*

Mrs. John J. Jones (Geraine)

Grandmother's Pound Cake

1¼ cups butter, not margarine
2 cups sugar
5 eggs

2 cups flour
½ teaspoon vanilla
1 teaspoon lemon juice

Mix softened butter with sugar. Add eggs 1 at a time. Beat. Add flour, vanilla and lemon juice. Beat until smooth. Bake in greased 10 inch tube pan at 350° for 45 minutes or until done.

Mrs. Bobby Greenwood (Judy)

Variation: Decrease butter to 1 cup, vanilla to ½ teaspoon. Omit 1 teaspoon lemon juice. Add 6 ounce package chocolate chips, 1 cup flaked coconut, 1 cup chopped pecans.

TOPPING:
¾ cup sugar
¾ cup water

¼ cup margarine
1 teaspoon almond extract

In saucepan, combine sugar and water. Boil 3 minutes. Remove, add margarine and almond extract. Blend. Pierce cake with meat fork and spread topping with pastry brush. Super moist. Freezes well.

Mrs. James E. Keeling (Betty)

Prune Cake

1½ cups sugar
1 cup Wesson oil
3 eggs
1 teaspoon soda
1 teaspoon baking powder
1 cup buttermilk
1 teaspoon salt

1 teaspoon allspice
1 teaspoon nutmeg
1 teaspoon cloves
2 cups flour
1 cup cooked, mashed prunes
1 cup chopped pecans

BROWN SUGAR FROSTING:
1 cup firmly packed brown sugar
½ cup milk

2 tablespoons butter
3 tablespoons Crisco
2 cups sifted powdered sugar

Cream together sugar and oil. Add eggs, 1 at a time, mixing well. Add soda and baking powder to buttermilk; combine with egg mixture. Sift salt, allspice, nutmeg, cloves, flour and add to creamed mixture, mixing well. Stir in prunes and pecans. Pour into two 9 inch layer pans or 1 greased and floured 9x13 inch pan. Bake layers at 350° for 35 to 40 minutes or larger pan for 45 to 50 minutes. Cool 10 minutes in pan and finish cooling on rack. Frost with brown sugar frosting.

FROSTING: Mix sugar, milk, butter and Crisco in saucepan and boil for 1 minute. Beat in powdered sugar until mixture is smooth. Spread between layers and on top and sides of cake. *These recipes were given to me at my bridal tea 26 years ago and I've never found one better for either. Guests always give compliments and want the recipes.*

Mrs. Lee Radford (Betty)

Sugarplum Cake

2 cups sugar
2 cups self-rising flour
1 cup oil
3 eggs

2 jars (4½ ounces each) baby food plums with tapioca
1 teaspoon cinnamon
1 teaspoon cloves
1 cup chopped pecans

Mix all ingredients and pour into a generously greased 10 inch Bundt pan coated with sugar. Bake at 325° for 1 hour or until done. Cool for 10 minutes before removing from pan. Serves 12.

Mrs. L.A. Rowlett (Jo)

Pumpkin Jelly Roll

3 eggs
1 cup sugar
⅔ cup pumpkin
1 teaspoon lemon juice
¾ cup flour

1 teaspoon baking powder
½ teaspoon salt
2 teaspoons pumpkin pie
spice
1 cup chopped pecans

FILLING:
1 package (8 ounces) cream
cheese
1 cup powdered sugar

¼ cup butter or margarine
½ teaspoon vanilla

Beat eggs on low speed of mixer for 5 minutes. Add sugar slowly and beat. Fold pumpkin and lemon juice into sugar mixture. Fold in flour, baking powder, salt and pumpkin pie spice. Put wax paper in 15x10 inch jelly roll pan and pour batter into pan. Sprinkle with pecans or other nuts. Bake at 375° for 15 minutes. Remove and put on towel sprinkled with powdered sugar. Pull off wax paper and roll up. Let cool.

FILLING: Mix together all ingredients. Unroll jelly roll, spread with filling and roll again. Refrigerate. *A pleasant change from pumpkin pie at Thanksgiving.*

Mrs. Duane Uhri (Delores)

Sour Cream Pound Cake

1 cup butter
3 cups sugar
6 eggs, separated
1 carton (8 ounces) sour
cream

¼ teaspoon soda (can use ½
teaspoon)
3 cups flour
1 to 2 teaspoons vanilla
1 teaspoon almond extract

Cream well butter and sugar. Add 1 egg yolk at a time. Mix soda and sour cream and add alternately with flour to butter mixture. Fold in beaten egg whites and flavorings. Bake in lightly greased 10 inch Bundt pan for 1 to 1½ hours at 300°.

Mrs. Rex Corey (Robyn)

Linda's Pumpkin Cake

1 cup butter	1 teaspoon allspice
2¾ cups sugar	1 teaspoon cloves
3 eggs, beaten	1 teaspoon cinnamon
3 cups flour	1 tablespoon vanilla
½ teaspoon baking powder	1 cup buttermilk
1½ teaspoons salt	1 can (16 ounces) pumpkin
1 teaspoon soda	1 cup pecans
1 teaspoon nutmeg	

GLAZE:

½ cup sugar	½ cup orange juice

Cream butter and sugar. Add eggs and mix well. Combine all dry ingredients. Stir into batter alternately with buttermilk and vanilla. Stir pumpkin into batter. Add pecans and pour into 10 inch Bundt pan. Bake at 350° for 1½ hours. Let cool for 20 minutes. Remove from pan and add glaze. *The best pumpkin cake I've tasted.*

GLAZE: Combine sugar and orange juice. Boil 5 minutes. Poke holes in cake. Dribble glaze over cake.

Mrs. Bill Heaton (Gladys)

Pineapple Nut Pound Cake

½ cup flaked coconut	1 package (18.5 ounces)
½ cup chopped nuts	super moist yellow cake
2 tablespoons butter or	mix
margarine, melted	¾ cup water
1 can (13½ ounces) crushed	¼ cup vegetable oil
pineapple	3 eggs

Mix coconut, nuts and margarine and sprinkle in pan. Drain pineapple, reserving ¼ cup juice. Beat cake mix, water, reserved pineapple juice, oil and eggs on low speed. Beat 2 minutes on medium speed. Pour batter into greased and floured 10 inch Bundt pan. Spoon pineapple evenly over batter. Bake in 350° oven for 45 to 50 minutes or until done. Cool about 20 minutes and remove from pan.

Mrs. Tom J. Lymenstull (Wanda)

Pumpkin Cake

2 cups sugar	2 teaspoons baking powder
1¼ cups cooking oil	2 teaspoons cinnamon
2 cups canned pumpkin	1 teaspoon salt
4 eggs	1 cup coconut
2 cups flour	1 cup chopped nuts
2 teaspoons soda	

ICING:

¼ cup butter, softened	2½ cups powdered sugar
2 packages (3 ounces) cream cheese, softened	1 teaspoon vanilla

Mix sugar, oil, pumpkin and eggs. Sift together flour, soda, baking powder, cinnamon and salt. Add to sugar mixture. Fold in coconut and chopped nuts. Pour batter into greased 1 pound coffee cans, filling until half full. Bake at 350° for 35 to 40 minutes. Yields approximately 5 loaves. *Batter may be baked in loaf pans.*

ICING: Mix well butter, cream cheese, sugar and vanilla. Spread on cooled cake.

Mrs. Jerry L. Ewing (Claudette)

Snowballs

1 quart vanilla ice cream	2 cups Baker's Angel Flake coconut, toasted

HOT CHOCOLATE SAUCE:

1 square (3 ounces) semisweet chocolate, cut in small pieces	½ cup strong coffee

Scoop 6 balls of ice cream with 2½ inch scoop. Dip scoop in hot water between each scoop. Freeze on wax paper lined baking sheet. On another sheet spread coconut and toast until golden for 10 to 12 minutes at 350°, stirring occasionally. Cool. Roll balls in coconut; freeze until ready to use.

SAUCE: Melt chocolate in top of double boiler with coffee and keep warm over hot water. If sauce is too thick, add a little coffee or cognac. Yields 1½ cups. Serve over Snowballs.

Mrs. Eugene E. Frantz (Mary)

Bavarian Orange Cake

1 cup margarine	Rind of 1 lemon, grated
1 cup sugar	2 cups flour
3 eggs, separated	1 teaspoon baking powder
¾ cup sour cream	½ teaspoon soda
Rind of 1 orange, grated	1 cup ground walnuts

ORANGE CREAM CHEESE FROSTING:

1 package (3 ounces) cream cheese, softened	1½ cups powdered sugar, sifted
1 tablespoon margarine, softened	1 to 2 teaspoons milk, if needed
¼ teaspoon grated orange peel	

Cream well margarine and sugar with mixer. Add egg yolks, one at a time, beating well after each addition. Stir in sour cream, orange and lemon rinds. Sift together on wax paper: flour, baking powder and soda. Add to creamed mixture, ½ cup at a time. Fold in walnuts. Beat egg whites and salt until stiff. Fold into batter gently but thoroughly. Pour into buttered and floured 10 inch tube pan and bake at 350° for 50 minutes. Let stand 5 minutes. Turn out on rack. Frost with orange cream cheese frosting.

FROSTING: Beat cream cheese, margarine and peel until light and fluffy. Gradually add sugar, beating until fluffy and of spreading consistency. If too thick, add milk and blend.

Mrs. Mary H. Frantz

Orange Ice

2 cups water	2 teaspoons finely grated orange rind
2 cups sugar, scant	6 to 8 fresh mint leaves, optional
2 cups orange juice	
⅓ cup lemon juice	

Soak sugar in water while grating orange rind. (A few crushed fresh mint leaves may be steeped in this water and removed later.) Add orange juice, lemon juice and orange rind. Stir until sugar is dissolved. Freeze in 4 ounce Dixie cups. Hammer in popsicle sticks when firm or freeze in ice tray with cube dividers. Cubes may be broken and beaten in strong mixer to make sherbet.

Mrs. L. B. Terry (Jeane)

Mandarin Orange Cake

1 box (18.5 ounces) yellow butter recipe cake mix
4 eggs

1 cup oil
1 can (11 ounces) mandarin oranges, cut

UNCOOKED ICING:
1 box (3 ounces) vanilla instant pudding mix
1 can (11 ounces) crushed pineapple, drained

1 carton (8 ounces) Cool Whip

Combine cake mix, eggs, oil and mandarian oranges. Mix well. Bake in 2 greased and floured 9 inch cake pans for 20 minutes at 350°. Remove from pans and cool.

ICING: Mix pudding and crushed pineapple. Fold in Cool Whip. Place icing on cake and refrigerate until ready to serve. Serves 12 to 16.

Mrs. Charles E. Allen (Bettie)

Variation: For icing, use 1 package (12⅛ ounces) cheese cake filling mix and 1 cup sour cream instead of 1 box vanilla instant pudding mix.

Mrs. Lynn Blair (Yvonne)

Homemade Peach Ice Cream

2 cans (14 ounces each) Eagle Brand milk
½ cup Karo syrup
1 pint half-and-half
Dash salt

1 teaspoon vanilla
1 quart fresh peaches, cut in chunks or 1 can (29 ounces), mashed
Milk

Mix all ingredients except milk. Pour into 1 gallon freezer container and add milk to fill within 1½ inches of top. Ice cream is ready when freezer quits.

Mrs. Don Bowen (Carolyn)

Jam Cake

1	cup butter	1	teaspoon soda
2	cups sugar	1	teaspoon cinnamon
4	eggs	1	teaspoon cloves
1	cup jam or preserves	3	cups flour
1	cup buttermilk	1	cup nuts

Cream butter and sugar. Beat in eggs. Add jam, buttermilk, soda, cinnamon and cloves. Gradually add flour. Mix in nuts. Pour in greased and floured tube cake pan. Bake at 350° for 1½ hours.

Variation: Cake may be baked in 2 loaf pans for approximately 1 hour. Strawberry, peach, blackberry jam or a combination of these jams are excellent for this cake recipe. Serves 12 to 16.

Mrs. Robert Clark (Sylvia)

White Cloud Cake

1	package (18.25 ounces) Duncan Hines white cake mix	1	can (3½ ounces) Baker's Angel Flake coconut
1	carton (8 ounces) Cool Whip	1	can (15 ounces) cream of coconut

Bake cake according to package instructions in 9x13 inch cake pan. While still warm, pierce cake with fork, pour cream of coconut over cake and sprinkle coconut on top. Cool. Spread on Cool Whip and refrigerate 6 to 8 hours. Will keep in refrigerator for several days. Serves 12.

Mrs. William Watson (Elizabeth)

Fudge Cupcakes

½ cup margarine
1 square Baker's
   unsweetened chocolate
2 eggs

1 cup sugar
¾ cup flour
1 teaspoon vanilla
½ cup pecans, optional

Melt margarine and chocolate over low heat. Beat together eggs, sugar and flour and add chocolate mixture. Add vanilla. Place cupcake liners in a 12 muffin tin. Divide batter equally. Bake 30 minutes at 350°. *If desired, place pecans on top before baking.*

Mrs. William B. Heye (Joan)

Toll House Cupcakes

½ cup butter or margarine,
   softened
6 tablespoons sugar
6 tablespoons firmly packed
   brown sugar
½ teaspoon vanilla

1 egg
1 cup plus 2 tablespoons
   flour
½ teaspoon soda
½ teaspoon salt

TOPPING:
½ cup firmly packed brown
   sugar
1 egg
⅛ teaspoon salt

½ teaspoon vanilla
1 package (6 ounces)
   chocolate chips

Combine and beat until creamy: butter, sugars, vanilla and egg. Sift together flour, soda and salt and mix with creamed mixture. Spoon by rounded tablespoon into cupcake paper lined pan. Bake at 375° 10 to 12 minutes. Remove from oven and put about 1 tablespoon of topping on each cupcake. Bake at 375° for 15 minutes.

TOPPING: Combine sugar, egg, salt and vanilla and beat until thick. Stir in chocolate chips. Yields 16 cupcakes.

Mrs. James D. Murphy (Rosemary)

Caramel Icing

1　cup firmly packed brown
　　sugar
½　cup granulated sugar
⅓　cup milk
2　tablespoons shortening

2　tablespoons butter
1　tablespoon Karo syrup
Pinch salt
1　teaspoon vanilla

Combine all ingredients except vanilla and slowly bring to rolling boil for 1 minute. Remove from heat and cool. Add vanilla and beat until creamy.

Mrs. H. Smith (Alyne)

Cooked Chocolate Icing

1　cup sugar
¼　cup cocoa
¼　teaspoon salt

¼　cup milk
1　teaspoon vanilla
¼　cup butter or margarine

Mix together in saucepan sugar, cocoa and salt. Add milk, vanilla and butter and let stand 1 minute. Cook on medium high heat until it comes to a boil. Boil for 1 minute. Remove from heat and beat until creamy. Spread immediately on cake. *It does not take much beating to get it to right consistency for spreading. Inexpensive!*

Aggie Mom

Cooked White Frosting

1　cup milk
¼　cup flour
Pinch salt
½　cup Crisco
1　cup sugar

2　teaspoons vanilla
½　cup margarine
1　can (3½ ounces) Baker's
　　Angel Flake coconut

Mix together milk, flour and salt. Cook, stirring constantly, until thick. *Prepare first and allow to cool thoroughly before baking cake.* Beat shortening and sugar at high speed until fluffy. Add cooled mixture and continue beating until light and fluffy. Stir in vanilla. Ice cooled cake and garnish with coconut. *Use with Jerry C. Cooper's Maroon and White Cake in Celebrity Section!*

Mrs. Glinn H. White (Bettyeann)

Cream Cheese Icing

1 package (8 ounces) cream
  cheese
3 tablespoons milk
1½ cups powdered sugar

Beat cream cheese with milk until smooth. Add cinnamon, vanilla and powdered sugar and beat until creamy. Frost when cake is cool.

Aggie Mom

Cheesecake I

6 tablespoons margarine or
  butter, melted
1 package (individual)
  graham crackers
2 tablespoons sugar
1½ teaspoons cinnamon

FILLING:
3 packages (8 ounces each)
  cream cheese
1 cup sugar
3 eggs
½ teaspoon vanilla

CRUST: Roll crackers until fine; add sugar and cinnamon. Mix well. Add melted butter and press into 9 or 10 inch spring form pan.

FILLING: Beat cream cheese until fluffy. Gradually add sugar. Beat in eggs one at a time. Add vanilla. Pour into crust. Bake at 375° for 20 minutes until set in middle. Cool and refrigerate at least 12 hours. Serves 8 to 12.

Mrs. Sydney D. Carter (Margaret)

Variation: CRUST: Decrease butter to 2 tablespoons, sugar to 1 tablespoon and cinnamon to ½ teaspoon.

FILLING: Use 4 eggs and ¼ teaspoon lemon juice and ¼ teaspoon vanilla.

TOPPING:
1 pint sour cream
3 tablespoons sugar
¼ teaspoon vanilla
Dash lemon extract

Combine all ingredients and place carefully on top of filling. Bake 10 minutes. Cool; refrigerate. *Freezes well.*

Mrs. Gerald E. Dixon (Jane)

Cheesecake II

LEMON THIN CRUST:

¼ cup butter

2 tablespoons sugar

½ box lemon thins, crushed

FILLING:

4 packages (8 ounces each) Kraft cream cheese, softened

1½ cups sugar

2 tablespoons flour

⅛ teaspoon salt

6 to 7 large eggs

2 to 3 tablespoons vanilla

TOPPING #1:

1 pint sour cream

4 tablespoons sugar

1 teaspoon vanilla

TOPPING #2:

1 box (10 ounces) frozen strawberries or blueberries

or

1 can (8 ounces) pineapple

3 to 4 tablespoons Minute Tapioca

¼ cup sugar, optional

LEMON THIN CRUST: Mix butter and sugar. Add crushed lemon thin cookies to butter mixture. Pat in greased spring form pan and set in refrigerator until cake is mixed.

FILLING: Mix sugar, flour, salt and set aside. Mix cream cheese until smooth and gradually add sugar mixture. Add one egg at a time, beating after each addition until all eggs are added. Add vanilla and pour in spring form pan which has been lined with lemon thin crust. Bake 1 to 2 hours at 225° until set but not brown. Leave in oven with door ajar until cool. *Do not over cook.*

TOPPING #1: *After cake is done, mix sour cream, sugar and vanilla and spoon on top. Bake 10 minutes more or until set.*

TOPPING #2: *Combine Minute Tapioca, sugar and fruit of your choice. Cook until tapioca is dissolved. Cool. Add to cake in place of sour cream topping.*

Aggie Mom

Miniature Cherry Cheesecake

1 box vanilla wafers
2 packages (8 ounces each) cream cheese
¾ cup sugar
2 eggs
1 tablespoon lemon juice
1 teaspoon vanilla
1 can cherry pie filling

Place vanilla wafer in bottom of paper cupcake holders. Mix together remaining ingredients except pie filling. Fill cupcake holders ¾ full with mixture. Bake at 350° for 15 minutes. Chill. Top with cherries from can of cherry pie filling shortly before serving.

Mrs. Emogene Greenwell

Chocolate Almond Cheesecake

1½ cups chocolate wafer crumbs
2 cups blanched almonds, lightly toasted and chopped
⅓ cup sugar
¾ cup butter, softened
3 packages (8 ounces each) cream cheese, softened
1¼ cups sugar
4 eggs
⅓ cup whipping cream, unwhipped
¼ cup Amaretto
1 teaspoon vanilla
2 cups sour cream
1 tablespoon sugar
1 teaspoon vanilla

Combine chocolate wafer crumbs, 1½ cups almonds, sugar and butter. Press on bottom and sides of 9½ inch buttered spring form pan. In large bowl, cream together cream cheese and sugar; beat in eggs, one at a time, beating well after each addition. Add whipping cream, Amaretto and vanilla and beat mixture until light. Pour batter into shell and bake in preheated 375° oven for 10 minutes. Reduce heat to 275° and bake 1 hour or more until cake is set in middle. Remove from oven and let set for 5 minutes. In bowl, combine sour cream, sugar and vanilla. Spread mixture evenly on cake. Return to oven and bake 5 minutes more. Transfer to rack; cool. Remove sides of pan and press ½ cup toasted almonds around edge and top.

Mrs. Jack Starry (Dorothy)

Jackie's Chocolate Cheesecake

CRUMB CRUST:
1 package (8½ ounces)
  chocolate wafers
⅓ cup butter, melted

2 tablespoons sugar
¼ teaspoon nutmeg

CHEESE FILLING:
3 eggs
1 cup sugar
3 packages (8 ounces each)
  cream cheese, softened
1 package (12 ounces) semisweet chocolate chips,
  melted

1 teaspoon vanilla
⅛ teaspoon salt
1 cup sour cream

TOPPING:
1 cup whipping cream,
  whipped

2 tablespoons powdered
  sugar

CRUST: Crush wafers into fine crumbs and mix with butter, sugar and nutmeg. Press evenly over bottom and sides of 9 inch springform pan. Refrigerate.

FILLING: In mixing bowl beat eggs with sugar until light. Beat in cream cheese until smooth. Add melted chocolate, vanilla, salt and sour cream. Beat until smooth and pour in crust; bake at 350° for 1 hour or until cake is firm. Cool in pan on wire rack. Refrigerate over night, covered.

TOPPING: Beat cream with powdered sugar until stiff. Remove sides of pan. Put cream through decorative tip or put spoonful of cream on top of each serving. Serves 16.

Mrs. J. Hal Brown (Eva Gay)

Sparkly Sherbet

60 ounces carbonated
   beverage of your choice,
   orange, lemon-lime or
   strawberry
1 can (14 ounces) sweetened
   condensed milk

1 can (8 ounces) fruit of
   your choice, crushed
   pineapple or Mandarin
   oranges

Mix together beverage, milk and fruit. Freeze in ice cream freezer.

Aggie Mom

Boston Cream Pie

CAKE:
2 egg whites
½ cup sugar
2¼ cups flour
1 cup sugar
3 teaspoons baking powder

1 teaspoon salt
⅓ cup salad oil
1½ teaspoons vanilla
2 egg yolks
1 cup milk

FRENCH CUSTARD FILLING:
⅓ cup sugar
1 tablespoon flour
1 tablespoon cornstarch
¼ teaspoon salt

1½ cups milk
1 egg yolk, slightly beaten
1 teaspoon vanilla

CHOCOLATE GLOSS:
½ cup sugar
1½ tablespoons cornstarch
1 ounce unsweetened
   chocolate
Dash salt

½ cup boiling water
1½ tablespoons butter
½ teaspoon vanilla

CAKE: Beat egg whites until foamy. Gradually beat in ½ cup sugar. Beat until stiff and glossy. Sift dry ingredients into another bowl. Add salad oil, ½ cup milk and vanilla. Beat 1 minute at medium speed. Add remaining milk and egg yolks. Beat 1 minute. Gently fold in egg white mixture with down up over motion. Bake in paper lined 9 inch cake pans at 350° for 25 minutes. Cool.

FILLING: Mix dry ingredients. Gradually stir in milk. Cook and stir until mixture thickens and boils. Cook and stir 2 to 3 minutes longer. Stir little of hot mixture into egg yolk. Return to hot mixture, stirring constantly. Bring just to boiling. Add vanilla and cool. Beat with wire whisk until smooth. Fill between layers and refrigerate.

GLOSS: Combine sugar, cornstarch, chocolate, salt and water in small saucepan. Cook and stir until blended and thickened. Remove from heat and add butter and vanilla. Pour over top layer while still hot and let drip down sides.

Aggie Mom

Cherry Meringue Dessert

COOKIE CIRCLE:

1¼ cups flour
¼ teaspoon salt
½ teaspoon baking powder
⅓ cup shortening
⅓ cup sugar
2 eggs, separated
1 tablespoon milk
½ cup chopped pecans

CHERRY FILLING:

1 can (16 ounces) red tart pitted cherries, reserve juice
2 tablespoons cornstarch
½ cup sugar
¼ teaspoon almond extract

MERINGUE:

2 egg whites, beaten
½ teaspoon vanilla
¼ teaspoon cream of tartar
4 tablespoons sugar

COOKIE: Sift together flour, salt and baking powder; set aside. Cream shortening and sugar. Blend in unbeaten egg yolks and milk. Beat well. Add dry ingredients. Stir until mixture forms a dough. Press into bottom of well greased 9 inch round cake pan. Reserve 2 tablespoons pecans for top. Sprinkle remainder of nuts over dough. Bake at 375° for 12 to 15 minutes. Cool.

FILLING: Drain cherries into bowl, reserving ¾ cup juice. Blend together cornstarch and sugar in saucepan. Add reserved cherry juice and stir until sugar dissolves. Cook over low heat, stirring constantly, until thick and clear. Remove from heat and add almond extract and cherries. Cool.

MERINGUE: Beat egg whites with vanilla and cream of tartar until soft peaks form. Gradually add sugar, beating until stiff and glossy. Transfer cookie circle to cookie sheet. Drop meringue by tablespoons all around edge, on top of cookie. Fill center with cherry filling and sprinkle chopped pecans over this. Bake at 350° for 12 to 15 minutes. *Delicious for ladies' luncheons or bridge club dessert.* Serves 8.

Mrs. Edward A. Long (Susan)

Coconut Torte

1 package (5½ ounces) Bis-Kit	1 can (3½ ounces) Baker's Angel Flake coconut
1 box (16 ounces) brown sugar	1 cup nuts, chopped
4 eggs	2 teaspoons vanilla
	Whipped topping, optional

Mix well all ingredients. Spread in greased and floured 9x13 inch pan. Bake 30 to 35 minutes in 350° oven. Serve with whipped topping. Serves 12 to 24.

Mrs. S. G. Evetts (Darlene)

Chocolate Mousse

1 package (4 ounces) German's sweet chocolate or semisweet chocolate	Dash salt
4 eggs, separated	1 teaspoon vanilla
¼ cup Land O Lakes unsalted, sweet butter, softened	6 tablespoons sugar
	Whipped cream, sweetened
	Vanilla or creme de cacao

In saucepan, cover chocolate bar with 2 inches of very hot tap water. Place lid on pan and let stand 5 minutes until chocolate is soft. When chocolate is soft, not dissolved, pour off water. Add egg yolks. Stir with whisk and cook over low heat until thick. Remove from heat. Add butter, salt and vanilla. Mix well. Cool but do not allow to become cold. Beat egg whites and gradually add sugar. Mix 1 tablespoon of egg whites into chocolate mixture. Fold in rest of egg whites. Pour into compote or individual serving dishes. Cover with Saran and refrigerate. Top with sweetened whipped cream, to which vanilla or creme de cacao has been added. Serves 6.

Mrs. Emagene Greenwell

Lemon Sponge Pudding

½ cup sugar
2 tablespoons flour
½ teaspoon salt
2 egg yolks, lightly beaten
1 cup milk

2 tablespoons lemon juice
2 teaspoons grated lemon rind
2 egg whites
2 cups whipping cream

Mix together sugar, flour and salt in large bowl. Add beaten egg yolks with milk. Add lemon juice and rind. Beat egg whites until stiff. Fold in. Pour into greased 1 quart souffle dish. Place in pan of hot water. Bake in 350° oven for 45 minutes. Chill. Serve with whipped cream. Serves 4.

Mrs. Jack McAuliff (Betty)

English Trifle Dessert

1 pound cake (16 ounce size)
1 cup strawberry preserves
¾ cup Dry Sack or cooking sherry

½ cup almond slices
2 cups custard sauce
1 cup whipping cream, optional

CUSTARD SAUCE:

⅔ cup sugar
2 tablespoons flour
½ teaspoon salt

6 egg yolks
1 quart milk
1 tablespoon vanilla

Cut cake in finger thickness slices and then half each slice. Rub the bottom of a bread loaf pan with preserves. Place cake slices in pan about 1 inch apart. Add more preserves; sprinkle Dry Sack; add custard; sprinkle almonds. Repeat 3 times and top last layer with strawberries. Chill overnight.

SAUCE: Combine in double boiler sugar, salt and flour. Beat egg yolks slightly and add to dry ingredients. Add ¾ cup milk and mix well, so there are no lumps. Add more milk little by little until full quart is used. Add vanilla. Mixture will thicken. Cool before using. *Our Aggie's favorite dessert.*

Mrs. T. B. Dellinger (Maria)

Tarte Aux Poires (Pear Tarts)

Pâte-Sucrée Short Dough Recipe for Tarte:

½ pound butter	12 pears, skinned
4 ounces sugar	1 pound sugar
1 egg	5 pints water
5 egg yolks	1 vanilla bean or 1 teaspoon
1 teaspoon vanilla	vanilla
1 pound flour	

Combine butter, sugar, egg, egg yolks and vanilla. Add flour and mix well. Place in refrigerator for 3 hours.

To prepare pears, remove skins and cut in half lengthwise. Prepare syrup by mixing and heating sugar, water and vanilla. Cook pears in syrup until done. Strain and let dry. Then add the creme d'almond, pears and meringue.

CREME d'ALMOND:

½ pound almond powder	2 ounces soft sweet butter
6 ounces sugar	1 drop almond extract
4 eggs	

MERINGUE:

4 egg whites	1 drop vanilla
8 ounces sugar	

CREME d'ALMOND: Combine almond powder, sugar, eggs, butter and almond extract. Remove dough from refrigerator. Roll and place in tart mold. Add creme d'almond. Arrange pear halves in circular pattern around mold toward the middle. Bake for 35 minutes at 350°.

MERINGUE: Beat together egg whites, sugar and vanilla until stiff. Place in pastry bag. Squeeze meringue on top of each pear half in tart mold. Bake for 4 minutes at 450°.

Mrs. Marie LaCombe

SPICE HINTS:
Apple pie—cinnamon
Cherry pie—mace or nutmeg
Chocolate cake—cinnamon, nutmeg, cloves
Grapefruit halves—ginger, coconut
Peach pie—cinnamon

Pears—sugar, cinnamon
Pineapple—cinnamon
Rice pudding—apple pie spice
Spice cake—instant coffee
Sugar cookies—anise

Old Indiana Persimmon Pudding

2 cups persimmon pulp
3 eggs
1¼ cups sugar
1½ cups flour
1 teaspoon baking powder
1 teaspoon soda
½ teaspoon salt

½ cup butter or margarine, melted
2½ cups milk
2 teaspoons cinnamon
1 teaspoon ginger
½ teaspoon nutmeg

Mix all ingredients. Batter will be thin. Pour into 13x18 inch glass dish. Bake for 1 hour at 325°. Pudding is done when a knife blade inserted into pudding comes out clean. This is a creamy tasting pudding, more the consistency of a souffle. The spices may be decreased or omitted as desired. *I have substituted peach pulp and also had a delicious pudding.* Serves 6 to 8.

Mrs. T. B. Dellinger (Maria)

Strawberry Pretzel Dessert

3 tablespoons sugar
2 cups broken pretzel sticks
¾ cup butter, melted
1 package (8 ounces) cream cheese
½ cup powdered sugar
1 carton (9 ounces) Cool Whip

2 cups miniature marshmallows
1 package (6 ounces) strawberry Jell-O
1 cup boiling water
1½ cups cold water
1 package (10 ounces) frozen strawberries

Prepare in layers. First layer: Mix sugar, pretzels and butter. Press in 9x13 inch pan. Bake at 350° for 15 minutes. Cool. Second layer: Mix cream cheese and powdered sugar. Fold in Cool Whip and marshmallows. Spread over cooled pretzel mixture. Third layer: Dissolve Jell-O in boiling water. Add cold water and frozen strawberries. Refrigerate until mixture begins to jell. Spread over second layer. Serves 12 to 15. *For a festive appearance, add green food color to second layer.*

Mrs. Merle Gorman (Sunie)

Choco-Mint Freeze

1¼ cups (about 30) finely crushed vanilla wafers
4 tablespoons butter or margarine, melted
1 quart peppermint stick ice cream, softened
½ cup butter or margarine

2 squares (2 ounces) Baker's unsweetened chocolate
3 egg yolks, well beaten
1½ cups sifted powdered sugar
½ cup pecans, chopped
1 teaspoon vanilla
3 egg whites

Mix crumbs with 4 tablespoons butter. Reserve ½ cup mixture and press remaining into 9 inch square pan. Spread with softened ice cream and freeze. Melt ½ cup butter and chocolate. Stir into egg yolks and mix with powdered sugar, pecans and vanilla. Beat until smooth. Beat egg whites until stiff and fold into chocolate mixture. Spread over ice cream. Top with reserved crumb mixture. Freeze. Makes 9 large servings. *Can be made way in advance and kept frozen until 30 minutes before serving.*

Mrs. Robert Stauch (Janet)

Jean's Chocolate Cinnamon Ice Cream

4 squares (1 ounce each) Baker's unsweetened chocolate
2 cans (14 ounces each) condensed milk
2½ cups sugar
1 tablespoon flour (cornstarch or arrowroot may be used)

¼ teaspoon salt
5 eggs
2 tablespoons vanilla
2 teaspoons cinnamon
2 pints whipping cream, unwhipped

Melt chocolate in top of double boiler. Add condensed milk. Beat with egg beater until smooth. Mix in sugar, flour and salt until thoroughly blended. Stir until thickened. Cook covered 10 minutes. Beat eggs slightly; stir in milk mixture and return to double boiler. Cook 1 minute. Cool. Strain if necessary. When completely cold and ready to make ice cream, add vanilla, cinnamon and cream. Freeze in home freezer. Makes ½ gallon. *Excellent home made ice cream.*

Mrs. Jack Starry (Dorothy)

Chocolate Ice Cream

1　can (14 ounces) sweetened
　　condensed milk
⅔　cup Hershey's syrup

2　cups whipping cream,
　　whipped

In large bowl, stir together sweetened condensed milk and syrup. Fold in whipped cream. Pour into individual parfait glasses. Cover. Freeze.

Mrs. Rex Corey (Robyn)

Frozen Strawberry Dessert

TOPPING AND BASE:

½　to ¾ cup butter
1　to 1¼ cups flour

¼　to 1 tablespoon firmly
　　packed brown sugar
½　to 1 cup chopped pecans

FILLING:

1　package (10 ounces) frozen
　　strawberries
2　egg whites
1　cup sugar

1　tablespoon lemon juice
1　teaspoon vanilla
½　pint whipping cream,
　　whipped

TOPPING AND BASE: Mix lightly all ingredients and place in 9x13 inch baking pan. Bake at 400°, stirring occasionally until golden brown, about 15 minutes. Use ½ on bottom of pan and save rest for top of filling.

FILLING: Place all ingredients except whipping cream in bowl and beat 20 minutes. Fold in whipped cream and pour into pan. Top with remaining crumbs. Freeze 8 hours. Serves 12 to 15.

Mrs. George Kardell (Roe)

Confections & Condiments

CANDY

Records from ancient times show candy has been known as far back as 2000 B.C. Sugar from the Orient was first refined in 1470 by a candy-maker in Venice, and the modern candy industry was born. In America sugar from maple tree sap provided candy during colonial times. With the invention of a revolving steam pan in 1850, large amounts of candy could be produced at low cost.

No other country produces more candy than the United States, and Aggies consume their fair share of the energy producing goodies. So take a creative tour through a "popular demand" section of our Hullabaloo!

Date Loaf Candy

1 cup milk	½ teaspoon salt
3 cups sugar	1 teaspoon vanilla
3 tablespoons white Karo syrup	½ teaspoon almond extract, optional
1 cup pitted dates	2 cups nuts
1 tablespoon butter	

Combine milk, sugar and Karo in large saucepan. Cook over medium heat, stirring and not allowing sugar crystals to adhere to sides of pan. Cook to firm ball stage, 248°, when tested in water. Add dates and just heat through, as high temperatures cause a bitter, undesirable taste in dates. Remove from heat. Add butter, salt and allow to cool. Add vanilla. Add almond extract, if desired. Beat until creamy. Add nuts. Pour mixture along one side of a warm damp cloth. Shape into a long loaf about an inch in diameter and roll up in the cloth. When cool and firm, cut in slices and store in an airtight container. *Dates should be as fresh as possible, not dry.*

Mrs. Charles D. Price, Jr. (Joyce)

Divinity

2 egg whites
2½ cups sugar

½ cup water
½ cup white corn syrup

Beat egg whites in large bowl until stiff. Set aside. Cook sugar, water and corn syrup together until it bubbles and sugar is melted. Pour ½ cup of syrup mixture over beaten egg whites and mix slightly. Continue cooking syrup until it spins a long thread or until it is 254° on candy thermometer. Slowly pour syrup over egg whites, beating as it is poured, using an electric mixer if possible. Beat until it holds it shape. Drop by teaspoonfuls on wax paper. Press a pecan or walnut half on each piece. *Food coloring may be added during beating. Store in tin boxes to retain a fresh, moist taste.*

Mrs. H. Smith (Alyne)

Fudge Candy Ring

1 package (6 ounces) Nestle's semisweet chocolate morsels
1 package (6 ounces) Nestle's butterscotch morsels
1 can (14 ounces) Eagle Brand sweetened condensed milk

1 cup coarsely chopped walnuts
½ teaspoon vanilla
1 cup walnut halves
Maraschino cherries, optional

Melt chocolate and butterscotch morsels with sweetened condensed milk in top of double boiler over hot, not boiling water. Stir occasionally until morsels melt and mixture begins to thicken. Remove from heat. Add chopped walnuts and vanilla. Blend well. Chill about 1 hour until mixture thickens. Line bottom of 9 inch pie pan with 12 inch square of foil. Place ¾ cup walnut halves in bottom of pan, forming a 2 inch wide flat ring. Spoon chocolate mixture in small mounds on top of nuts to form ring. Decorate with remaining nuts. Add maraschino cherries, if desired. Chill in refrigerator until firm enough to slice. Cut into ½ inch slices. Yields 36 slices.

Mrs. M. D. Davison (Mickey)

Sour Cream Fudge
Velvety smooth...sweet, but tangy, too!!

2 cups sugar	2 tablespoons butter or
½ teaspoon salt	margarine
1 cup sour cream	½ cup broken pecans or
	other nuts

Combine sugar, salt and sour cream. Cook, stirring occasionally, to soft ball stage 236°. Add butter. Cool at room temperature without stirring, until it becomes lukewarm 110°. Beat until mixture loses gloss and add nuts. Spread in buttered 8 inch square pan. When firm, cut in squares. Yields 24 pieces.

Aggie Mom

Martha Washington Bonbons

½ cup margarine	1 quart pecans (4 cups),
2 boxes (1 pound each)	chopped fine
powdered sugar	1 tablespoon vanilla
1 can (14 ounces) Eagle	1½ blocks paraffin
Brand sweetened	6 squares semisweet
condensed milk	chocolate

Mix first five ingredients and roll into small balls. Melt paraffin and chocolate in a double boiler. Dip balls in paraffin mixture and place on wax paper.

Mrs. Ralph Plumlee (Stella)

Orange Balls

1 box (12 ounces) vanilla	¾ cup powdered sugar
wafers, crushed	¾ cup Baker's flaked coconut
½ cup frozen orange juice	½ cup chopped nuts
concentrate, thawed and	
undiluted	

In large bowl mix all ingredients. Work together with hands to make a smooth mixture. Shape into 1 inch balls. Store in covered container in refrigerator. May be rolled in powdered sugar.

Mrs. Gerald E. Dixon (Jane)

Patience

2 cups sugar
1½ cups Pet evaporated milk
3 tablespoons butter

1 cup sugar
½ cup nuts, optional
Dash salt

Cook 2 cups sugar, milk and butter until it forms a soft ball in water. Caramelize 1 cup sugar in heavy saucepan. Add caramelized sugar to first mixture and cook until it forms a soft ball. Remove from stove and beat until creamy. Add nuts, if desired and a pinch of salt. Pour into greased pan to cool and cut into squares before it hardens. *More nuts may be added if desired.*

Mrs. Ralph Plumlee (Stella)

Peanut Butter Surprise

½ cup crunchy peanut butter
1 cup graham cracker crumbs
1 cup chopped pecans
1 can (3½ ounces) flaked coconut

1 pound powdered sugar, sifted
1 cup butter, melted
1 package (6 ounces) semisweet chocolate morsels
½ block (2 ounces) paraffin

Combine peanut butter, graham cracker crumbs, pecans, coconut and sugar. Add melted butter and mix. Shape into 1 inch balls. Chill 15 minutes. In small saucepan melt paraffin and chocolate over low heat. Put toothpick in each ball and dip in warm chocolate until covered. Place on wax paper. Yields 5½ dozen.

Mrs. Homer Green (Wilma)

Peanut Brittle

2 cups sugar	2 tablespoons butter
1 cup light corn syrup	1 teaspoon baking soda
3 cups raw Spanish peanuts	

Combine sugar and corn syrup in a heavy saucepan. Cook over low heat, stirring constantly until it comes to a full boil. Add peanuts and butter. Continue cooking to 302° on candy thermometer, stirring frequently. Candy should be rich caramel brown color. Remove from heat and stir in baking soda. Immediately spread thin on a large piece of buttered foil.

Mrs. Richard Williams (Wanda)

Delectable Pralines

2 cups sugar	¼ teaspoon baking soda
½ cup milk	1 teaspoon vanilla
½ cup corn syrup	2 cups pecans, halves or
2 tablespoons margarine	pieces

Combine sugar, milk, corn syrup, margarine and soda in saucepan. Place over moderate heat, stirring gently until sugar dissolves. Cook to soft ball stage, 238° on candy thermometer, and remove from heat. Add vanilla and beat until creamy. Stir in pecans. Drop from spoon onto wax paper. Yields 36 pralines.

Mrs. Jack McAuliff (Betty)

Pralines

1 box (3⅝ ounces) butterscotch pudding, not instant	½ cup sugar
	½ cup Pet evaporated milk
	2 tablespoons butter
1 cup brown sugar	2 cups pecans

Mix all ingredients except pecans. Cook 5 to 8 mintues, until mixture comes to soft ball stage when tested in water. Beat until creamy and add pecans. Drop by teaspoonfuls on wax paper. Let harden.

Mrs. Ralph Plumlee (Stella)

Southern Pralines

2¼ cups sugar	2 teaspoons vanilla
2 tablespoons sour cream	1 teaspoon rum flavoring
1 cup buttermilk	2½ cups pecans
1 teaspoon baking soda	

In heavy Dutch oven combine sugar, sour cream, buttermilk and baking soda. Cook over medium heat, stirring constantly. Mixture will foam, then turn a caramel color after 7 to 9 minutes. Continue cooking to soft ball stage 234°. Add flavorings and pecans. Beat with wooden spoon until it begins to thicken and becomes tacky. Drop onto buttered foil and cool. If candy becomes too thick, add a little hot water to thin it.

Mrs. Richard Williams (Wanda)

Susan's Pretzel Bark

1 pound white chocolate	½ cup broken pretzel sticks

Melt chocolate on very low heat in a Teflon pan. When completely melted, stir in pretzels. Line a cookie sheet with foil, shiny side up, and spread warm chocolate to sides. Let cool. Break into small pieces.

Mrs. James Thompson (Charlotte)

Special Nuts

1 cup sugar	½ teaspoon cloves
¼ cup water	Dash salt
½ teaspoon nutmeg	2 cups pecans or walnut
1 teaspoon cinnamon	halves

Mix sugar, salt, spices and water in saucepan. Cook to a soft ball stage and then add nuts. Remove from heat and stir until mixture becomes sugary and nuts coated. Pour out on wax paper. Let dry.

Mrs. James P. Newberry (Mary Jane)

Spiced Hot Pecans

3 tablespoons butter	¼ teaspoon garlic powder
3 tablespoons Worcestershire sauce	¼ teaspoon red pepper
	Dash Tabasco sauce
1 teaspoon salt	1 pound pecan halves
½ teaspoon cinnamon	

Melt butter with seasonings. Add pecans and stir until coated. Bake on cookie sheet at 300° for 20 to 25 minutes, stirring often. Yields 4 cups pecans.

Mrs. Bruce Lowry (Elena)

Spiced Sweet Pecans

1 egg white	¼ teaspoon allspice
2½ tablespoons water	¼ teaspoon cloves
¾ cup sugar	¾ teaspoon salt
1 teaspoon cinnamon	3 to 3½ cups pecan halves
¼ teaspoon nutmeg	

Beat egg white and water until frothy. Add sugar, cinnamon, nutmeg, allspice, cloves and salt. Blend well. Stir in pecans and coat well. Remove pecans and place on cookie sheet lined with buttered foil. Bake at 275° for 45 minutes. Stir gently after 20 minutes and again in 15 minutes to cook on all sides. Cool and store in airtight container. Yields 4 to 4½ cups.

Mrs. Bruce Lowry (Elena)

Sugar Peanuts

1 cup sugar	4 cups raw peanuts
1 cup water	

Combine sugar and water in saucepan. Cook until sugar is dissolved. Add peanuts. Cook until all syrup is gone, stirring frequently. Spread peanuts on cookie sheet. Bake at 300° for 1 hour, stirring every 15 minutes. Cool and store in sealed container.

Mrs. Jay D. Smith (Berniece)

Oven-Made Caramel Corn

5 quarts popped corn	½ cup light corn syrup
¾ cup margarine	1 teaspoon salt
1 cup sugar	½ teaspoon baking soda
1 cup brown sugar	

Spread popped corn in large roaster. Put in oven at 250° to keep warm and crisp. Combine margarine, sugars, corn syrup and salt in 2 quart heavy saucepan. Cook on medium heat, stirring until sugar dissolves. Continue to boil to firm ball stage 248° about 5 minutes. Remove from heat and stir in baking soda. Syrup will foam. Take popped corn from oven and pour hot caramel mixture over it in a fine stream. Stir to mix well. Return to oven for 45 to 50 minutes, stirring every 15 minutes. Cool. Store in airtight containers and keep in a cool place. Yields 5 quarts.

Mrs. James E. Doherty (Clara June)

Granola Breakfast Cereal

4 cups quick cooking oats	1 cup slivered almonds or
⅓ cup brown sugar	other nuts
½ cup wheat germ	½ cup soy nuts, not beans
½ cup coconut	¼ cup sunflower seeds
¼ cup sesame seed, hulled or	⅓ cup vegetable oil
unhulled	¼ cup honey
	1 teaspoon vanilla

Heat dry oats on ungreased cookie sheet at 350° for 10 minutes. Stir. Add brown sugar, wheat germ, coconut, sesame seed, almonds, soy nuts, sunflower seeds and mix. Dribble oil, honey and vanilla over all and mix well again. Bake on cookie sheet at 350° 20 to 25 minutes. Stir often to insure toasting evenly to a light brown.

Variation: Raisins and/or chopped dates may be added after baking.

Mrs. John H. Vandeven (Norma)

Barbecue Sauce

2 tablespoons butter
1 medium onion, finely chopped
2 tablespoons chopped celery
2 tablespoons vinegar
1 tablespoon brown sugar
1 cup catsup
1 cup water

3 tablespoons Worcestershire sauce
4 tablespoons lemon juice
½ teaspoon salt
½ teaspoon celery salt
½ teaspoon onion salt
½ teaspoon garlic salt
1 teaspoon hickory smoke sauce

Brown onion in butter. Add chopped celery and cook for 5 minutes. Add remaining ingredients and cook slowly for 15 minutes. May be refrigerated and kept for 2 weeks. Yields 1 quart.

Mrs. James P. Licandro (Marie)

Smokehouse Barbecue Sauce

2 bottles (48 ounces each) catsup
7 cups water
3 tablespoons Liquid Smoke
1 tablespoon salt
5 tablespoons sugar
1 cup brown sugar

4 tablespoons Worcestershire sauce
1 medium onion, sliced
1½ tablespoons garlic powder
1 tablespoon red pepper
1½ tablespoons allspice
¾ tablespoon chili powder
3 to 5 bay leaves

Mix all ingredients and bring to a rolling boil. Turn down and simmer for an hour. Yields 5 quarts.

Mrs. Glinn H. White (Bettyeann)

Bechamel Sauce

4 tablespoons butter	1 cup whipping cream
4 tablespoons flour	1 teaspoon salt
1 cup milk	⅛ teaspoon white pepper

In heavy saucepan, melt butter over moderate heat. Remove pan from heat and stir in flour. Pour in milk and cream all at once, whisking constantly until flour partially dissolves. Return pan to high heat and cook, stirring constantly. When sauce comes to a boil and is smooth, reduce heat. Simmer for 2 or 3 minutes longer until sauce is thick enough to coat heavily wires of the whisk. Remove pan from heat and season with salt and white pepper.

Marie LaCombe

Chili Sauce
Makes the kitchen smell great!

1 gallon ripe tomatoes, peeled and chopped	5 tablespoons salt
½ gallon chopped onions	1 quart vinegar
2 or 3 hot green peppers, whole or sliced	1 tablespoon cinnamon
½ cup sugar	¼ teaspoon allspice
	¼ teaspoon cloves

Prepare tomatoes and onions, using a food processor if you have one. Mix everything in a large canning kettle that will hold 2 to 3 gallons. Simmer uncovered about 2 hours until sauce is thickened, stirring every 5 to 10 minutes to keep it from sticking to bottom of kettle. Pour sauce into 12 hot, sterilized pint jars and seal with sterilized lids. Cool filled jars on counter and store in cool place. Yields 2 gallons. *This is delicious on black-eyed, purple hull, cream peas, and on Spanish omelets.*

Mrs. Lee Radford (Betty)

Cocktail Sauce

1 bottle (12 ounces) Heinz chili sauce

1 bottle (14 ounces) Heinz tomato catsup

2 tablespoons vinegar or lemon juice

1 teaspoon Lawry's seasoned salt

3 or 4 tablespoons horseradish

4 or 5 dashes Tabasco sauce

Mix all ingredients and refrigerate. *Must use Heinz for right consistency.*

Mrs. Ralph Plumlee (Stella)

Cocktail Sauce for Boiled Shrimp

1 bottle (14 ounces) catsup

3 tablespoons fresh lemon juice

1 tablespoon horseradish

1 teaspoon Worcestershire sauce

1 teaspoon salt

½ teaspoon Spice Islands Beau Monde seasoning

Combine all ingredients. Serve with boiled shrimp.

Mrs. Jack McAuliff (Betty)

Easy Mornay Sauce

¼ cup butter

½ cup flour

2 cups milk

1 pound Velveeta cheese, grated

½ can (6 ounces) beer

Melt butter, add flour and cook until bubbly. Add milk and cook until smooth. Add grated cheese and cook until melted. Beat with electric beater for 15 minutes. Add beer a little at a time as you beat.

Mrs. John B. Isbell (Charlene)

Tartar Sauce

2   cups chopped onion
2   cups dill pickle relish

2   cups Kraft mayonnaise
⅓   cup lemon juice

Mix all ingredients and refrigerate. Yields 6⅓ cups.

Mrs. Ralph Plumlee (Stella)

Tomato Sauce

2   tablespoons olive oil
½   cup finely chopped onion
2   cups Italian plum or whole
    pack tomatoes, not
    drained
3   tablespoons tomato paste

1   tablespoon finely cut fresh
    basil
1   teaspoon sugar
Salt and fresh ground black
    pepper

Using stainless steel saucepan, heat olive oil. Add onion and cook over moderate heat until soft, but not browned. Add tomatoes, tomato paste, basil, sugar, salt and a few sprinklings of pepper. Lower heat and simmer with pan partially covered for about 45 minutes, stirring occasionally. Press sauce through a fine sieve, into a bowl or pan. Season to taste and serve hot.

Marie LaCombe

Spiced Peaches

1   can (29 ounces) peach
    halves, drained and juice
    reserved
½   cup sugar

½   cup peach juice
¼   cup vinegar
8   to 10 whole cloves
1   stick cinnamon

Combine sugar, juice, vinegar and spices in a saucepan. Bring to a boil and simmer 10 minutes. Add fruit and heat thoroughly. Put in a single layer in refrigerator dish. Be sure to cover fruit with syrup. Cover and refrigerate overnight.

Mrs. Charles D. Price, Jr. (Joyce)

Cucumber Pineapple Marmalade
If you give it, give the recipe, too!

2	cups cucumbers, peeled and chopped very fine
½	cup crushed pineapple
⅓	cup (about 3 lemons) lemon juice

2	tablespoons chopped lemon rind
4	cups sugar
	Few drops green food coloring, optional
1	package Certo Fruit Pectin

Place cucumbers in saucepan. Add lemon juice, rind, crushed pineapple, sugar and food coloring. Mix well. Bring to a full rolling boil over high heat and boil hard 1 minute, stirring constantly. Remove from heat and stir in Certo Fruit Pectin. Skim off foam with a metal spoon. Ladle into sterilized canning jars with 2 piece lids leaving ⅛ inch space at top. Process in water bath as follows: after ladling into jars, wipe around tops with a clean cloth. Put lids on and tighten securely, but not completely. Place jars on rack in kettle or canner and cover with water to 1 inch over.

Mrs. T. B. Dellinger (Maria)

Pineapple Strawberry Jam
A quick and easy gift!

1	package (10 ounces) frozen strawberries, thawed
2⅓	cups (20 ounces) crushed pineapple, undrained

¼	cup water
1	box Sure-Jell fruit pectin
3½	cups sugar
1	block paraffin

Mix strawberries, pineapple, water and fruit pectin in a 4 quart saucepan. Bring to a boil over high heat, stirring constantly. Add sugar and bring to a rolling boil. Boil 1 minute. Remove from heat. Stir and skim off foam for 5 minutes. Ladle into sterilized jelly glasses. Melt paraffin over low heat. Pour at least ¼ inch paraffin on top of jam in each glass. No need to refrigerate unless storing for a long time.

Mrs. Frank S. Covaro (Genie)

Microwave

MICROWAVE

Microwave cooking was discovered by accident in 1945 when a scientist placed a chocolate bar beside a radar vacuum tube when he was testing. In 1947 the first model, the Radarange, became available to restaurants and hotels but was not used in homes because of the high cost. By 1967 Amana Radaranges were made available to the public and by the 1970's many companies were manufacturing microwave ovens. Now many American families own one of these energy saving, quick cooking ovens. Texans particularly find microwave ovens beneficial, because they create little heat on hot summer days.

Generally, cooking takes much less time in microwave ovens than electric or gas ranges. A microwave oven will defrost frozen food, heat cooked food or cook food. Cooking takes place on the outer edges of food first; therefore, food should be arranged in a circle or with the dense portion of food on the outside of the dish. Stirring helps to distribute heat and thus reduce cooking time. Microwaving in a covered dish causes food to cook quicker also. Another feature of these ovens is that most foods do not brown when cooked in microwave ovens.

Heating baby food or warming formula in a microwave can be a modern miracle for a new mom. Blanching vegetables for freezing and jelly making are performed with ease in a microwave. Softening cheeses, melting chocolate and margarine, making Jell-O and brewing a cup of tea are only the beginning steps to enjoying your microwave oven. The following recipes are a few favorites of Aggie Moms.

Peanut Brittle

1　cup sugar	1　tablespoon butter
2　cups raw peanuts	1　teaspoon vanilla
½　cup white Karo syrup	1　teaspoon soda
⅛　teaspoon salt	

Combine sugar, peanuts, syrup and salt in a deep 1½ quart bowl and mix well. Microwave on HIGH for 8 minutes. Stir in butter and vanilla. Microwave on HIGH for 2 more minutes. Add soda and stir well. Spread thin on a lightly buttered cookie sheet. Cool. Break into pieces and store covered.

Mrs. Bob Cannon (La Joyce)

Quickies

POTATO HALVES

Wash, slice potato in half. Season cut side with seasoning salt and butter. Place cut side down on dish and microwave on HIGH 6 to 8 minutes or until tender. Serve.

CORN ON THE COB

Shuck, silk and wash corn. Wrap in Saran Wrap and seal ONE end only. Place in dish. Microwave on HIGH one ear for 3 minutes. Butter and serve.

APPLES

Wash, remove cores from apples. Fill centers with 1 teaspoon brown sugar, 1 teaspoon butter, dash of cinnamon and a few raisins. Microwave on HIGH 5 minutes or until apples are tender. Time depends on the number of apples.

POTATO CASSEROLE

Peel, wash and slice potatoes thinly. Place in microwave dish. Salt and pepper to taste. Cover with whipping cream. Microwave on MEDIUM until tender. Top with shredded cheese. Serve hot. 1 quart serves 4.

JELL-O WITH FRUIT

Heat 1 cup water in microwave on HIGH for 1½ minutes. Add Jell-O and stir until dissolved. Add 1 cup cold water and 1 cup any drained fruit desired. Place in footed glasses and refrigerate until set. Top with spoon of whipped topping. Serves 4 to 6.

CHICKEN BREAST

Coat 1 chicken breast with crushed corn flakes. Microwave on HIGH for about 3 minutes. Serve. Allow more time when more pieces of chicken are cooked.

Heat 1 cup water in microwave on HIGH for 1 minute. Add instant coffee, hot chocolate or tea bag for a quick drink.

Since casseroles will not brown, toppings of grated cheese, crushed potato chips or sauces may be added to give a nice finished touch.

Sugared honey may be liquified by heating in microwave for 30 seconds or more.

Party Bread Sticks

10 thin sesame bread sticks
5 slices bacon, cut in half
   lengthwise

½ cup Parmesan cheese

Roll one side of bacon strip in cheese. Roll cheese side of bacon against bread stick diagonally. Place sticks on microwave baking sheet lined with paper towel. Microwave on HIGH for 4½ to 6 minutes. Roll in cheese again. Yields 10 sticks.

Variation: Use 20 small bread sticks. Various flavors of sticks may be used.

Mrs. Frank S. Covaro (Genie)

Carrots and Dill

1 pound carrots, sliced
1 tablespoon butter
2 tablespoons catsup

½ teaspoon dill weed
¼ teaspoon salt

Combine ingredients. Mix well and microwave on HIGH for 8 minutes. Stir and microwave on HIGH for 7 minutes or until tender. Serves 6. *Use no water.*

Mrs. C. S. Clements (Carole)

Scalloped Potatoes and Ham

1½ cups milk
2 cups leftover chopped ham
4 cups sliced potatoes
⅔ cup chopped onion
2 tablespoons flour

1 teaspoon salt
¼ teaspoon pepper
2 tablespoons butter
Paprika

Warm milk in 2 cup measure. In 3 quart casserole put a layer of ham. Add a layer of potatoes and onions. Sprinkle with flour, salt and pepper. Dot with butter. Add another layer of each. Pour warm milk over mixture. Sprinkle paprika on top. Cook uncovered on HIGH for 10 minutes, then cook on ROAST for 15 minutes or until potatoes are tender. Let stand 2 minutes before serving. Serves 12 to 14.

Mrs. J. A. Stockard (Sue)

Mother's Squash Casserole

1	package (6 ounces) Mexican corn bread mix	1/8	teaspoon salt
3	packages (10 ounces each) frozen squash	1	can (10¾ ounces) cream of chicken soup
1	onion, chopped		Sage to taste
1	tablespoon butter	1/8	teaspoon pepper
		1	cup grated Cheddar cheese

Bake corn bread mix according to package directions. Microwave squash and onion together in a large dish on HIGH for 15 to 20 minutes or until tender. Drain excess liquid and mash. Add butter, salt, soup, sage, pepper and crumbled corn bread. Mix until blended. Pour into a 2 quart baking dish. Microwave on HIGH for 15 minutes. Remove from oven and top with grated cheese. Serves 10 to 12. *Can be used as a substitute for dressing.*

Variation: ½ cup cheese may be added to casserole.

Mrs. Bob Cannon (La Joyce)

Cheesy Meat Loaf

1½	pounds ground beef	½	cup milk
1	egg, slightly beaten	¼	cup chopped onion
1	tablespoon Worcestershire sauce	1/3	cup dry bread crumbs
¼	teaspoon pepper	1	cup grated Cheddar cheese
¼	teaspoon salt	1	can (4 ounces) mushroom pieces, drained

TOPPING:

5	tablespoons brown sugar	½	cup catsup
1	teaspoon dry mustard		

Combine beef, egg, Worcestershire sauce, pepper, salt, milk, onion and bread crumbs. Mix well. Roll out on wax paper into rectangular shape about ½ inch thick. Sprinkle cheese and mushrooms on top of beef mixture. Roll lengthwise like a jelly roll by picking up edge of wax paper and allowing meat to roll over on itself. Place on platter and microwave on a carousel or turn occasionally for 25 to 30 minutes on ROAST.

TOPPING: Blend brown sugar, mustard and catsup. Spread over top of loaf as soon as it comes out of microwave. Serves 6 to 10.

Variation: Substitute Monterey Jack for Cheddar cheese.

Mrs. John Vandeven (Norma)

Meat Loaf

1 can (8 ounces) tomato sauce	1 medium onion, chopped
¼ cup brown sugar	¼ cup cracker crumbs
¼ cup vinegar	1½ teaspoons salt
1 teaspoon mustard	¼ teaspoon pepper
1 egg, beaten	2 pounds ground beef

Combine tomato sauce, brown sugar, vinegar and mustard. Add beaten egg, onion, cracker crumbs, salt and pepper. Mix well with ground beef and shape into oval loaf with a depression in the middle. Microwave uncovered on ROAST for 25 to 30 minutes or until done in the center. Allow to stand 10 minutes before serving. Serves 8 to 10.

Mrs. J. A. Stockard (Sue)

Banana Pudding

2 cups sugar	1 tablespoon vanilla
4 cups milk	1 box (16 ounces) vanilla wafers
6 tablespoons cornstarch	
4 eggs, beaten	4 bananas

Combine sugar, milk and cornstarch. Microwave on HIGH 10 to 12 minutes, stirring every 3 minutes. When mixture begins to thicken, stir in eggs. Microwave on MEDIUM 3 to 5 minutes, stirring each minute until thick. Remove from oven. Stir in vanilla. Line 2 quart dish with wafers. Cover with slices of banana, then half of pudding. Repeat layers. Decorate top with cookie crumbs or a design of whole cookies. Cool before serving. When serving, top each portion with a spoon of whipped cream. Serves 8 to 10.

Variations: This recipe may be used to make pineapple pudding. Reduce sugar to 1½ cups. When pudding is cooked, add 1 can (15¼ ounces) drained, crushed pineapple. Coconut pudding may be made by adding 1 can (3½ ounces) shredded coconut after the pudding is cooked.

Mrs. Johnny E. Graham (Sara)

Hershey Chocolate Pie

1 (8 ounces) Almond
   Hershey bar
1 heaping teaspoon instant
   coffee
¼ cup boiling water

1 carton (8 ounces) Cool
   Whip
1 graham cracker crust (8
   inch)

Melt Hershey bar over hot water or microwave for 2 minutes on ROAST. Add instant coffee to water that has been warmed in microwave on HIGH for 1 minute. Cool and add to melted chocolate bar. Stir gently and cool. Fold into Cool Whip. Pour into graham cracker crust and refrigerate. Serves 6 to 8.

Mrs. Durwood Pickle (Elizabeth)

Chocolate Pie

2 baked (9 inch) pie shells,
   cooled
3 cups sugar
4 cups milk

6 tablespoons cornstarch
½ cup cocoa
6 egg yolks, beaten
2 teaspoons vanilla

MERINGUE:
6 egg whites
½ teaspoon cream of tartar

1 teaspoon vanilla
¾ cup sugar

Combine sugar, milk, cornstarch and cocoa. Microwave on HIGH about 12 minutes, stirring every 3 minutes. When mixture begins to thicken, stir in egg yolks. Continue to microwave on MEDIUM for 3 to 4 minutes, stirring each minute until thick. Remove from oven. Stir in vanilla. Pour into prepared crust. Top with meringue. *Begin warming milk in microwave while preparing other ingredients.*

MERINGUE: *Beat egg whites, cream of tartar and vanilla until foamy. Slowly add sugar, continuing to beat until stiff peaks form. Spoon onto pies. Bake in REGULAR OVEN 8 to 10 minutes at 400°. Serves 14.*

Mrs. Johnny E. Graham (Sara)

Martha's Raspberry Delight

1 cup water
2 packages (3 ounces each) raspberry Jell-O
1 can (16 ounces) jellied cranberry sauce
1 carton (16 ounces) sour cream
1 cup chopped walnuts

Place water in 2 cup glass container. Microwave on HIGH for 2 minutes. Add Jell-O to hot water and stir until dissolved. Mash cranberry sauce and combine with sour cream. Add Jell-O to cranberry mixture and stir in chopped walnuts. Pour into lightly greased mold. Refrigerate until firm. Serves 8.

Mrs. George D. Neal (Carolyn)

Carrot Cake

1½ cups sugar
1 cup oil
1½ teaspoons vanilla
3 eggs, beaten
1½ cups unsifted flour
¾ teaspoon salt
1½ teaspoons soda
3 teaspoons cinnamon
2½ cups grated raw carrots
¾ cup chopped walnuts
¾ cup raisins

CREAM CHEESE FROSTING:
2 cups powdered sugar
1 package (3 ounces) cream cheese
3 tablespoons butter
1 teaspoon vanilla
1 tablespoon half-and-half

In large bowl mix sugar, oil and vanilla. Add eggs and blend. In another bowl combine flour, salt, soda and cinnamon. Stir into egg mixture, then fold in carrots, walnuts and raisins. Pour batter into greased and floured microwave tube cake pan. Microwave on HIGH for 16 minutes, turning every 4 minutes. Cool and remove from pan. Frost with Cream Cheese Frosting.

FROSTING: Combine all ingredients in 2 quart dish. Microwave on HIGH for 1 minute. Beat with electric mixer until blended. Drizzle over cake. If mixture is too thick to drizzle, blend in a little more half-and-half. Serves 12 to 16.

Mrs. Fred Randall (Darlene)

Cheesecake

¼ cup butter or margarine	2 tablespoons sugar
1 cup graham cracker crumbs (about 12 crackers)	¼ teaspoon cinnamon

FILLING:

2 packages (8 ounces each) cream cheese	2 teaspoons vanilla
	¼ teaspoon salt
1 can (14 ounces) Eagle Brand milk	2 eggs

CRUST: Place butter in 9 inch round glass baking dish and microwave on ROAST for 1 minute or until melted. Stir in cracker crumbs, sugar and cinnamon. Press mixture over bottom and sides of dish. Let cool.

FILLING: Place cream cheese in medium glass mixing bowl. Microwave on WARM for 8 minutes or until softened. Beat cheese with electric mixer until light and fluffy. Beat in milk, vanilla and salt. Add eggs and beat well. Pour into pie shell and microwave on SIMMER for 16 to 18 minutes or until almost set in center. Chill several hours before serving. *May be topped with a can of chilled cherry or blueberry pie filling before serving.* Serves 8.

Mrs. Bob Cannon (La Joyce)

Hot Fudge Sauce

3 squares unsweetened chocolate	1 can (14 ounces) Eagle Brand milk
1 teaspoon margarine	2 teaspoons vanilla

Place chocolate squares and margarine in a 1 quart dish. Microwave on HIGH for 1½ minutes. Stir until chocolate is dissolved. Stir in Eagle Brand milk. Microwave on HIGH for 1½ minutes. Stir and microwave on HIGH for 30 seconds. Remove from oven and add vanilla. Serve warm over ice cream. Store sauce covered in refrigerator. When rewarming, add 2 tablespoons of milk if a thinner consistency is desired.

Mrs. George D. Neal (Carolyn)

Graham Toffees

1 tablespoon butter or margarine	½ cup chopped pecans or walnuts
9 cinnamon graham crackers	½ cup milk chocolate or semisweet chocolate chips
½ cup butter or margarine	
½ cup firmly packed brown sugar	

Microwave 1 tablespoon butter in 8 inch square dish on HIGH 30 seconds or until melted. Spread over bottom and sides of dish. Line bottom of dish with crackers. Combine ½ cup butter and sugar in 4 cup measure or bowl. Microwave on HIGH for 1 minute. Beat with wire whisk until smooth. Microwave on HIGH for 2 minutes. Pour over crackers and spread evenly. Sprinkle with nuts. Microwave on HIGH until mixture boils 1 minute. Rotate ¼ turn every 30 seconds. Cool 2 minutes. Sprinkle with chocolate. When chocolate is soft, spread evenly. Loosen edges and remove from dish. Cut in pieces. For crisp toffee store in refrigerator. Yields 12 to 16 bars.

Mrs. Frank S. Covaro (Genie)

Party Mix

½ cup butter or margarine	2 cups shredded wheat biscuits
2 tablespoons Worcestershire sauce	2 cups shredded rice biscuits
Tabasco sauce to taste	1 cup salted mixed nuts
½ teaspoon salt	1 cup thin pretzel sticks
2 cups shredded corn biscuits	

In a deep 3 quart glass casserole, melt butter on HIGH for 1 minute. Add Worcestershire sauce, Tabasco sauce and salt. Stir to combine. Mix remaining ingredients and stir into butter mixture. Microwave on HIGH uncovered, stirring frequently, for 6 to 7 minutes or until cereal is crisp and well coated with butter mixture. Spread mixture on a tray lined with paper towels and allow to cool before serving. Store in airtight container. Yields 8 cups.

Mrs. Kenneth D. Cheairs (Dorothy)

Let's Have a Party

LET'S HAVE A PARTY

Parties and holidays bring memories of fun times and great food. Cooking can be fun, especially when sharing recipes. This collection of recipes is presented to people who love to cook, who have to cook and who want to know how to cook.

The beginning of *Hullabaloo in the Kitchen* started with Aggie Moms sharing their recipes with each other at the monthly luncheon meetings. We hope our favorite recipes bring you pleasure and that they will soon become your favorites, too.

Backyard Corn and Sausage Roast
Annual Event in South Bend, Indiana

GRILLED BRATWURST:
Simmer Bratwurst *slowly* in one bottle of beer with one peeled onion until all the beer has evaporated. Place over charcoal, turning regularly, until browned evenly.

ROASTED CORN:
Soak several dozen ears of sweet corn in their shucks overnight in a large tub of salted water. Place unshucked corn on grill over charcoals and cover with burlap that has been soaked in water. As the corn roasts, you will need to keep the burlap wet with a fine spray from your backyard hose. Check ears periodically until tender and done. Shuck, roll in butter, salt to taste and enjoy with Bratwurst, favorite salad or slaw, sourdough bread and Apple Walnut Goodness.

APPLE WALNUT GOODNESS:
For a delightful aroma that fills the kitchen!

1 unbaked (10 inch) deep dish pie crust with top crust	1 cup coarsely chopped walnuts
6 (your favorite) apples, peeled, cored and sliced	1 cup firmly packed brown sugar
1 cup raisins	¼ to ½ cup butter
	Cinnamon or allspice to taste

Layer apples, raisins and walnuts in pie crust. Top with brown sugar, dot with butter and sprinkle with cinnamon or allspice. Cover with top crust, crimp or flute edges and make holes in a pretty pattern in top crust to let out steam. Brush top with softened butter and bake 40 to 50 minutes or until golden brown at 350°. *Serve warm with cream or cinnamon sauce.*

CINNAMON SAUCE:

1½ teaspoons cornstarch
1 cup milk
1 tablespoons margarine

½ teaspoon salt
Cinnamon
Brown sugar

Mix cornstarch and milk until smooth. Add margarine and salt. Bring to boil over medium heat, stirring constantly. Boil one minute. Add brown sugar and cinnamon to taste.

Mrs. Lowell McMann (Joan)

Sweet Party Mix

1 pound margarine or butter
1 teaspoon garlic powder
1 tablespoon Worcestershire sauce
1 teaspoon Lawry's seasoned salt
1 cup sugar

1 box (12 ounces) rice chex
1 box (12 ounces) corn, wheat or bran chex
1 box (10 ounces) thin pretzel sticks
1 cup mixed nuts or peanuts

Over medium heat, in a very large pot, combine butter, garlic powder, Worcestershire sauce, salt and sugar. Stir until sugar is dissolved. Remove from heat and add cereals, nuts and pretzels. Toss until well coated. Spread on 2 lipped cookie sheets and bake 1 hour at 250° stirring every 15 minutes to prevent sticking. Store in airtight containers. Yields 2 gallons.

Mrs. Frank S. Covaro (Genie)

Cranberry Balls

2 packages (8 ounces each) cream cheese, softened
1 can (16 ounces) whole cranberry sauce, well drained

1 cup chopped nuts
¾ cup coconut

Combine cream cheese, cranberry sauce and nuts. Mix well and chill for one hour. Form into balls and roll in coconut. Chill and serve. Yields 72 balls. *A pretty and festive appetizer for the holidays.*

Mrs. Jack Starry (Dorothy)

Cheese or Ham Puffs
(Kaas of Ham Seesjes)

½ cup butter
1 cup boiling water
1 cup flour

¼ teaspoon salt
4 eggs

Add butter to boiling water in saucepan. Stir until butter is melted, keeping water at boil. Add all flour and salt at once. Stir vigorously until mixture is smooth and forms a ball that does not separate. Cool slightly. Add eggs one at a time, mixing well after each addition. Drop small amount, size of walnut, on greased baking sheet. Bake in preheated 450° oven for 15 to 20 minutes, until golden yellow. Allow to cool and fill with one of the following fillings. Yields 24 puffs.

CHEESE FILLING:

5 tablespoons butter
3 cups grated Gouda cheese
4 eggs, well beaten

Salt to taste
Dash red pepper

Cream butter, blend in grated cheese and eggs. Add salt, red pepper and mix. Use pastry bag or small spoon to fill puffs.

HAM FILLING:

3 tablespoons butter
3 tablespoons mayonnaise
5 ounces ham, finely chopped
1 small onion, finely chopped

1 tablespoon parsley, chopped finely
1½ teaspoons curry powder
Dash Maggi seasoning liquid

Cream butter and mix with mayonnaise, ham, onion, parsley, curry powder and Maggi. Cut open puffs and fill. Yields 24 puffs.

Mrs. Jack Starry (Dorothy)

Shred Cheddar or Swiss cheese and freeze in packages. Measure out for recipe and return to freezer.

Cranberry Party Salad

1 pound ground cranberries
1½ cups sugar
1 can (20 ounces) crushed
  pineapple

1 bag (16 ounces) miniature
  marshmallows
4 ounces Cool Whip
1 cup chopped pecans

Combine cranberries, sugar, pineapple and marshmallows. Refrigerate overnight. Drain. Add Cool Whip and pecans. Chill. Serves 10 to 12.

Mrs. S. G. Evetts (Darlene)

Seafoam Salad

1 package (3 ounces) lime
  Jell-O
1 can (14 ounces) crushed
  pineapple, drained
1 package (8 ounces) cream
  cheese, softened

1 jar (6 ounces) maraschino
  cherries, drained
1 cup chopped nuts
½ pint whipping cream,
  whipped

Drain pineapple, reserving juice. Add water to juice to make 1 cup. Heat liquid to boiling. Add Jell-O and stir to dissolve. Chill until slightly set. Beat cream cheese until smooth. Stir in pineapple, cherries and nuts. Cool, but do not let mixture set. Fold in whipped cream and pour into 9 inch square pan or into a 4 cup mold. Chill until firm. Serves 9.

A&M Mothers' Club Luncheon

Coleslaw

1 large head cabbage,
  shredded
1 large green bell pepper,
  chopped
¾ cup sugar

1 teaspoon mustard
1 teaspoon celery seed
1½ teaspoons salt
¾ cup white vinegar
½ cup corn oil

Set aside shredded cabbage and chopped green pepper. Combine sugar, mustard, celery seed, salt and vinegar. Bring to a boil. Remove from heat and add corn oil. Pour over slaw and refrigerate for 24 hours. Serves 10 to 12. *Double recipe for large group.*

A&M Mothers' Club Luncheon

Copper Pennies

2	pounds sliced carrots, slightly cooked	1	can (10¾ ounces) condensed tomato soup
1	medium onion, thinly sliced	½	cup corn oil
1	medium green pepper, diced	¾	cup white vinegar
		1	teaspoon dry mustard
2	cans (16 ounces each) white hominy, drained	1	teaspoon Worcestershire sauce
1	cup sugar	¼	teaspoon salt
		¼	teaspoon pepper

Combine carrots, onion, green pepper and hominy in a large bowl. Mix remaining ingredients and pour over vegetable mixture. Chill overnight. Serves 6 to 8. *Keeps well for 2 weeks.*

A&M Mothers' Club Luncheon

Marinated Vegetables

½	cup vegetable oil	1	can (16 ounces) sliced carrots, drained
1	teaspoon salt		
¾	cup white vinegar	1	jar (2 ounces) chopped pimientos, drained
1	cup sugar		
1	can (16 ounces) French green beans, drained	2	cups chopped celery
		½	cup chopped bell pepper
1	cup shoe peg corn	¼	cup chopped onion
1	cup tiny English peas		

Combine vegetable oil, salt, vinegar, and sugar. In a saucepan bring to full boil. Remove from heat and set aside. Combine beans, peg corn, English peas, carrots, pimientos, celery, bell pepper and onion. Mix well and pour hot mixture over vegetables. Refrigerate. Serves 8 to 10. *Will keep indefinitely.*

Mrs. George D. Neal (Carolyn)
Mrs. Ralph Plumlee (Stella)

Three Bean Salad

1 can (16 ounces) cut green beans	⅓ cup wine vinegar
1 can (16 ounces) cut wax beans	⅓ cup salad oil
1 can (16 ounces) kidney beans	⅓ cup sugar
1 medium onion, sliced thin	1 teaspoon salt
1 small bell pepper, chopped	½ teaspoon pepper
	½ teaspoon celery seed
	¼ teaspoon basil

Drain beans well. Add onion and bell pepper. Mix remaining ingredients. Pour over bean mixture and refrigerate for several hours before serving. Stir several times. Serves 10 to 12.

A&M Mothers' Club Luncheon

Chicken Artichoke Salad

6 to 8 cooked chicken breasts	4 cups mayonnaise
2 boxes (8 ounces each) chicken Rice-A-Roni	8 green onions, chopped
4 jars (3½ ounces each) chopped marinated artichokes	1 medium size bell pepper, chopped
	2½ cups ripe olives, sliced

Cut chicken into bite size pieces. Cook Rice-A-Roni slightly using directions on box. Drain liquid from artichokes and mix liquid with mayonnaise. Combine all ingredients. Chill overnight. Serves 12 to 16.

Mrs. Jack McAuliff (Betty)

To freshen air in house, boil 1 tablespoon whole cloves in pan of water for few minutes.

Chicken Salad Deluxe

4 quarts cooked chicken or turkey	1½ cups coarsely chopped walnuts
1 cup finely minced onion or 1 bunch scallions, snipped	3 cups mayonnaise
	½ cup white wine vinegar
	1½ cups chicken broth
6 cups sliced celery with tops	2 teaspoons salt
	¼ teaspoon pepper
1 dozen hard cooked eggs diced, optional	

Day before, cook chicken or turkey and debone. Chop into large pieces and refrigerate. Prepare onions, celery and eggs. Refrigerate. At least 2½ hours before serving, combine mayonnaise, vinegar, broth, salt and pepper. Toss with all other ingredients. Refrigerate until serving time. Serves 25. *Arrange on beds of lettuce and garnish with watercress or parsley.*

Mrs. H. Smith (Alyne)

Hot Potato Salad

6 large potatoes, boiled in skins	6 green onions, chopped
¼ cup butter	1 can (10¾ ounces) cream of mushroom soup
Salt and pepper to taste	½ pound rat cheese
1 jar (4 ounces) pimientos	

Peel potatoes and combine with butter, salt, pepper, pimientos, onions, soup and cheese. Place in 375° oven until salad bubbles. Serves 12.

Mrs. Rodney W. Kelly (Pat)

SPICE HINTS:
Cheese dishes—sage, marjoram
Cheese sauce—mustard
Cottage cheese—onion salt, dill, caraway seed
Cream cheese—basil, parsley flakes

AGGIE VICTORY DINNER

Aggie hearts are elegantly warmed by a fall setting as shown in the lovely home of Mr. & Mrs. R. Warren Sexton '54, supporters of all Texas A&M activities. Exquisite arrangements for a festive holiday feast make Aggies cherish thoughts of home, entwined with invigorating memories of Texas A&M University.

Variety spices the palates of Aggies of all ages. Accentuating the cozy arrangement are hearty fare and inviting "nibblers," perfect for enjoying an Aggie football victory in full measure. Dallas Aggie Moms take special pride in preparing tasteful meals and keeping their love for Texas A&M University as warm as the hearth fire.

COLOR PHOTOGRAPHY:
Rick Cook, Designer
Michael Wilson, Photographer
Mrs. Rosanne Green, Food Stylist
Lambert's Landscape: Plants
Jim Gallemore '54, The Hickory Point: Barbecued Ribs
Croissant Royale French Bakery: Bread
Mrs. Charlene Isbell, Original Cake Designs: Cake

TONIGHT'S DINNER includes: New Orleans Shrimp (p. 121), Cheese Ball (p. 118), Relish Tray with Confetti Dip (p. 112), Party Bread Sticks (p. 338), Spinach Salad IV (p. 171), Corn on the Cob, Bread, Barbecued Ribs, Aggie Cake, Sangria Punch (p. 135), Popcorn (p. 361) and Fudge Candy (p. 323).

Hot Curried Fruit

2 cans (16 ounces each) fruit salad
2 cans (16 ounces each) unsweetened pineapple chunks

2 bananas, sliced
¼ cup flour
¼ cup brown sugar
1 teaspoon curry powder

Drain fruit and save juices. Mix flour, brown sugar and curry powder with juice to make a thick base. Add fruit and some of the juice, making sure it is not too runny. Cook over heat and stir for 1 hour. Serve hot. Serves 10.

Mrs. Henry Rose (Iolanda)

Scalloped Pineapple
Really Different

2 cups (8 slices) bread, crusts removed
1 can (3½ cups) pineapple chunks, in heavy syrup, undrained
2 cups sugar

3 eggs
½ cup cream or evaporated milk
½ cup melted butter (not margarine)

Toast and cube bread. Toss with sugar. Beat eggs and cream together. Add to bread. Add pineapple and butter. Toss lightly. Put in greased 9 inch square dish and bake at 350° about 45 minutes or until golden brown. *May be doubled and baked in 9x13 inch dish. Great with ham or pork. Use cookie sheet under shelf in case of spillage in oven.*

Mrs. Frank S. Covaro (Genie)

SPICE HINTS:
Deviled eggs — savory, mustard
Omelet — basil
Scrambled eggs — savory
Tomato omelet — oregano

Brunch Eggs

1 cup (4 ounces) Canadian bacon, diced
¼ cup green onion, chopped
3 tablespoons butter or margarine
12 eggs, beaten
1 can (3 ounces) mushroom pieces, drained

1 recipe cheese sauce
4 teaspoons butter or margarine, melted
2¼ cups (3 slices) soft bread crumbs
⅛ teaspoon paprika

In skillet cook Canadian bacon and onion in 3 tablespoons butter until onion is tender and transparent. Add eggs and scramble until set. Set aside.

CHEESE SAUCE:
2 tablespoons butter or margarine
2 tablespoons flour
½ teaspoon salt

⅛ teaspoon pepper
2 cups milk
1 cup (4 ounces) processed American cheese, shredded

Melt butter. Stir in flour, salt and pepper. Using a medium to low heat add milk and stir until thick. Add cheese and stir until melted. Slowly fold eggs and mushrooms into cheese sauce. Put in greased 9x13 inch glass pan. Mix butter, crumbs and paprika. Scatter over top of eggs. Bake in 325° oven for 25 to 30 minutes. Serves 10 to 12. *This may be put in refrigerator after preparing and baked the next day.*

Mrs. Hal Smith (Aletta)

Cheese, Bread and Egg Dish

7 slices white bread, buttered
1 cup grated cheese
2 eggs
1 cup milk

1 teaspoon salt
¼ teaspoon paprika
⅛ teaspoon red pepper
¼ teaspoon dry mustard

Cut 2 slices of bread in triangles and the remaining 5 slices in cubes. In buttered 8 inch square baking dish beginning with bread, alternate layers of bread and cheese. Combine remaining ingredients. Pour over bread and cheese. Place triangles of bread upright around edge of baking dish to form a crown. Bake at 350° for 25 minutes. Serves 4.

Mrs. Tom J. Lymenstull (Wanda)

Eggs Day Ahead

3   dozen eggs
½   cup milk
¼   pound butter, divided
¼   pound Cheddar cheese,
     grated

2   cans (10½ ounces each)
     cream of mushroom soup
½   cup sherry

Mix eggs and milk. Add half of butter to skillet and soft scramble eggs. Heat remaining ingredients in saucepan. In lightly greased 3 quart rectangular baking dish, layer eggs and sauce. Cover and refrigerate for one day. Bake at 275° for 50 minutes. Serves 14 to 15. *For brunch serve with sausage, fruit and muffins.*

Marie LaCombe

Egg Puff
Delicious for breakfast, lunch or supper!

17   thin slices day old white
      bread
6   large eggs
2   cups milk
2   cups half-and-half
1¼ teaspoons salt
¼   teaspoon pepper
1½ teaspoons dry mustard

2   teaspoons Worcestershire
     sauce
½   pound grated sharp
     Cheddar cheese
1   to 2 pounds Owens
     sausage, browned and
     crumbled, optional

Trim crust from bread. Spread one side of bread generously with butter. Cut bread into 1 inch cubes. In a large bowl, beat eggs well. Add milk, half-and-half, salt, pepper, mustard, Worcestershire sauce and set aside. Butter bottom and sides of a 3 quart casserole or 9x13 inch pan. Layer ⅓ of bread cubes, sausage and ⅓ of grated cheese. Repeat layers. Pour egg mixture over all being sure all bread is well moistened. Cover and refrigerate overnight. Bake in 325° oven about one hour or until fluffy and golden. Serves 10 to 12.

Mrs. Robert Fredrickson (Mary Ann)

Savory Eggs

2 cups grated American cheese	1 to 2 teaspoons prepared mustard
¼ cup margarine or butter	1 cup half-and-half
½ teaspoon salt	12 eggs, beaten
¼ teaspoon pepper	

Sprinkle cheese in greased 9x13 inch pan. Dot with butter. Combine remaining ingredients. Mix well. Pour over cheese. Bake 20 mintues at 325°. Stir through mixture and bake 15 to 20 minutes longer. Serves 6 to 8. *Mixture may be prepared ahead and refrigerated until ready to bake. Great to serve at New Year's brunch with sausage, biscuits and black-eyed peas.*

Mrs. John J. Jones III (Geraine)

Do Ahead Sausage Souffle

6 slices soft bread, cubed	2 cups evaporated milk, divided
2 cups shredded Cheddar cheese	½ teaspoon dry mustard
1 pound cooked sausage links, cut in thirds	1 can (10¾ ounces) mushroom soup
4 eggs	

Spread bread evenly in bottom of well greased 2 quart baking dish or 9x13 inch pan. Sprinkle cheese over bread and arrange sausage on top. Beat eggs with 1½ cups milk. Mix remaining ½ cup milk with mustard and soup. Pour egg mixture over first layer. Top casserole with soup mixture. Cover tightly. Refrigerate overnight. Place in cold oven. Bake 300° about 1 hour or until puffy and brown. Serve immediately. Serves 6.

Variation: One pound bulk sausage, cooked and crumbled, may be used.

Mrs. T. Eugene Zachary (Nancy)

Bacon and Egg Quiche

8 eggs	2 unbaked (10 inch) pie
1 pound bacon	shells
1 cup grated Monterey Jack	Salt
cheese	Pepper
1 cup grated Cheddar cheese	Seasoned salt
24 ounces half-and-half	

Fry bacon until crisp and crumble into bottom of pie shells. Mix grated cheeses together and sprinkle over bacon. Add half-and-half, salt, pepper and seasoned salt to eggs. Beat and pour egg mixture over cheese and bacon. Bake in preheated oven for 1 hour at 325°. Serves 12 to 16.

Variation: Milk may be used.

Mrs. Sam Harting (Sandra)

Quiche

1 unbaked (10 inch) pie shell	1 tablespoon chopped chives
4 slices bacon, cooked crisp	⅛ teaspoon nutmeg
and crumbled	½ pound Monterey Jack
1½ cups ham or Canadian	cheese, grated
bacon, optional	4 eggs
¾ cup grated Parmesan	2 cups half-and-half
cheese	Salt and pepper to taste

Prick pie shell. Partially bake at 350° for 10 minutes. Combine bacon, Parmesan cheese, chives and nutmeg. Set aside. Place Monterey Jack cheese in pie shell. Cover with bacon mixture. Beat eggs, cream and seasonings. Pour into pie shell. Bake at 350° for 40 minutes or until knife inserted in quiche comes out clean. Serves 6.

Mrs. Rex Corey (Robyn)

Crabby Cheese
Much better than it sounds

½ pound fresh mushrooms,
 sliced
2 tablespoons butter
2 tablespoons flour
1 can (10¾ ounces) chicken
 broth
1 can (10¾ ounces) cream
 of mushroom soup

1 package (8 ounces) Old
 English cheese slices
1 package (6 ounces)
 Wakefield crabmeat,
 thawed
2 ounces dry Sherry
English muffins or pastry
 shells

Sauté mushrooms in butter. Remove mushrooms and add flour to butter and juice to make a thick roux. Slowly add chicken broth and allow to thicken. Add cream of mushroom soup and bring to very slow boil. Reduce heat and add Old English cheese slices. Allow these to melt completely. Add crabmeat and mushrooms. Just before serving, stir in Sherry. Serve over toasted English muffins or in pastry shells (Aggies prefer muffins). Serves 4 to 6. *Good for brunch or luncheon. Aggies love this with eggs and hash browns.*

Mrs. Bruce Johnston (Pat)

Chicken Broccoli Casserole

1 package (10 ounces) frozen
 chopped broccoli
2 to 3 cups cooked diced
 chicken
2 cans (10¾ ounces each)
 cream of chicken soup,
 undiluted
1 cup mayonnaise

1 tablespoon lemon juice
½ to 1 teaspoon curry
 powder, depending on
 taste
1 cup grated American
 cheese
1 box plain croutons

Cook broccoli and drain. Add soup, mayonnaise, lemon juice and curry powder to chicken and broccoli. Place in a greased 1½ quart casserole. Sprinkle with cheese and croutons. Bake uncovered at 325° for 30 to 40 minutes. Serves 6 to 8.

Aggie Mom

Green Chili Casserole

2 cans (4 ounces each) whole green chilies (do not use green peppers or pablano peppers)	2 eggs
	½ cup milk
	1 can (10¾ ounces) cream of chicken soup
½ pound longhorn cheese, cut into thin strips	Garlic salt
½ pound longhorn cheese, grated	½ pound Monterey Jack cheese, grated
	Paprika

Slit chilies open and remove seeds. Stuff chilies with strips of longhorn cheese and place in a greased 9x13 inch baking dish, side by side. Beat eggs and milk and add cream of chicken soup, garlic salt and Monterey Jack cheese. Pour over chilies. Sprinkle with longhorn cheese and paprika for color. Bake at 350° for 45 minutes or until set. Serves 4 to 6.

Mrs. Bruce Johnston (Pat)

Mexican Casserole

1 pound ground beef	1 teaspoon salt
1 medium onion, chopped	1 teaspoon chili powder
1 can (15 ounces) Ranch Style beans	1 package (8 ounces) tortilla chips
1 can (10¾ ounces) mushroom soup	1 pound Cheddar cheese, grated
1 can (10 ounces) Rotel tomatoes and green chilies, chopped	

Brown ground beef and onions. Drain. Add beans, soup, tomatoes, green chilies, salt, chili powder and simmer for 10 minutes. Line greased 3 quart casserole with chips and cheese. Spoon half of mixture onto chips and cheese. Repeat layers. Bake at 300° for 30 minutes. Serves 6 to 8.

A&M Mothers' Club Luncheon

SPICE HINTS:
Hamburger — basil, curry powder
Ham loaf — rosemary
Meat balls — savory, mustard, garlic salt
Pork chops — sage, thyme

Mexican Ground Beef Casserole

2	pounds ground beef	1	can (10¾ ounces) cream of mushroom soup
1	large onion, chopped	1	can (10¾ ounces) cream of chicken soup
1	can (4 ounces) chopped green chilies	1	soup can milk
1	can (4 ounces) taco sauce	1	package soft tortillas
		2	cups cheese, grated

Brown meat and onion in skillet. Drain fat and add green chilies, taco sauce, mushroom soup, chicken soup and milk. Grease a 9x13 inch casserole. Cut tortillas into small pieces and layer in casserole with meat mixture. Repeat. Bake for 1 hour at 325°. Add grated cheese on top shortly before baking is complete. Serves 6 to 8. *Freezes well.*

A&M Mothers' Club Luncheon

Aggie Barbecue Hamburger Mix

4	pounds ground beef	½	teaspoon pepper
4	medium onions, chopped	3	tablespoons Worcestershire sauce
3	garlic cloves, minced		
2	cups chopped celery and tops	2	bottles (12 ounces each) catsup
4	teaspoons salt		

Brown ground beef, stirring to mix well. Remove and place in electric roaster. Sauté onion, garlic and celery. Add to meat. Mix salt, pepper, Worcestershire sauce and catsup and add to meat mixture. Simmer 20 minutes. Serves 40. *Great filling for hot buns.*

Mrs. R. C. Bischofhausen (Pat)

SPICE HINTS:
Beef stew — basil, mixed herbs
Fried chicken — paprika, thyme, marjoram

Aggie Spaghetti and Meatballs

MEATBALLS:

4 pounds ground beef	3 cups bread crumbs
1 quart minced onions	6 eggs
6 cloves garlic, minced	3 tablespoons salt
1 cup chopped parsley	3 teaspoons black pepper
3 cups grated Parmesan cheese	

Mix all ingredients for meatballs adding a little water if too dry. Shape into 50 meatballs. In baking pan, place meatballs one layer deep and bake 450° for 30 minutes. Put balls and drippings in roasting pan.

SAUCE:

5 cups chopped onions	3 tablespoons salt
10 cloves garlic, minced	1 teaspoon black pepper
½ cup vegetable oil	1 teaspoon crushed red pepper
5 cans (28 ounces each) tomatoes	5 cans (6 ounces each) tomato paste
5 cups water	4 pounds spaghetti
1 cup chopped parsley	Grated cheese
½ teaspoon dried basil	
2½ teaspoons dried thyme	

Cook onion and garlic in oil for 5 minutes. Add tomatoes, water, sauce, seasonings and simmer for 30 minutes. Pour over meatballs and bake covered for 1½ hours at 350°. Serve over cooked spaghetti and top with grated cheese. Serves 25 *or rather 25 Aggie servings.*

Mrs. R. C. Bischofhausen (Pat)

Variations for Popcorn

BLUE CHEESE:
Melt 1 cup butter. Stir in 1 package blue cheese salad dressing mix. Toss with 6 quarts popped corn.

PARMESAN CHEESE:
Melt ¼ cup butter. Pour over 2 quarts popped corn. Add ½ cup Parmesan cheese.

Mrs. Jean Gross

Luscious Apricot Bars

⅔ cup dried apricots	¼ teaspoon salt
½ cup soft butter or margarine	1 cup firmly packed brown sugar
¼ cup sugar	2 eggs, beaten
1⅓ cups sifted flour, reserve ⅓ cup	½ teaspoon vanilla
½ teaspoon baking powder	½ cup chopped nuts

Rinse apricots. Cover with water and boil 10 mintues. Drain, cool and chop. Set aside. Mix butter, sugar and 1 cup flour until crumbly. Pack into greased 8 inch square pan and bake at 350° for 25 minutes. Sift ⅓ cup flour, baking powder and salt. Beat brown sugar into eggs and add flour mixture. Add vanilla, nuts and apricots. Spread over baked layer. Bake 30 minutes or until done. Cool in pan and cut into bars. Serves 16 to 32 depending on size you desire. Roll in powdered sugar.

Mrs. L. A. Rowlett, Jr. (Jo)

Pumpkin Bars

2 cups sugar	½ teaspoon nutmeg
2 cups flour	½ teaspoon salt
2 teaspoons baking powder	4 eggs
1 teaspoon soda	1 cup cooking oil
2 teaspoons cinnamon	1 can (16 ounces) pumpkin

FROSTING:

4 teaspoons sugar	¼ cup Crisco
4 teaspoons water	2 cups powdered sugar
Dash of salt	1 egg
¼ cup margarine	1 teaspoon vanilla

Mix by hand sugar, flour, baking powder, soda, cinnamon, nutmeg and salt. Add eggs, oil, pumpkin and mix with electric mixer. Bake in 11x17 inch pan for 25 to 30 minutes. Cut in desired size bars.

FROSTING: In saucepan boil sugar, water and salt until dissolved. Cool. Mix together with margarine, Crisco, powdered sugar, eggs and vanilla Beat until smooth and spread on bars. Serves 36.

A&M Mothers' Club Luncheon

Jewish Apple Cake

3	teaspoons sugar	1	cup Crisco oil
2	teaspoons cinnamon	2⅓	teaspoons vanilla
6	to 7 medium apples (about 5 cups)	4	eggs, slightly beaten
		3	cups sifted flour
2	cups sugar	3	teaspoons baking powder
¼	cup orange juice	¾	cup nuts, chopped

Mix together 3 teaspoons sugar and cinnamon. Peel apples and slice thin. Mix sugar and cinnamon mixture through apples. Combine 2 cups sugar, orange juice, oil, vanilla and eggs. Beat with mixer 8 or 10 minutes. Sift together flour and baking powder. Add to sugar and egg mixture. Fold in nuts. Grease and flour a 10 inch bundt pan. Pour one half of batter into pan. Cover with one half apple mixture. Repeat with remainder of batter, then remainder of apples. Preheat oven to 350°. Bake for 1½ hours. Oven heat may vary; test for doneness. Cool in pan, turn out and dust with powdered sugar, if desired.

Mrs. T. B. Dellinger (Maria)

Eggnog For Forty

24	egg yolks	1	quart whipping cream
2	cups sugar	2	quarts milk
1	quart bourbon	1	quart vanilla ice cream
1	pint brandy, optional	24	egg whites, stiffly beaten

Beat egg yolks and sugar until thick and lemon colored. Add bourbon and brandy and stir well. Blend in cream and milk. Add ice cream and mix well. Add stiffly beaten egg whites. Place in refrigerator to chill. Serves 40.

Mrs. John B. Isbell (Charlene)

Dessert for 16

½ cup butter
2 cups powdered sugar
6 eggs, separated
½ cup sugar
1 can (20 ounces) crushed pineapple, drained

1 cup nuts
1 pint whipping cream, whipped
1 teaspoon vanilla
1 box (12 ounces) vanilla wafers

Cream butter and powdered sugar. Add egg yolks, pineapple and nuts. Beat egg whites until fluffy, adding sugar a little at a time until stiff. Fold in beaten egg whites and whipped cream. Put crushed wafers on bottom of two 9 inch square pans. Pour in mixture and top with crushed wafers.

Mrs. Jerry L. Ewing (Claudette)

Layered Cookie

1 cup sugar
1 cup butter
1 egg, beaten
½ cup milk
1 can (3½ ounces) Bakers Angel Flake coconut

1 cup graham cracker crumbs
1 cup chopped pecans or walnuts
1 teaspoon vanilla
Whole graham crackers

Combine sugar, butter, egg and milk. Cook over low heat until boiling, stirring constantly. Remove from heat and add crumbs, coconut and nuts. Line bottom of 9x13 inch pan with whole graham crackers. Spread mixture over graham crackers in pan. Top with another layer of graham crackers. Spread with frosting and refrigerate at least 4 hours. Cut into squares or bars to serve.

FROSTING:
1 box powdered sugar
1 teaspoon vanilla
½ cup butter

6 tablespoons evaporated milk

Combine powdered sugar, vanilla, butter and evaporated milk. Mix well and spread on cookies. Chopped pecans may be sprinkled across top.

Aggie Mom

KITCHEN CHART
OF
PAN AND BAKING DISH SIZES

Common Kitchen Pans

4 cup baking dish:
   9 inch pie plate
   8 inch layer cake pan
   7⅜x3⅝ inch loaf pan

8 cup baking dish:
   8x8 inch square pan
   11x7 inch baking pan
   9x5 inch loaf pan

6 cup baking dish:
   8 or 9 inch layer cake pan
   10 inch pie plate
   8½x3⅝ inch loaf pan

10 cup baking dish:
   9x9 inch square pan
   11¾x7½ inch baking pan
   15x10 inch jelly-roll pan

12 cup baking dish and over:

13½x8½ inch glass baking pan	12 cups
13x9 inch metal baking pan	15 cups
14x10½ inch roasting pan	19 cups

Special Baking Pans

Brioche pan:

9½x3¼ inch pan	8 cups

Charlotte mold:

6x4¼ inch mold	7½ cups

Melon mold:

7x5½x4 inch mold	6 cups

Ring molds:

8½x2¼ inch mold	4½ cups
9¼x2¾ inch mold	8 cups

Springform pans:

8x3 inch pan	12 cups
9x3 inch pan	16 cups

Tube pans:

7½x3 inch Bundt pan	6 cups
9x3½ inch Kugelhupf tube or Bundt pan	9 cups
9x3½ inch angel cake pan	12 cups
10x3¾ inch Bundt pan	12 cups
10x4 inch Kugelhupf tube pan	16 cups
10x4 inch angel cake pan	18 cups

EQUIVALENT MEASUREMENTS

Dash .... Less than ⅛ teaspoon
3 teaspoons .... 1 tablespoon
4 tablespoons.................... ¼ cup
5⅓ tablespoons.................. ⅓ cup
8 tablespoons.................... ½ cup
16 tablespoons.................. 1 cup
2 tablespoons (liquid)............. 1 ounce
1 cup.......................... 8 fluid ounces
2 cups .... 1 pint (16 fluid ounces)
4 cups .... 1 quart
2 pints........................ 1 quart
4 quarts .... 1 gallon
⅛ cup .... 2 tablespoons
⅓ cup .... 5 tablespoons plus 1 teaspoon
⅔ cup .... 10 tablespoons plus 2 teaspoons
¾ cup .... 12 tablespoons

COMMON FOOD EQUIVALENTS

Ingredient	Amount	Approximate Measure
Coconut, flaked or shredded	3½ ounce can	about 1⅓ cups
	7 or 8 ounce package	about 2⅔ cups
Orange		
juice	1 medium	⅓ to ½ cup
peel, grated	1 medium	1 to 2 tablespoons
Nuts, shelled		
almonds	1 pound	3½ cups
peanuts	1 pound	3 cups
pecans	1 pound	4 cups
walnuts	1 pound	4 cups
Sugar		
brown	1 pound	2¼ cups (firmly packed)
granulated	1 pound	2¼ cups
powdered	1 pound	about 4 cups

INGREDIENT SUBSTITUTIONS

INGREDIENT	AMOUNT	SUBSTITUTES
Baking Powder	1 teaspoon	¼ teaspoon soda plus ⅝ teaspoon cream of tartar
Butter	1 cup	⅞ to 1 cup hydrogenated fat plus ½ teaspoon salt, or ⅞ cup oil plus ½ teaspoon salt, or ⅞ cup lard plus ½ teaspoon salt
Chocolate, Semisweet	6 ounce package	2 squares unsweetened chocolate plus 2 tablespoons shortening and ½ cup sugar
Chocolate, Unsweetened	1 ounce or square	3 tablespoons cocoa plus 1 tablespoon fat
Cocoa	¼ cup or 4 tablespoons	1 ounce (square) chocolate and omit 1½ teaspoons shortening called for in recipe
Corn Syrup	1 cup	1 cup sugar plus ¼ cup liquid (use whatever liquid is called for in recipe)
Cornstarch (for thickening)	1 tablespoon	2 tablespoons all-purpose flour, or 2 tablespoons, or 6 teaspoons quick cooking tapioca
Flour, All-Purpose (for thickening)	1 tablespoon	½ tablespoon cornstarch, potato starch, rice starch, or 1 teaspoon granular tapioca, or 2 to 3 teaspoons quick cooking tapioca

INGREDIENT SUBSTITUTIONS

INGREDIENT	AMOUNT	SUBSTITUTES
Milk, Buttermilk	1 cup	1 cup yogurt
Milk, Buttermilk or Sour	1 cup	1 cup sweet milk minus 1 tablespoon plus 1 tablespoon lemon juice or vinegar (allow to stand 5 to 10 minutes), or 1 cup sweet milk plus 1¾ teaspoons cream of tartar
Milk, Sweetened Condensed	1 can (about 1⅓ cups)	⅓ cup plus 2 tablespoons evaporated milk, plus 1 cup sugar, plus 2 tablespoons plus 2 teaspoons butter. Heat until sugar and butter are dissolved.
Sugar, White	1 teaspoon	⅛ teaspoon noncaloric sweetener solution or follow manufacturer's directions
Sugar, White	1 cup	1 cup corn syrup minus ¼ cup of liquid in recipe, or 1⅓ cups molasses minus ⅓ cup of liquid in recipe, or 1 cup brown sugar, firmly packed, or 1 cup honey and reduce liquid in recipe by ¼ cup, or 1¾ cups powdered sugar, packed (do not use when baking), or 1 cup molasses, plus ¼ to ½ teaspoon soda. Omit baking powder.

OLD MAIN

"Old Main," the prominent landmark of the Texas A&M University campus in early times, presents a study in contrast to stately buildings and the beautiful campus enjoyed today.

THE FIGHTIN' TEXAS AGGIE BAND

"The Fightin' Texas Aggie Band" tradition dates back to 1894, when a generous professor endowed a $100 contribution to sponsor 13 members playing borrowed instruments. Today, the Band is over 300 members strong and extends its reputation for unequaled excellence in precision and spirit in music.

INDEX

374

D

NOTES

HULLABALOO IN THE KITCHEN
Dallas A&M University Mothers' Club
P.O. Box 796212
Dallas, Texas 75379

Please send me _____copies of **Hullabaloo In The Kitchen** @ $12.95 each _____

Postage and handling @ 2.00 each _____

Texas residents add 5% sales tax @ .65 each _____

Dallas Area Rapid Transit Authority residents
add 1% additional sales tax after January 1, 1984 @ .13 each _____

Total Enclosed _____

Name _____

Address _____

City _____ State _____ Zip _____

Make checks payable to **Hullabaloo In The Kitchen**
All proceeds from the sale of this cookbook will be returned to Texas A&M University
for scholarships and student activities.

HULLABALOO IN THE KITCHEN
Dallas A&M University Mothers' Club
P.O. Box 796212
Dallas, Texas 75379

Please send me _____copies of **Hullabaloo In The Kitchen** @ $12.95 each _____

Postage and handling @ 2.00 each _____

Texas residents add 5% sales tax @ .65 each _____

Dallas Area Rapid Transit Authority residents
add 1% additional sales tax after January 1, 1984 @ .13 each _____

Total Enclosed _____

Name _____

Address _____

City _____ State _____ Zip _____

Make checks payable to **Hullabaloo In The Kitchen**
All proceeds from the sale of this cookbook will be returned to Texas A&M University
for scholarships and student activities.